Howard Garrett's
Texas Trees

Howard Garrett's
Texas Trees

A Lone Star Book
Published by Traylor Trade Publishing
An imprint of The Rowman and Littlefield Publishing Group, Inc.
4501 Forbes Boulevard, Suite 200
Lanham, Maryland 20706

Distributed by National Book Network

Library of Congress Catalog-in-Publication Data

Garrett, Howard, 1947–
    [Texas trees]
      Howard Garrett's Texas trees / Howard Garrett.
        p. cm.
    Includes bibliographical references (p.)
    ISBN 0-89123-076-9 (cloth : alk. paper)
    1. Trees—Texas. 2. Trees—Texas–Identification. I. Title

    SB435.52.T4 G38 2002
    635.9'77'09764—dc21
                  2002007118

To Naud Burnett

The man who taught me

the importance of trees.

CONTENTS

INTRODUCTION, xiii

SELECTING, PLANTING, AND MAINTAINING
YOUR TREES, 1

FAMILY NAMES, 16

THE TREES, 19

The author's garden in the fall.

INTRODUCTION

My love affair with trees began early. As a kid, I climbed everything that stood still, but trees were my favorite obstacles. My two favorite trees were a catalpa and a mimosa, both smooth-barked trees in our yard in Pittsburg, Texas. Unfortunately, mimosa trees are weak and dying out across the country. The catalpa is still on my good tree list, even though most of the rest of the world considers it a trash tree. Well, that's what this book is about—horticultural details as well as my opinions on whether and how to use the various trees available in Texas.

After I grew up and quit climbing them, trees became enormously important to me for another reason. During my conversion to organics in the late 1980s, I was astonished to find how well trees responded to the organic method. Once residential and commercial projects ceased using high nitrogen, synthetic fertilizers and toxic chemical pesticides, the trees on these projects almost immediately took on a better appearance and started to grow at a faster rate than before the change. The one tree that taught me the most is a ginkgo in my own backyard in the Lakewood area of Dallas. See the entry on ginkgos for the full story, but my experience proved to me that trees grow better under an organic program. I didn't understand the details in the beginning—I just knew it was working. Now I do understand the secret. That wonderfully simple secret is actually no secret at all. In general what happened is that I discovered Mother Nature's plan—a perfect plan that is in some ways too simple for most folks to buy into at first.

The secret? Imitate nature as closely as you can: (1)Select adapted plants and plant them correctly at the proper time and in the right location. (2)Don't do anything that hurts the life in the soil.

It's really that simple. You will find the details of this basic plan in the first chapter, and then special instructions for particular trees under the appropriate entries.

I hope you will find this book easy to use, but I encourage your suggestions. Welcome to the common sense approach to dealing with Texas' most wonderful plants—the trees.

Howard Garrett

Texas ash in the late winter.

Chinese pistachio in the autumn.

Big tooth maple in the fall.

SELECTING, PLANTING, AND MAINTAINING YOUR TREES

Texas is a big place with a huge range of climate, soil, and water quality. There are many trees that can grow here—trees native to Texas as well as those that have been introduced from other states or countries and have adapted to certain parts of our state. The color photos in this book as well as the horticultural requirements mentioned will help you make good choices for your property. My goal is to increase your enjoyment of your trees and reduce the millions of dollars wasted annually through improper tree selections and poor horticultural practices.

Trees are the most important landscape plants because of their high initial cost and their long-term potential to increase property value and improve the quality of any site. When and how to plant trees is crucial. Fall is the ideal time to plant most new trees. The reason? Cool weather shuts down the growth of treetops, but roots of all permanent plants have a growth spurt in the fall. If planted correctly, they will be subject to less stress during this time of the year. Even so, successful planting can be done 12 months a year if proper procedures are used.

SELECTION

The most important factor in planting and growing trees is the selection of adapted trees (i.e., trees that are suitable for the area where they are to be planted). If you plant silver maple, Arizona ash, mimosa, fruitless mulberry, poplar, or Siberian elm, I can't help you. Ill-adapted trees have no chance of producing long-term beauty in Texas or anywhere else. They will be a maintenance problem and a great frustration. These trees should never be considered. Yes, they are included in these pages but only because I want you to learn why they are bad choices.

Now let's consider some good choices. There's a second group of trees that will grow well in Texas—but only in certain conditions and certain soils. Acid soil-loving trees such as dogwood, sweetgum, pin oak, water oak, willow oak, and the straight-trunked east Texas pines prefer deep, sandy, highly organic soils. These trees and others are good choices if planted in the right soil and the right part of Texas. Sweetgum and bald cypress will do well in black clay soils but only if the soils are deep.

If white rock is near the surface, these trees will be yellow and sickly, and there is no way to reverse the process.

Trees that are best for wet soils include willow, birch, and bald cypress. Trees that enjoy almost desert conditions include Chisos oak, eldarica pine, Arizona cypress, and Parkinsonia.

There is a third group of trees that are more foolproof and less demanding than the second group. These trees, which are nearly perfect for sandy as well as black and white soils, include bur oak, chinkapin oak, live oak, shumard red oak, native pecan, and Texas ash. There are many other choices that will grow—in various conditions—and they are listed alphabetically by their common name because that's how they are referred to in the trade and by homeowners.

HOW TO PLANT TREES PROPERLY

People don't grow trees. Trees grow in spite of people. For the most part, trees are tough, durable, and easy to plant and transplant if handled in a sensible and natural way.

To plant any tree (shade, fruit, big, little, native, or introduced), here's the plan:

1. **Dig a wide, ugly hole.** Dig a very wide, rough-sided hole, three to four times wider (especially at the soil surface) than the tree ball. Square-shaped holes also work. The point is to prevent the roots from circling in the hole. In other

Planting adapted trees is the single most important part of successful tree management. This east Texas pine tree was planted in black clay soil—a poor choice.

A wide, ugly hole undergoing the "perk" test.

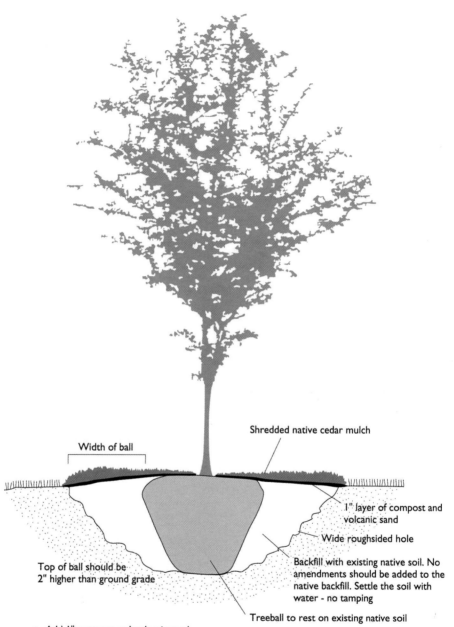

Width of ball

Shredded native cedar mulch

1" layer of compost and volcanic sand

Wide roughsided hole

Top of ball should be 2" higher than ground grade

Backfill with existing native soil. No amendments should be added to the native backfill. Settle the soil with water - no tamping

Treeball to rest on existing native soil

- Add 1" compost and volcanic sand.
- Add 3–5" native cedar mulch. Do not pile mulch on trunks.
- Do not stake trees.
- Do not wrap tree trunks.
- Do not thin or top trees.

Note: Remove any soil that has been added to the top of root balls.
       Expose the actual top of the root ball.

words, do not dig small, smooth-sided holes. The width of the bottom of the hole isn't important, but the depth of the hole should be exactly the same as the height of the ball. Measure— don't guess. It's better to dig a little shallow rather than too deep. If a little bit of the ball is sticking out of the ground after planting, that's okay, but when you over dig and have to put backfill under the ball, the tree can settle and drown. If you set the ball too low in the first place, that can be even worse.

2. **Run a "perk" test.** This tests the porousness or "percolation" of the soil. If time allows, dig and fill the hole with water before planting. Plant the next day only if the water has drained from the hole—unless you have selected a wet soil-loving tree.

These roots were improperly cut at planting time, and the tree died.

Cutting pot-bound roots.

3. **Treat the root system.** Container-grown trees often have root-bound or pot-bound balls. If so, cut the outer edge of the roots (using a knife or a screwdriver to rip the roots loose) and don't worry about hurting the tree. Balled and burlapped trees don't need this treatment. Not only do tightly bound roots have great difficulty breaking away and growing into the surrounding soil, they also prevent moisture from getting into the root ball.

4. **Backfill with existing soil.** Backfill with nothing except soil that came out of the hole. No bark, no peat moss, no compost, no foreign soil, and no fertilizer go into the backfill. You don't want the backfill to be different—especially not softer—than the surrounding native soil.

Remove ropes, wires, and burlap. (Burlap can remain on the sides and bottom of tree balls.) Backfill with existing soil only.

The procedures for transplanting and planting new trees are identical.

Best topdressing mulch for trees is shredded native cedar.

Apply a thin layer of lava sand or other volcanic rock on top of backfill before the mulch is applied.

After planting trees, mulch with compost and shredded tree trimmings.

Entire beds can be mulched when trees are planted close together.

This will create a "pot effect," which makes proper watering difficult and encourages roots to circle in the hole. Circling roots can eventually kill the tree. Settle the soil with water—don't tamp with feet, 2x4s, or anything else. Simply let the weight of the water settle the soil naturally.

5. **Mulch the top of the ball.** After the backfill is settled and leveled with the surrounding grade, cover the disturbed area with a 1-inch layer of a 50/50 mix of compost and lava sand. Any volcanic rock material can be used if lava sand isn't available, and earthworm castings can substitute for the compost. In fact, earthworm castings are a high-quality form of compost. Finally, add a 3-inch or greater layer of shredded tree trimmings. Native cedar is the best choice. By the way, native cedar is a sloppy term for our native junipers, which you can read about later under the heading of "Cedar."

Example of bad tree wrapping. None should be used.

Think an insect could figure out how to get through this protective wrapping?

6. Do not wrap or stake. The ill-advised technique of staking trees was probably started years ago by those who planted bare-rooted trees and mistakenly put soft potting soil in the hole as backfill. Wrapping material around tree trunks probably got started because it looked important. Landscape contractors have admitted to me that brown paper wrap, tree stakes, guy wires, and even the troublesome watering rings are added to newly planted trees for no other reason than to impress the homeowner. Never mind the fact that all these additions are detrimental to the young trees.

Tree staking with wires, ropes, or cables cuts into the bark or at least crushes the cambium layer (even when rubber hoses are used) and causes stress and long-term injury. Staking also prevents the natural movement of the tree in the wind, which prevents the development of trunk caliper and trunk strength.

I have asked many people, including contractors, landscape architects, and others, what is the purpose of wrapping gauze, paper, cardboard, or burlap around the trunks of newly planted trees. The answers range all over the place but include protection from insects, diseases, lawn mowers, weed eaters, and sunburn. Some tree wrappers admit that the only reason they do so is that everyone else does it. Look at the bark under some tree wrapping that's been in place awhile, and you'll see that the cover actually encourages and protects insects and diseases and causes weak, shriveled bark—just like when you leave a bandage on your finger too long. The only possible reason to wrap tree trunks is the rare possibility of sunburn to the trunks of thin-barked trees. If you're worried about that, use a whitewash of 50/50 white latex paint and water. The tree will grow it off naturally. Tree Trunk Goop (see Appendix 2) could also be used.

Trees planted properly don't need the stakes, the wrapping, or the expense.

7. Do not build water dikes. If you plant your trees correctly, these things aren't necessary. Supposedly these water ring-dike things form a dish that makes watering more efficient. The problem with that thought process is that when trees are backfilled with the existing native soil and a thick layer (3–5 inches) of

Improper staking and wrapping.

Improper staking and water ring construction.

Damage from staking connections.

Tops should never be cut back from newly planted or existing trees.

This shows proper staking, wrapping, water rings, and cutting back—there is none.

mulch is tossed down on top of the disturbed area, moisture will stay in the root zone for a long time without the cost or inconvenience of the water rings. If you build water rings around the trees, you have to tear them down at some point or you'll have "watering bumps" around your trees forever.

8. Do not cut back the top. Thinning out the tops of transplants and new trees is another old-time procedure that just doesn't make sense. Alleged experts still recommend cutting away as much as 50% of the top growth to compensate for root loss. I've planted lots of trees, including fruit trees, and they always establish and start to grow better when all of the limbs are left on the tree. Dr. Carl Whitcomb has proven this with his plant research. See the bibliography for information on his books and research. Trees need foliage to collect sunlight, manufacture food, and grow. There are two exceptions in Texas—live oaks and yaupon hollies transplanted from the wild respond positively to a thinning of about 40% of the top. Why? I don't know. I haven't figured it out yet.

HOW TO PROTECT AND MAINTAIN TREES

Protecting Existing Trees

It is essential to tree health to protect the tree root systems by leaving the grade and the drainage pattern, both surface and underground, intact (especially if there is construction on the property). Although tree roots grow out far

Minimum protection for an escarpment live oak on a residential construction site.

Protecting a newly planted Texas ash from animals.

Protecting a tree grove on a commercial site.

beyond the drip line of the foliage, protecting the area from drip line to trunk will give most trees a fair chance of survival. Installing a physical barrier such as a wire or wood fence is the only method that keeps automobile and foot traffic, fill soil, and construction debris off a tree's root system. Establish an envelope that is needed for access and construction activity, build a sturdy fence on that line, and keep people, machines, and materials out of that area. It is also worth the time and money to cover the entire site, inside and outside the fence, with a thick layer (8–12 inches) of shredded tree trimmings mulch, shredded native cedar being the best choice.

Pruning

Remember that trees don't need much pruning. Thinning every year is not good for trees. Pruning is for your benefit, not the tree's. If tree limbs are against the house or in your way or if more light is needed for plants under trees, prune some limbs away, but don't be fooled into thinking that it is good for the tree. It's not. It's just good for your

This is a proper pruning cut protecting the branch collar. Notice no pruning paint or wound dressing.

interests. Also, when cuts need to be made, avoid making flush cuts. Homeowners who prune trees and make flush cuts aren't foolish—just misinformed. People who recommend flush cuts are the fools. Cuts that are made flush against the tree trunk or larger limbs severely damage the tree. Flush cuts remove the branch collar, which is the swollen ring of tissue extending from the trunk. This ring of tissue is nature's healing device. It is part of the trunk or the large limb, not part of the limb being pruned away. After the pruning, the branch collar expands and grows over the pruning cuts to seal off or compartmentalize the wounds to prevent rot and insect attack. There's an easy way to tell if you have made your pruning cuts too close—the pruning wound will be oval. If the cut is round, that's perfect, just as nature intended.

As stated, most trees don't need pruning, but a few do—again for your benefit. With proper management, the injury will be minor. Some fruit trees such as peaches need regular pruning to encourage large fruit production and to make harvesting easier,

Improper flush cut on a cedar elm.

These properly made cuts are healing nicely.

A gutted elm and resulting storm damage.

but ornamental fruit trees don't require any. When a tree is drastically thinned, artificially "lifted," or severely cut back, the tree is hurt. A good rule of thumb for trimming trees is to try to copy nature's pruning techniques. Pruning a tree into an artificial shape is a waste of money, has ugly results, and is usually detrimental to the health of the plant. If you can't decide whether to trim or not, don't! Remember that any cut into the living tissue hurts the plant. Pruning is done for your benefit, not for the trees' benefit. If the trees didn't want the limbs and foliage, they wouldn't be there.

A common pruning mistake is to "lift" or "raise" the tree by removing lower limbs. Low limbs add grace and beauty to the tree. Removing them unnecessarily causes stress and leads to other health-related problems. "Lifting" doesn't even necessarily allow more light to reach the grass or other plantings beneath the tree. If the top of the tree has not been thinned, a solid canopy still exists and no significant increase of light to the ground plane has been created. It's best to remove only dead or damaged limbs, limbs that are rubbing, limbs with mistletoe or disease, and in certain

Storm damage to an overpruned maple.

cases enough of the canopy to allow shafts of sunlight all the way through the tree to the plants growing beneath. Limbs that are hitting the house,

o *11* *oo*

the car in the driveway, or you as you walk by can be removed. But remember—it's for your benefit.

Pruning paint should NOT be used. Damaged living tissue will always heal faster if exposed to fresh air. Pruning paint will seal moisture and disease spores into a protected environment and actually increase the spread of pathogens. Some arborists still recommend painting the cuts on oak trees in oak wilt areas. I'm not sold on that idea. It's better to simply avoid pruning oaks in the spring and early summer when the trees are the most susceptible to the disease. If you must prune in the spring, go ahead and take their advice on applying wound dressing if you want to, but use Lac Balsam or natural shellac instead of the black tar-like products.

Cavities are a confusing tree subject. Still, the tree business people recommend filling cavities with various materials from foam to concrete. Arborists who know their business agree with me and recommend leaving the cavities open—even those that hold water. It is a mistake to drill a hole at an angle from the bottom of a water-holding cavity to the outside of the tree. The idea behind the drilling is to keep the water drained from the hole, but all this procedure does is violate the protective barrier the tree can build for itself. Now diseases can easily begin their dirty work and your tree has a whole new problem.

Cabling

Cabling is another expensive technique that in most cases is unnecessary and detrimental to trees. Drilling holes in limbs and connecting them with metal cables is pretty silly. Cabling simply moves the stress points from one position to another. Cables are unsightly, expensive, and create an artificial tension in trees that can actually lead to more ice and wind breakage instead of less.

The only time cabling should be used is to keep a weak crotch from splitting. In that case, proper cabling runs horizontally between vertical limbs or trunks and keeps them from splitting the tree in half. Removing one of the weak sides is a far better approach than cabling. Cabling should never be

The proper way to treat a cavity—leave it open.

Cabling to hold up low-slung limbs is detrimental to the tree and dangerous to people and nearby construction.

used to attempt to hold up weak or low hanging limbs. These low slung limbs usually have great tensile strength and don't need any help. Even in severe ice storms, they bend to the ground under the weight of the ice but then spring back when the ice melts. Limbs most sensitive to ice storm damage are the vertical limbs, especially on trees that have been overpruned or gutted (where large interior limbs have been removed leaving an artificially airy appearance).

See the text for the best way to control mistletoe.

Mistletoe

Are there any magic silver bullets yet to eliminate this aerial weed called mistletoe? No, but there are some techniques that help to keep it in control. Mistletoe is a plant parasite that primarily attaches to limbs or trunks of low quality, stressed trees. Common targets include hackberry, bois d'arc, Siberian elm, Arizona ash, honey locust, box elder, and other weak trees. Quality trees in stress from environmental problems are also subject to mistletoe attack.

Removal is not practical at this time with any chemical or organic spray, so the only choice is removal by pruning. Infected limbs should be cut away completely if possible. If that can't be done, notch into the limb or trunk to remove the entire rooting structure of the mistletoe and paint the wound with black pruning paint to prevent resprouting. This is the only time I recommend painting cuts, especially with black wound dressing. Shooting the mistletoe out with a shotgun works pretty well if you live in the country, but improving the tree's health by improving the soil is the best preventative. To get rid of the removed mistletoe, compost it, hang it over the doorways for the holidays, or chop it up and sprinkle it on fire ant mounds. Yep, it works. You can also make a fire ant mound drench from soaking mistletoe in water to make a tea.

Mulching

Trees should be mulched at the time of planting, and additional mulch should be added each year unless a green cover crop exists across the root system. When trees are planted in turf, use a 3–4-inch layer of shredded mulch over the root ball to prevent the competition of grass roots, to maintain soil moisture, and to keep the soil temperature at the proper level. When trees are planted in beds, the entire bed should be mulched. Don't pile mulch up on the trunks of trees. That can keep the tree bark moist and lead to problems.

Fertilizing

Trees need very little fertilizer, but when it is used, the amount should be based on the surface area of ground rather than the diameter of the tree trunk. Organic programs feed the soil rather than the plants, so the amount of fertilizer is related to the amount of soil area, not the number, kind, or size of the plants. I normally fertilize once in the early spring and again in the early summer with an organic fertilizer at the rate of 10–20 pounds per 1,000 square feet. A third application is sometimes needed in the fall, but this procedure is more for the plants around the trees than for the trees themselves. Fertilizer should be spread on the surface of the soil rather than put in deep holes around the trees. The root system of trees is much more shallow than most people realize. Most of the roots are located in the top 12–19 inches of soil. Most of the feeder roots are in the top 7 inches of soil. It is also beneficial to broadcast lava sand or other volcanic rock blends under trees at the rate of 40–80 pounds per 1,000 square feet. If you live near a volcano, this isn't necessary.

Watering

Watering depends on the soil type, climate, plant varieties, and sun exposure. If trees are planted in the fall using the natural techniques, one thorough watering at planting may be all that is ever needed. It is critical for farmers and ranchers to plant and water well at this time so the tree will survive when irrigation water is not available.

On the other hand, newly planted trees in landscape projects should be thoroughly soaked every other week or so in the hot growing season and maybe once a month in the cooler seasons. This watering should be done in addition to the regular watering of the grass areas or planting areas surrounding the trees. Obviously, rain will alter this schedule. Once trees are established, a regular watering of the surrounding planting areas is normally enough. If trees are planted properly, little supplemental watering is needed except during the heat of the summer. During periods of extreme drought, the soaking procedure may need to be used again on introduced trees. On the other hand, marginal trees, planted properly and grown under an organic program, will have huge root systems and healthy populations of beneficial mycorrhizal fungi on the roots. As a result, those trees have the ability to access water and nutrients from the soil even in the harshest of conditions. If native trees are used, even the summer watering may not be needed.

Pest Control

Primary pest control results from planting adapted trees properly. Healthy trees have a natural resistance to insect pests and diseases. Sprays for insects and diseases should be applied only after pests are seen, and only environmentally safe alternatives to toxic poisons should be used—and that does not mean diazinon, Dursban, Orthene, Kelthane, Sevin, or any other toxic chemical poison. Even problem flare-ups of pests can be controlled with food products that are beneficial to the soil and the environment.

Aphids, for example, can be controlled with a strong blast of water and the release of ladybugs. Ladybugs (ladybird beetles), green lacewings, and trichogramma wasps provide excellent control of aphids, spider mites, worms, and other small

Releasing trichogramma wasps to control various caterpillar pest problems.

Texas Forest Service recommends toxic fungicide treatment to the root flare of a live oak.

Here the chemical fungicide has been applied incompetently.
See Appendix 3 for the Sick Tree Treatment.

insects. Beneficial insects should be released at dusk after wetting all the foliage or at daybreak when dew is on the foliage. Heavy infestations can be knocked back with garlic-pepper tea (see Appendix 2), and for serious pest infestations add citrus oil.

Most fungal problems can be controlled by spraying Garrett Juice (see Appendix 2) plus garlic tea. Potassium bicarbonate can be added for tougher problems. The use of horticultural cornmeal will shut down most minor fungal diseases that pop up. This is available in many feed stores and organic garden centers. Mulching plants with shredded native cedar will also help reduce insect pests and diseases. The Sick Tree Treatment (see Appendix 3) should be used for severe tree problems.

Trees are easy to grow in Texas if you use a few simple, common sense approaches and make some smart selections. I hope this book will help you with those decisions and techniques.

FAMILY NAMES

Aceraceae ....Maple Family	Lauraceae ....Laurel Family
Anacadiaceae ....Sumac or Cashew Family	Lythraceae ...Crape Myrtle or Loosestrife Family
Aquifoliaceae ....Holly Family	Magnoliaceae ....Magnolia Family
Arecaceae ....Palm Family	Meliaceae ....Mahogany Family
Betulaceae ....Birch Family	Moraceae ....Mulberry Family
Bignoniaceae ...Catalpa or Trumpet Vine Family	Myricaceae .....Wax Myrtle or Bayberry Family
Boraginaceae ....Borage Family	Oleaceae ....Olive Family
Caprifoliaceae ....Honeysuckle Family	Pinaceae ....Pine Family
Cercidiophyllaceae ....Katsuratree Family	Platanaceae ....Sycamore Family
Cornaceae ....Dogwood Family	Rhamnaceae ....Buckthorn Family
Cupressaceae .....Cypress or Redwood Family	Rosaceae ....Rose Family
Ebenaceae ....Persimmon or Ebony Family	Rutaceae ....Citrus or Rue Family
Elaeagnaceae ....Oleaster Family	Salicaceae ....Willow Family
Ericaceae ....Heath or Blueberry Family	Sapindaceae ....Soapberry Family
Euphorbiaceae ....Spurge Family	Sapotaceae ..Chicle, Sapote, or Sapodilla Family
Fabaceae ......Legume, Bean, or Pulse Family	Simaroubaceae ....Quassia Family
Fagaceae ....Beech Family	Sterculiaceae ......Chocolate or Cacao Family
Ginkgoaceae ....Ginkgo Family	Tiliaceae ....Linden Family
Hamamelidaceae ....Witch Hazel Family	Ulmaceae ....Elm Family
Hippocastanaceae ....Buckeye Family	Verbenaceae ....Vervain Family
Juglandaceae ....Walnut Family	

TREE PLANTING
EPIDEMIC

One thing that's really fun about my job is learning new stuff all the time. Sometimes it's not good stuff. I have been stunned to discover what a huge number of trees have been planted too low. There seems to be several reasons why this problem exists. Many trees have simply been set too low in the planting operation. Holes were too deeply dug. Other trees were planted at about the right level, but settled due to the wrong backfill or weak rootballs. But one of the most common causes of deep tree planting problems starts at the growing operations and sometimes in the nurseries. As trees grow, they are stepped from seedlings to 1 gallon pots and then to increasingly larger containers. Often during this process more and more soil is added to the top of the root ball. Why, I don't know. By the time the tree is ready to plant, it may be several inches deep in the container. That fact combined with the planting mistakes often puts the true top of the root ball several inches underground. This covering of the tree ball with soil can also happen on field grown trees by the cultivating plows. Trees that are planted too low have several problems. Soil above the root ball shuts off oxygen to the feeder roots and carbon dioxide can't escape from the soil. Roots that do grow often circle and grow primarily in the soft, loose textured, added soil. The coiling roots can girdle trees several years after planting. Then also there is a girdling action from the soil moisture on the bark of the tree. A frustrating part of the problem is that the damage doesn't start to show up until sometimes 10–15 years after planting, when the tree is trying to mature and offer its beauty and shade. The symptoms can also show up the first few years. Watch for poor top growth, light colored foliage and a thinning canopy.

It's easy to tell if a tree has been planted too low. The trunk will go straight into the ground like a telephone pole instead of having a distinctive flair at the soil surface. The solution is relatively easy too. Remove the excess soil down to the true top of the original root ball. This work can be done by homeowners with a hard rake or by professional arborists with a special tool called an air spade. It is basically a sand blaster with a customized nozzle that blows the soil away from roots without injuring them. Girdling roots can be pruned away if needed at this time. If the excavation down to the top of the ball is not too deep, the area can be left concaved and lightly mulched with shredded tree trimmings. If the soil removal leaves a deep hole, a grate may have to be added that can serve as an arbor for ground cover. The long-term solution to this problem is to plant your trees according to my drawing on page 3, leaving the actual root ball 2 inches higher than grade and backfill with native soil only. With this technique not even settling will leave the tree too deep in the ground.

THE TREES

Wright acacia.

Acacia, Catclaw

COMMON NAMES: Catclaw Acacia, Catclaw, Acacia, Wright Acacia, Wright's Acacia, Joint-vetch, Una De Gato, Huisachillo, Tree Catclaw, Texas Catclaw, Devil's Claw

BOTANICAL NAME: *Acacia greggii* var. *wrightii*

PRONUNCIATION: ah-KAY-shuh GREG-ee-eye, WRITE-ee-eye

FAMILY: Fabaceae (Legume, Bean, or Pulse Family)

TYPE: Deciduous tree

HEIGHT: 15–30 feet

SPREAD: 10–12 feet

FINAL SPACING: 10–15 feet

NATURAL HABITAT AND PREFERRED SITE: Catclaw acacia is native to south Texas and the Trans-Pecos and grows in rocky, well-drained soils requiring a minimum amount of water. Catclaw acacia has adapted to a variety of soils as far north as Abilene and Dallas.

IDENTIFICATION: Catclaw acacia is a large shrub or small tree with feathery foliage and fragrant flowers in the spring. It is thorny and thicket-forming, with a spreading, irregular overall form.

FLOWERS AND FRUIT: The flowers are off-white to creamy yellow and are cylindrical spikes ¾–1½ inches long. They bloom primarily in the spring. The fruit is a legume, usually curling and contorted, 2–5½ inches long. It starts forming in July and stays on the tree into the winter. The seeds are dark brown and shiny, ¼–⅓ inch long. It comes into bloom in the mid spring or later, usually after heavy rains.

FOLIAGE: The leaves are compound, 1–3 inches long.

BARK: The young bark is thin, gray to brown in color. On older trunks it separates into thin, narrow scales. The twigs are armed with short ¼-inch spines.

CULTURE: Catclaw acacia is extremely drought tolerant and needs little fertilizer. It can grow in rocky soils but adapts to fairly heavy clay soils as well if they are well-drained.

PROBLEMS: The biggest problem is that it is not widely available.

PROPAGATION: It can be grown from seed, cuttings, and transplanting. Because seed is covered with a hard seed coat, mechanical or acid scarification is sometimes necessary. Seed will germinate in 7–12 days with proper conditions and warm soil temperatures. Without scarification, germination may take as long as a month. Cuttings can be made from softwood or semi-hardwood taken in the late spring or early summer. Due to its taproot, transplanting is difficult on all but very small seedlings.

INSIGHT: The catclaw acacia flowers are fragrant and make a superb honey. **Wright acacia** (*Acacia wrightii*) and **Gregg acacia** (*A. greggii*) are extremely similar but can be distinguished by the following: the seed pods of Gregg acacia are quite contorted and the leaflets of Wright acacia are the larger of the two. *Shinners & Mahler's Illustrated Flora of North Central Texas* says that both plants are *A. greggi*, but catclaw is variety *A. greggii* and Wright acacia is variety *A.g. wrightii*.

Anacua foliage.

Anacua

COMMON NAMES: Anacua, Sandpaper Anacua, Sandpaper Tree, Knockaway, Knackaway, Manzanita, Manzanillo

BOTANICAL NAME: *Ehretia anacua*

PRONUNCIATION: eh-REE-shah ah-NOK-you-ah or ah-NOK-wha

FAMILY: Boraginaceae (Borage Family)

TYPE: Almost evergreen shade tree

HEIGHT: 30–40 feet, up to 50 feet

SPREAD: 30 feet

FINAL SPACING: 30–40 feet

NATURAL HABITAT AND PREFERRED SITE: Anacua is native to southern Texas, primarily the Gulf prairies and marshes, the Rio Grande Plains, and the Edwards Plateau along the Balcones escarpment in Comal, Hays, and Travis counties. It grows in full sun in alkaline soils with good drainage, but it can also survive in slightly acid sands and clays. In sandy soils it tends to sucker (or sprout from the base), causing thickets. It could be introduced fairly successfully as far north as Austin.

IDENTIFICATION: The crown is very dense and creates heavy shade. Mature trees often have a distinctive, gnarled appearance and are often multi-trunked. Anacua is mostly evergreen, although it loses some of its foliage in the winter.

FLOWERS AND FRUIT: Anacua blooms from the late fall through the winter into the early spring depending on rain and climate. It may have more than one blooming period. The flowers are pure white and fragrant. The spring-ripening fruits are bright orange drupes about the size of hackberries. They are ¼ inch wide and contain 2 seeds. The fruit doesn't stay on the tree long because it is a favorite of birds and other wildlife. Anacua rarely sets and keeps flowers and fruit in areas north of San Antonio.

FOLIAGE: The foliage is dark green—almost evergreen—and has a rough sandpaper texture. The shape of the leaves is elliptical.

BARK: The bark is heavily textured and deeply furrowed. It separates into thin, gray or reddish scales with age.

CULTURE: Anacua needs plenty of water to establish and then becomes very drought tolerant. After establishment it can be killed by over watering or poor drainage. Very little, if any, fertilizer is needed.

PROBLEMS: Very few problems exist other than those caused by poor drainage, improper planting, or environmental damage.

PROPAGATION: It can be grown from seed, cuttings, or transplants. Seed will germinate within 30 days if first stratified in moisture and cold temperatures. Anacua can be rooted from young wood or suckers as well as softwood cuttings on the current year's growth.

INSIGHT: Anacua is a great honeybee attractant and food source for wildlife. There are terrific specimens growing around the Alamo in San Antonio. There is one currently alive at the Dallas Discovery Gardens.

Anacua at the Alamo.

Arizona ash in the fall showing its best quality.

Ash, Arizona

COMMON NAMES: Arizona Ash, Velvet Ash, Modesto Ash, Desert Ash, Leather Leaf Ash, Smooth Ash, Tumi Ash, Fresno, Standley Ash

BOTANICAL NAME: *Fraxinus velutina*

PRONUNCIATION: FRAK-suh-nus vel-ou-TEE-na

FAMILY: Oleaceae (Olive Family)

TYPE: Deciduous shade tree

HEIGHT: 30 feet or greater

SPREAD: 30 feet

FINAL SPACING: Do not plant.

NATURAL HABITAT AND PREFERRED SITE: Arizona ash grows naturally in the high mountains and cool canyons of the Trans-Pecos and along streams, rivers, and dry streambeds. It is a plant that likes protected places where there is almost constant water. It is native to El Paso County, Culberson County, the Guadalupe Mountains, and the drainage creeks of Jeff Davis County and other west Texas areas. Unfortunately, this tree has been planted in many residential areas because it is so easy to propagate and grow into a salable plant.

IDENTIFICATION: Arizona ash or velvet ash is a fast-growing tree. It has brittle wood, yellow fall color, and usually a lot of dead branches. It is quite attractive some years.

FLOWERS AND FRUIT: The flowers appear in clusters before the leaves emerge in the spring. Male and female flowers are on separate plants (dioecious). The flowers have no petals. The fruits are samaras (winged seeds) about 1–1½ inches long.

Arizona ash fall foliage.

FOLIAGE: The compound leaves are about 8–10 inches long with leaflets that are about 2–3 inches in length.

BARK: The bark is light gray to off-white in color. It is relatively smooth and uninteresting.

CULTURE: Arizona ash will grow in most any soil but needs a lot of water and light fertilization.

PROBLEMS: It is susceptible to all kinds of problems. First, it is short-lived. It is also very susceptible to insects, diseases, and freeze damage in the northern part of the state. It was introduced as a drought tolerant, low maintenance tree but is far from it. The only reason it is on the market is that it is easy to grow from seed or stem cuttings.

PROPAGATION: Don't.

INSIGHT: These photographs make it look like a pretty good tree, but don't be fooled. In its native habitat and occasionally in the rest of Texas, the fall color is outstanding, but the tree is simply not a good investment.

Fragrant ash. (Photo by Andy Wasowski.)

Ash, Fragrant

COMMON NAMES: Fragrant Ash, Flowering Ash, Fresno
BOTANICAL NAME: *Fraxinus cuspidata*
PRONUNCIATION: FRAK-suh-nus cus-pi-DA-tah
FAMILY: Oleaceae (Olive Family)
TYPE: Deciduous ornamental tree
HEIGHT: 10–20 feet
SPREAD: 8–12 feet
FINAL SPACING: 8–15 feet
NATURAL HABITAT AND PREFERRED SITE: It grows naturally in the canyons of the Devils and Pecos rivers along the Rio Grande Valley in Val Verde County and on the western Edwards Plateau. It primarily grows in the Trans-Pecos and far west Texas on mountain slopes and in canyons, primarily rocky soil conditions.
IDENTIFICATION: Fragrant ash has white flowers that are, in fact, very fragrant—it is the only ash with this kind of flower. It is more shrubby than tree-like and has long, thin leaflets on compound leaves.
FLOWERS AND FRUIT: The flowers have 4 white petals that appear as the leaves first emerge in the spring and are borne on clusters 3–4 inches long. In the spring, fragrant ash seems to be completely covered with a white blanket of flowers. The bloom period is generally in the spring from April to May. The fruits are drooping panicles of long samaras (winged seeds) on slender stems.
FOLIAGE: The leaves are compound, 3–6 inches long, made up of 5–7 leaflets that are delicate and narrow.
BARK: The bark is smooth and white to medium gray. On old trunks the bark starts breaking into short scales and irregular fissures.
CULTURE: Fragrant ash will grow equally well in slightly alkaline limestone soils or slightly acidic igneous soils. It even does well in the heavy black clay soils.
PROBLEMS: Poor availability in the nursery trade is the biggest problem.
PROPAGATION: It is best grown from seed. Seed may be planted in the fall immediately after harvest or stored at 41°F and planted in the spring.
INSIGHT: This gorgeous tree is at least as showy as flowering dogwood and should be planted much more in Texas.

Green ash.

Ash, Green

COMMON NAMES: Green Ash, Red Ash, Darlington Ash, Swamp Ash, River Ash, Water Ash

BOTANICAL NAME: *Fraxinus pennsylvanica*

PRONUNCIATION: FRAK-suh-nus pen-cil-VAN-ik-ca

FAMILY: Oleaceae (Olive Family)

TYPE: Deciduous shade tree

HEIGHT: 50–70 feet

SPREAD: 40–50 feet

FINAL SPACING: 20–50 feet, if planted at all

NATURAL HABITAT AND PREFERRED SITE: A wide-ranging tree in Texas, green ash grows wild in the Piney Woods, Gulf prairies and marshes, Post Oak Savannah, Blackland Prairies, Cross Timbers, and Rio Grand Plains—basically the eastern half of the state. It also grows along the banks of the Canadian River in the Panhandle in Hemphill and Roberts counties. It can grow in a wide range of moist soils including limestone, clays, and sandy loams. It needs plenty of moisture. It grows along rivers and streams and even in swamps, flood plains, swales, and depressions.

IDENTIFICATION: It is an upright-growing, spreading, round-topped shade tree that has been reported to grow as tall as 80 feet. It has the typical compound leaves of the ash trees, but the leaflets are wider than Arizona ash leaflets and generally not as wide as Texas ash leaflets. Fall color is yellow as opposed to the multicolored foliage seen in Texas ash.

FLOWERS AND FRUIT: Male flowers are on one plant and female flowers on the other (dioecious), and they are nothing to get excited about. The fruits are samaras (winged seeds) in panicles or clusters—the typical winged seeds of ash trees.

FOLIAGE: The leaves are large and compound, 8–12 inches long, with usually 5–9 leaflets—7 is the most common number. The leaflets are very pointed.

BARK: The bark is brown to dark gray and fairly tight on the tree. The ridges or fissures are rather shallow.

CULTURE: Green ash grows in moist soil in nature and on a lot of residential properties, although I do not recommend it very highly. It is not a long-lived tree and is subject to several challenges.

PROBLEMS: Green ash is susceptible to aphids in the early summer, borers, and damage from drought. And it can experience fairly serious dieback during summer droughts.

PROPAGATION: Don't—unless you are interested in growing a problematic, short-lived tree.

INSIGHT: The green ash hybrids that are on the market are even less adapted in Texas than the parent plant. I've learned that the hard way on landscape projects.

Prickly ash foliage.

Ash, Prickly

COMMON NAMES: Prickly Ash, Hercules' Club, Toothache Tree, Tickle Tongue Tree, Pepper Bark

BOTANICAL NAME: *Zanthoxylum clava herculis*

PRONUNCIATION: zanth-OX-ih-lum CLA-va her-CUE-lis

FAMILY: Rutaceae (Citrus or Rue Family)

TYPE: Deciduous middle-sized tree

HEIGHT: 15–30 feet

SPREAD: 15–30 feet

FINAL SPACING: 10–15 feet, but seldom planted

NATURAL HABITAT AND PREFERRED SITE: Prickly ash is normally found along hedgerows, in thickets, and on edges of forests in east Texas but also spreading farther west. This interesting little tree is adapted to a wide range of soils and prefers full sun. According to *A Field Guide to Texas Trees* by Simpson, it is a tree of the Blackland Prairies, Piney Woods, Gulf prairies and marshes, and the Post Oak Savannah. It likes deep, heavy, alkaline clay soils but will also grow in the almost sterile sands. It shows up most often on the wood's edge or fence rows where the seeds have been planted by birds and other wildlife.

IDENTIFICATION: It is a shrubby small tree that rarely grows over 15 feet. The bark is gray-white with cork-based, nasty spines or thorns on the trunks and stems. It has very light, lacy foliage.

FLOWERS AND FRUIT: The flowers appear in the spring and are small, yellowish green clusters on the female plants. The fruit is a brownish follicle containing a single seed that ripens from the mid to late summer.

FOLIAGE: The foliage is compound and alternate, and each leaflet is lance-shaped and aromatic.

BARK: The bark is the most distinctive feature. It is smooth, has mottled light and dark spots, and features dramatic spines that are very wide at the base.

CULTURE: Prickly ash is very easy to grow in most any soil. Not really recommended for planting, it is easy to keep alive if it already exists on-site.

PROBLEMS: The foliage gets eaten by caterpillars, but the caterpillar that loves the foliage most is the giant swallowtail, so care should be given to protect these beautiful butterflies.

PROPAGATION: It can be done by seed or cuttings. Seed germinates in 20–40 days. This process can be helped by soaking in liquid seaweed or Garrett Juice (see Appendix 2) and then storing at 41°F for 30 days. Prickly ash can also be propagated by root cuttings taken in the late winter. Cut roots into links approximately 1 inch long and place them horizontally in potting soil. Moisten the soil and cover it with paper until growth begins on the roots, then plant. If protected through the winter, the plant should grow well in the spring.

INSIGHT: All parts of the tree, including the bark, will numb the gums and tongue when chewed or sucked. Native Americans used prickly ash or tickle tongue tree as a painkiller. They chewed the bark for toothaches and drank berry tea for sore throats. The bark and berries are stimulants and have historically been used to treat digestive problems, rheumatism, skin diseases, nervous headaches, varicose veins, and congestion. Prickly ash provides cover for wildlife, and the blooms help to make a delicious honey.

Prickly ash showing its thorny trunk and limbs.

Ash, Texas

COMMON NAMES: Texas Ash, Mountain Ash
BOTANICAL NAME: *Fraxinus texensis*
PRONUNCIATION: FRAK-suh-nus tex-EN-sis
FAMILY: Oleaceae (Olive Family)
TYPE: Deciduous shade tree
HEIGHT: 30–50 feet
SPREAD: 30–40 feet
FINAL SPACING: 20–40 feet

NATURAL HABITAT AND PREFERRED SITE: Texas ash grows natively in the limestone soils of north Texas, west to Palo Pinto County, and down to the Balcones escarpment of the Edwards Plateau. It is also native in Val Verde County at the far west end of its range. It grows in very low rainfall areas and can handle steeply sloped and very thin soils but will adapt to normal landscape conditions throughout Texas.

IDENTIFICATION: Texas ash is a beautiful shade tree that is graceful in the summer and has rich fall color that ranges from hues of yellow, orange, and gold to red and purple. It will often completely turn a brilliant scarlet red. The tree generally has a very neat rounded or oval form, which will spread with age.

FLOWERS AND FRUIT: Small, greenish yellow flowers bloom in the spring in clusters of samaras (winged seeds) that ripen in the fall.

BARK: The bark is smooth and very light in color—light gray to almost white in some cases when young. It gets darker and mildly fissured with age.

FOLIAGE: The foliage is composed of compound leaves, 8–13 inches long. The leaves have 3–7 leaflets (with 7 being the most common). The leaflets are rounded when young but become more pointed with age. The white ash, arguably the same tree, has dark lustrous color on the top of the leaves with a paler whitish color beneath.

CULTURE: Texas ash is very easy to grow in most soils unless over watered. It has very low water and fertilizer requirements but does need excellent drainage. It is also very easy to transplant from the wild.

PROBLEMS: Poor drainage is the biggest problem, which will lead to borers, root diseases, and other environmentally related pests.

PROPAGATION: Texas ash can be grown very easily from seed, cuttings, or transplants. Seed should be sown outdoors in the fall in beds or pots, planted ¼–½ inch deep in well-drained soil. The planting area for best results should be given light to medium shade in the afternoon for the first season. Cuttings will do best when taken very late in the winter as

Texas or white ash.

Texas ash summer foliage.

Texas ash in flower in the early spring.

buds are swelling just before flowering. Texas ash up to 6 inches in caliper can be transplanted successfully if handled properly. Books that recommend that trees be pruned back at transplanting time should be ignored. Not a twig should be cut away at transplanting.

INSIGHT: This is the most plentiful ash in Texas. Texas ash is very close kin to the **white ash** (*Fraxinus americana*); according to renowned native tree expert, the late Benny Simpson, the only difference between the white ash and Texas ash is that the seed of the white ash is slightly longer. *Shinners & Mahler's Illustrated Flora of North Central Texas* argues that the Texas ash may be the subspecies of white ash. I don't care—they both do very well here. I have recommended white ash cultivars in the past, but it is best in all cases to try to stick with native plants whenever possible.

Texas ash seed in the fall.

Typical Texas ash fall color.

Ash, Wafer

COMMON NAMES: Wafer Ash, Waferash, Hoptree, Common Hoptree, Skunkbush, Wahoo, Cola Dezorillo

BOTANICAL NAME: *Patellae trifoliata*

PRONUNCIATION: pat-TEA-lee-ah TRI-fole-ee-AH-tah

FAMILY: Rutaceae (Citrus or Rue Family)

TYPE: Deciduous small tree or bush

HEIGHT: 5–20 feet

SPREAD: 5–10 feet

FINAL SPACING: 6–12 feet

NATURAL HABITAT AND PREFERRED SITE: The wafer ash will grow almost throughout the entire state except for the extreme southern tip of Texas. It is often found in protected canyons, on the edges of woods, in fence rows, and along streams. It will grow in full sun, partial shade, or as a complete understory tree. It can take a wide range of soils and grows well in both moist conditions as well as dry, rocky sites.

IDENTIFICATION: The wafer ash is a very interesting small tree that has aromatic foliage (some people consider it to be offensively aromatic). It's a deciduous shrub or tree that grows to a maximum height of 25 feet. It has slender branches and pale compound leaves with 3 leaflets that vary in shape. The winged fruit is the most distinctive part of the little tree.

FLOWERS AND FRUIT: The flowers are greenish white, blooming in terminal panicles in the early spring. The fruits (samaras) follow and sport a distinctive, single, disc-shaped wing. The plant is usually unisexual or dioecious (male and female flowers on different trees). The seeds are flat and about ⅓ inch in diameter, surrounded by a papery wing. The ripe seeds will stay on the tree throughout the winter.

FOLIAGE: The leaves are alternate, trifoliate, and light green.

BARK: The bark is light in color and smooth.

CULTURE: Wafer ash is relatively easy to grow and should be used more. It is drought tolerant and can stand soils ranging from sandy to heavy clays and can even grow in rocky soil. It is adapted to full sun but does better with light shade as an understory tree. It needs very little, if any, fertilizer to survive and thrive.

PROBLEMS: Relatively few problems pop up when the tree is planted in an adapted site and given a moderate to light amount of water.

PROPAGATION: Best results come from harvesting the fruit in the late summer and early fall as the seed begins to dry, and then planting in pots or in the ground. It is not necessary to remove the wings. Seed

Wafer ash.

will normally remain viable for about 16 months. Partial shade is beneficial for the young seedlings as they develop. Stratification is normally not needed. Some people like to provide cold hours (at 41°F) for 3 months. The plant can also be propagated by budding, grafting, or layering. Softwood and semi-hardwood cuttings taken in the midsummer to late fall can be successful.

INSIGHT: Wafer ash is a good tree to provide food and shelter for wildlife. According to *Shinners & Mahler's Illustrated Flora of North Central Texas*, the fruit has been used in the past as a substitute for hop even though it is reported to contain alkaloids and other toxic ingredients.

River birch growing on the State Fairgrounds in Dallas.

River birch foliage.

Birch, River

COMMON NAMES: River Birch, Birch, Black Birch, Red Birch, Water Birch

BOTANICAL NAME: *Betula nigra*

PRONUNCIATION: BET-ew-la NI-gra

FAMILY: Betulaceae (Birch Family)

TYPE: Deciduous tree

HEIGHT: 30–50 feet

SPREAD: 15–20 feet

FINAL SPACING: 20–25 feet

NATURAL HABITAT AND PREFERRED SITE: River birch grows naturally along creeks, in bottomlands, and in other wet areas and prefers moist sandy or loamy soil. It occasionally grows in standing water in bogs. River birch loves the wetlands of the Piney Woods and the Post Oak Savannah. It grows near the running waters of rivers and creeks as well as beside the still waters of swamps, bays, and sloughs. According to Simpson (*A Field Guide to Texas Trees*), specimens have grown as high as 90 feet.

IDENTIFICATION: The most distinguishing characteristic of river birch is the bark, which is a dark red color and peels off in large sheets.

FLOWERS AND FRUIT: The flowers bloom in the early spring before the leaves emerge. Male and female flowers are borne separately and become winged nutlets about ⅛ inch long, which ripen from April to June.

FOLIAGE: The simple, alternate, deciduous leaves have serrated edges and are lustrous dark green above, tomentose (hairy) below. In most years river birch has pretty good yellow fall color.

BARK: The bark is a beautiful, flaking material that may be the most distinctive feature of the tree. It is dull reddish brown, peeling in curly, thin, papery strips.

CULTURE: River birch is relatively easy to grow in most soils given enough moisture, although the tree does not live very long. I don't recommend it for a major tree planting.

PROBLEMS: It has a short life and does not like the heat and highly alkaline soils in most parts of Texas.

PROPAGATION: It can be grown from seed or cuttings. Seed can be sown in the fall or in the following spring after storage in cold temperatures of around 40°F for 30–60 days. Cuttings are best taken in the late winter before bud break.

INSIGHT: River birch is a graceful tree, very good-looking in the garden, but it does not live a long time.

Bird of paradise.

Bird of Paradise

COMMON NAMES: Bird of Paradise, Bird of Paradise Bush, Mexican Poinciana, Pride of Barbados, Paradise Poinciana

BOTANICAL NAME: *Caesalpinia gilliesii*

PRONUNCIATION: kie-sal-PEEN-ee-ah gi-LISS-ee-eye

FAMILY: Fabaceae (Legume, Bean, or Pulse Family)

TYPE: Semi-tropical ornamental tree

HEIGHT: 8–15 feet

SPREAD: 10–15 feet

FINAL SPACING: 8–10 feet

NATURAL HABITAT AND PREFERRED SITE: This introduced tree was originally collected from Argentina, Brazil, and Chile. According to *Shinners & Mahler's Illustrated Flora of North Central Texas,* several Texas species (*C. drummondii, C. jamesii*) are now placed in the genus *Hoffmann seggia* and *Pomaria.* All these plants prefer full sun and well-drained soil. The fertility level is not important. They prefer the southern half of the state to avoid freeze damage. For use in the landscape, plant in full sun in an area where it will be protected from severe freezing weather.

IDENTIFICATION: Bird of paradise is a small, delicate ornamental tree with lacy foliage and long-lasting, colorful summer flowers.

FLOWERS AND FRUIT: The flowers are showy with open racemes and are usually yellow and red. The fruits are pods that are dark brown to black at maturity and often appear on the plant while it is still flowering. The pods are pubescent, which means fuzzy.

FOLIAGE: The leaves are delicate and compound with 11–29 pinnae (primary divisions of a pinnate leaf), each with many leaflets.

BARK: The bark is smooth and brownish gray.

CULTURE: Bird of paradise is relatively easy to grow and will be a perennial or permanent plant in the southern half of the state. It will sometimes freeze in the northern portion. It needs normal bed preparation and moderate water and fertilizer.

PROBLEMS: Other than freeze damage, I have seen almost no problems with this plant.

PROPAGATION: It is easy to grow from seed planted in the spring. I have never tried growing it from stem cuttings, but it should be easy in the late winter just before bud break.

INSIGHT: Mexican Poinciana (*Caesalpinia mexicana*) is a yellow flowering Texas native that grows wild in the far southern tip of the state. There are also red and orange varieties that have to be grown in the far southern part of the state or treated as annuals. It has been reported that the leaves of **Pride-of-Barbados** (*C. pulcherrima*) have been used as a fish poison in Central America and that the seeds have been used to poison criminals.

Black gum fall color.

Black gum foliage.

Black Gum

COMMON NAMES: Black Gum, Black Tupelo, Sour-gum
BOTANICAL NAME: *Nyssa sylvatica*
PRONUNCIATION: NI-sa sil-VA-ti-ca
FAMILY: Cornaceae (Dogwood Family)
TYPE: Deciduous shade tree
HEIGHT: 50–100 feet
SPREAD: 30–40 feet
FINAL SPACING: 30–40 feet
NATURAL HABITAT AND PREFERRED SITE: Black gum grows in swamps, moist woods, and streams in east Texas or Houston-area clays. It likes the fully drained soils of the Piney Woods, Gulf prairies and marshes, and other flood plain locations.
IDENTIFICATION: Black gum is a large, graceful tree with shiny foliage that turns a brilliant scarlet red in the fall. It has blue-black fruit that normally stays on the tree after the red foliage drops in the fall.
FLOWERS AND FRUIT: The flowers are unisexual. Both male and female flowers are yellow or white, forming in the early spring. The fruit is an elliptical, blue-black, fleshy drupe that ripens in the late summer through fall.
FOLIAGE: The simple, alternate leaves that are shiny and dark green in the summer, brilliant red in the fall. The leaves have smooth edges that are a little thicker than the rest of the leaf and range in length from 2–5 inches.

BARK: The bark is gray to dark brown or black with deeper fissures on older trunks.
CULTURE: Black gum is a beautiful tree that unfortunately can only grow in sandy acid soils such as those of east Texas. Don't even try to plant black gum in alkaline soils. It needs moist soil year round for best results and is relatively slow-growing.
PROBLEMS: It cannot grow in the black and white or other alkaline clay soils of the state.
PROPAGATION: It can be grown from seed, cuttings, or transplants. Seed needs to be sown immediately after collection in the fall or stratified for 30–60 days at about 40°F. Seed should be kept moist in storage and after planting. Seedlings will benefit from partial shade. Black gum can be propagated from cuttings, but it is not easy. Cuttings need to be taken in the late winter and kept under a mist system; percentage of success will be low. Transplanting is difficult because in sandy soil locations the root balls won't hold together. The best success will come from transplanting very small trees.
INSIGHT: *Nyssa sylvatica* also includes the **east Texas tupelo**. *Nyssa aquatica* is the **water tupelo** and *Nyssa sylvatica* var. *biflora* is the **swamp tupelo**. In the right conditions, all these trees can grow to an excess of 100 feet tall.

Black locust flowers.

Black Locust

COMMON NAMES: Black Locust, False Acacia, Bastard Acacia

BOTANICAL NAME: *Robinia pseudoacacia*

PRONUNCIATION: row-BIN-ee-ah SUE-doe-ah-KAY-see-ah

FAMILY: Fabaceae (Legume, Bean, or Pulse Family)

TYPE: Deciduous shade tree

HEIGHT: 40–50 feet

SPREAD: 40 feet

FINAL SPACING: 20–30 feet

NATURAL HABITAT AND PREFERRED SITE: Black locust is found in full sun, sandy roadsides, and fence rows but likes deep, well-drained calcarious (high calcium) soils. It is not native to Texas but has naturalized here quite well. Black locust is often seen in abandoned fields and old home sites. It is native to Georgia, Oklahoma, Arkansas, and northeast up to New York.

IDENTIFICATION: It is an upright and spreading tree with small, oval leaflets on large compound leaves that have yellow fall color. It is a fast-growing tree with fragrant, white flowers in the spring.

FLOWERS AND FRUIT: The flowers are fragrant and white in the late spring, from May to June. They are loose, hanging racemes, 4–5 inches or longer. The individual flowers are bonnet-shaped and about 1 inch long. The fruit is a legume that ripens in the fall. It is brown, flat, and of course bean-like since this plant is a legume. The seeds inside the pods are kidney-shaped.

FOLIAGE: The leaves are compound with small, oval leaflets that are yellow in the fall. The leaves are 8–14 inches long. There are 7–19 leaflets per leaf and the leaflets are ½–2 inches long.

BARK: The bark is a light gray to reddish brown, smooth when young but deeply ridged on mature trees. The trunk is sometimes twisted and has thorns that are paired or scattered individually. The twigs are zigzag in shape and very brittle.

CULTURE: Black locust grows fairly easily in most well-drained soils and requires a minimum amount of water and fertilizer.

PROBLEMS: Other than being short-lived, it has very few serious problems. It is susceptible to attack by locust borers and leaf miners, but both can be controlled with healthy soil and organic pest control.

Black locust tree in the spring.

PROPAGATION: It can be easily grown from seed. Seed germination can be increased by soaking the seed in hot water or liquid humate. Beds or pots should be kept moist but not wet. No mulch or shade is required. Damping off is somewhat of a problem, but it can be eliminated with the use of cornmeal in the potting soil.

INSIGHT: Once established black locust is very difficult to get rid of because of root sprouts. Its wood is one of the strongest and most durable in North America. The leaves close slightly at night, appearing to go to sleep. The inner bark, young leaves, and seeds are toxic to livestock and humans. Children have been poisoned by sucking fresh twigs or eating either the bark or seeds according to *Shinners & Mahler's Illustrated Flora of North Central Texas*. Black locust is a beautiful tree and should be more widely planted, particularly in small gardens and courtyards when flower color and fragrance are important and long life is not.

Bois d'Arc in the winter.

Bois d'Arc

COMMON NAMES: Bois d'Arc, Horse Apple, Osage Orange, Bow Wood, Hedge Apple, Bodark, Yellow Wood, Naranjo Chino

BOTANICAL NAME: *Maclura pomifera*

PRONUNCIATION: ma-CLUE-ra pom-IF-er-ah

FAMILY: Moraceae (Mulberry or Fig Family)

TYPE: Deciduous shade tree

HEIGHT: 40–60 feet

SPREAD: 40 feet

FINAL SPACING: Probably shouldn't plant in most cases.

NATURAL HABITAT AND PREFERRED SITE: Bois d'Arc needs full sun. It is native to Oklahoma, Louisiana, Missouri, and Texas and is plentiful throughout the Red River Valley. It favors stream bottoms and low areas and can become a weedy invader of disturbed land. Bois d'Arc is well-known for growing in fence rows and has been widely used as a windbreak plant because of its tendency to form thickets. Bois d'Arc does better in deep soils with more moisture than very shallow rocky soils offer. According to Simpson's *A Field Guide to Texas Trees*, it is difficult to tell where the plant is native because it has been planted in so many areas. Bois d'Arc reaches its largest size in the Red River and Trinity river valleys in northern Texas. It is definitely native to the great Blackland Prairies of Texas.

IDENTIFICATION: Male and female trees grow to about 50 feet in height and have strong spines on the stems. The leaves are bright green with yellow fall color. The fruit, which forms in the fall, is large, lime green, and wrinkled, 4–6 inches in diameter. It is called a horse apple. The horse apples form on the female plants only. You can often see Bois d'Arc leaning over in landscape situations because the root system has failed. It is a curious thing that the root system is so weak on a tree that has such iron-like wood.

FLOWERS AND FRUIT: The insignificant flowers form in the spring from April to June. The fruit is the large horse apple that looks a little bit like a lime green brain, 4–6 inches in diameter. It is loaded with juice that is milky and acidic.

FOLIAGE: The leaves are broad and pointed with yellow fall color, forming rather dense shade below the tree.

BARK: The bark is brown to orange—usually deeply furrowed with often interlacing, rounded ridges.

Bois d'Arc foliage and fruit in the summer.

CULTURE: Bois d'Arc is curious in that it grows very fast and easily, almost weed-like, but it is sometimes hard to keep healthy and alive in landscaping. Large chunks of the tree will often die, and borers frequently attack the iron-like wood, causing further problems. The root system seems shallow and not durable. It does not need very much water, although deep soils are much better than shallow rocky soils. It needs little to no fertilizer.

PROBLEMS: It is a very messy tree to have in a maintained garden. With its shallow root system, the Bois d'Arc will sometimes fall over in wet soils or high winds. Also, it is susceptible to borers and other related immune-system problems.

PROPAGATION: It is very easily grown from stem cuttings cut from branches or rather large limbs. It can also be grown from the fruit. The fruit is crushed, and the seed, after drying, is stratified by soaking in water for 30 days and then planted in the spring. According to Vines' *Trees, Shrubs, and Woody Vines of the Southwest,* a bushel of fruit will yield approximately 24,500 seeds weighing about 2 pounds, and if stored at 41°F, the seed will retain viability for 3 years or more.

INSIGHT: The Native American Osage Indians used Bois d'Arc to make war clubs and bows, hence the name. The invention of barbed wire reportedly came from someone seeing the thorns on the Bois d'Arc fence rows. The fruit, or horse apple, has historically been used to repel cockroaches and fleas. Horses actually do eat the fruit, which has caused some horses to die when it gets lodged in the animal's throat. Some people are allergic to the milky sap from the stems, leaves, and fruit and develop dermatitis. The foliage has been used to feed silkworms, and a yellow dye has been made from the root bark. The bark of the trunk has been used for tanning leather. In landscape situations Bois d'Arc generally should be removed to favor more desirable plants. The bright orange wood is often used for fence posts and construction material because it takes forever to rot.

Box elder.

Box Elder

COMMON NAMES: Box Elder, Ash-Leaf Maple, Arse, Fresno De Guajuco, Box-Elder Maple

BOTANICAL NAME: *Acer negundo*

PRONUNCIATION: A-sir nay-GOON-dough

FAMILY: Aceraceae (Maple Family)

TYPE: Deciduous shade tree

HEIGHT: 40–50 feet, up to 75 feet

SPREAD: 40–50 feet

FINAL SPACING: Do not plant too many, but it is a tree that I normally leave if existing on-site.

NATURAL HABITAT AND PREFERRED SITE: Native to Texas and Oklahoma and several other southern states northward to Canada, it seems to grow very well in most any soil and naturalizes easily but does prefer plenty of water.

IDENTIFICATION: Box elder differs from other maples by having 3–5 leaflets. It has yellow fall color.

FLOWERS AND FRUIT: Small, green flowers bloom in the spring before the leaves emerge. The fruits are double samaras (winged seeds) ripening from August through October, generally in drooping clusters, 6–8 inches long. The winged seeds are reddish brown, ½ inch long, and V-shaped.

FOLIAGE: The new growth is olive green and the mature foliage is bright pea green. It looks similar to poison ivy, but the box elder has opposite leaves instead of alternate leaves as poison ivy does. The leaves are 6–15 inches long and compound with usually 3–7 leaflets.

BARK: The bark is green and smooth when young. It later turns a pale gray to brown, dividing into narrow, rounded ridges with short scales and shallow fissures with age.

CULTURE: Box elder is easy to grow in a wide range of soils if moisture is available.

PROBLEMS: It is susceptible to dry conditions, insects, and heart rot. It also attracts the box elder bug, which is more of a nuisance than a serious problem.

PROPAGATION: It grows easily from seed after soaking in water. Seed should be planted in the spring and will germinate very quickly. Partial shade is helpful for the young seedlings.

INSIGHT: This is the most common maple growing wild in Texas. The beautiful, red and black box elder bug loves this tree but can be an irritation, although it does very little damage to the tree or any of the rest of your property.

Mexican buckeye.

Buckeye, Mexican

COMMON NAMES: Mexican Buckeye, Texas Buckeye, Monilla

BOTANICAL NAME: *Ungnaidia speciosa*

PRONUNCIATION: oong-NAD-ee-ah spee-see-OH-sa

FAMILY: Sapindaceae (Soapberry Family)

TYPE: Deciduous small tree

HEIGHT: 20 feet

SPREAD: 20 feet

FINAL SPACING: 10–20 feet

NATURAL HABITAT AND PREFERRED SITE: It grows wild on mountain slopes and in canyons across the Trans-Pecos as well as in central Texas, including as far north as Harris, Tarrant, and Dallas counties. Mexican buckeye grows well in limestone outcroppings but will adapt to normal garden soil in sun or shade. It primarily should be used as an understory tree. I have found it growing out of cracks in the solid granite at Enchanted Rock near Fredericksburg. It seems to grow the best west of the Brazos River and actually prefers alkaline soils.

IDENTIFICATION: Mexican buckeye is a shrub or small tree that can grow multi-trunked or single-stemmed. It normally has an irregular overall shape. It has purple flowers in the spring that bloom just after the redbud trees bloom. The flowers come out just before the foliage or as the immature foliage starts to emerge. It has brilliant yellow fall color and decorative three-compartment seed pods on its bare branches in the winter.

FLOWERS AND FRUIT: The flowers appear as the leaves emerge in the spring or just before. It has

Mexican buckeye growing out of solid granite at Enchanted Rock near Fredericksburg.

Mexican buckeye in spring bloom.

small, fragrant flowers that are often mistaken for the redbud, which blooms earlier in the spring. The flowers range in color from pink to purple and appear in closely attached clusters. The seeds are round, shiny black, and hard. The plant usually flowers in its third season.

FOLIAGE: It looks a little bit like the pecan, having compound leaves, 5–12 inches long, with 5–7 leaflets. Mexican buckeye has one of the most brilliant yellow fall color displays of all the trees that will grow in Texas.

BARK: The bark is very thin and light gray. It can be easily damaged by maintenance equipment. With age it becomes mottled gray to brown and develops shallow fissures.

CULTURE: Mexican buckeye is very easy to grow in sun or shade in any well-drained soil. It has slow to moderate growth and needs very little water and fertilizer. Although drought tolerant, it can also stand moist soils.

PROBLEMS: It has very few problems, if any at all. It is an ornamental tree that should be used much more. I guess the fact that the seeds are reported to be poisonous is a possible problem. The leaves and fruit have been reported to cause mild poisoning of livestock but are seldom browsed unless they are the only foliage around.

PROPAGATION: The shiny black seed can be harvested beginning in late the summer through October, when the capsules turn a dark reddish brown and crack open. After a short drying period, the seed can be planted into moist soil and will germinate within 3 weeks without any pretreatment. Seed will germinate best in warm soil. I have not had much luck at this point growing Mexican buckeye from cuttings.

INSIGHT: Mexican buckeye is not a member of the true buckeye family. Bees make an excellent honey from the flowers.

Mexican buckeye fall color.

Mexican buckeye fruit.

Scarlet buckeye in the Lakewood area of Dallas, growing in black and white soils.

Scarlet buckeye.

Buckeye, Scarlet

COMMON NAMES: Scarlet Buckeye, Red Buckeye, Firecracker Plant

BOTANICAL NAME: *Aesculus pavia* var. *pavia*

PRONUNCIATION: ESS-kah-lus PA-via

FAMILY: Hippocastanaceae (Buckeye Family)

TYPE: Deciduous ornamental tree

HEIGHT: 15–30 feet

SPREAD: 10–15 feet

FINAL SPACING: 8–15 feet

NATURAL HABITAT AND PREFERRED SITE: Scarlet buckeye is a large shrub or small tree usually growing as an understory tree in forests or thickets along streams in east and central Texas. It shows up in the acid soils of the Piney Woods and is found growing as far west as the Edwards Plateau. At home, grow it as an understory plant in well-prepared soil with filtered morning sun and afternoon shade.

IDENTIFICATION: Scarlet buckeye is a beautiful little tree that has compound leaves with 5 leaflets and bright red flowers in the early to late spring. The plant generally goes dormant and loses its leaves in midsummer. The defoliation seems to be less severe in partially shaded conditions.

FLOWERS AND FRUIT: The flowers form in the spring—usually March to May—in showy, red clusters. The fruit is a 1–2-inch capsule, light brown with 1–3 flattened or rounded seeds inside.

FOLIAGE: The leaves are compound and deciduous, usually with 5 leaflets but sometimes having only 3. The leaves commonly drop in midsummer during a dormant season caused by the heat. This leaf drop is also reported to be partly due to disease.

BARK: The bark is light gray to brown, very smooth on young branches, but older trunks will roughen and become flaky.

CULTURE: Scarlet buckeye is fairly easy to grow in well-prepared soil in morning sun or filtered light and requires a moderate amount of water and low amounts of fertilizer. The premature summer drop of foliage can possibly be eliminated with an intensely maintained organic program and the use of horticultural cornmeal.

PROBLEMS: Premature summer drop of foliage and foliage burn in full sun situations are the main problems. If the leaf drop is due to disease organisms, cornmeal will reduce or eliminate the problem.

PROPAGATION: Scarlet buckeyes germinate easily from fresh untreated seed. Roots will sometimes emerge from seed while in storage. There's no need for any pretreatment. Seed should be planted immediately after collection and will germinate in 3–30 days. The first season or two will be spent developing root systems, so don't expect to see much topical growth. I have a small scarlet buckeye in my front garden that is not yet 18 inches tall. It was planted four years ago. Scarlet buckeyes can also be grown from root cuttings taken in the late winter just before the new growth emerges. This is also a time to try stem cuttings. Keep them in moist potting soil and in a very humid environment.

INSIGHT: Scarlet buckeye is a very beautiful small tree that should be used more.

Texas buckeye at Enchanted Rock near Fredericksburg.

Buckeye, Texas

COMMON NAMES: Texas Buckeye, White Buckeye
BOTANICAL NAME: *Aesculus glabra*
PRONUNCIATION: ESS-kah-lus GLA-bra
FAMILY: Hippocastanaceae (Buckeye Family)
TYPE: Deciduous ornamental tree
HEIGHT: 20–40 feet
SPREAD: 10–20 feet
FINAL SPACING: 10–15 feet
NATURAL HABITAT AND PREFERRED SITE: Texas buckeye likes the hard granite sands of the Edwards Plateau, although it will also grow in deep soils from sand to heavy clays. It can grow in sun and part shade, but the best location is morning sun with afternoon shade.
IDENTIFICATION: Texas buckeye has an upright form with large compound leaves that almost completely defoliate in midsummer because of the heat and so-called fungal diseases.
FLOWERS AND FRUIT: The flowers are off-white to light yellow in terminal clusters, which appear after the leaves unfurl. The round, hairy, or warted fruit appears in the early summer. It often looks like a leathery capsule with blunt spines and contains 1–3 large, shiny seeds.
FOLIAGE: The large compound leaves have 7–9 leaflets and occasionally as many as 11. Fall color is yellow, with the leaves often turning in midsummer when the heat and/or fungal diseases defoliate the plant.

BARK: The bark is gray to black with narrow fissures.
CULTURE: Texas buckeye is easy to grow and should be used more often. It grows well in moderately prepared garden soil or in most native soils throughout Texas—other than in areas of high rainfall.
PROBLEMS: Summer defoliation is a problem. Regular waterings during the hot and dry part of the summer will normally help to prevent the defoliation.
PROPAGATION: Texas buckeyes germinate easily from fresh untreated seed. Roots will sometimes emerge from seed while in storage. There is no need for any pretreatment of seed. Plant immediately after collection. Seed will germinate any time from 3 days to 30 days. The first season or two will be spent developing root systems. Texas buckeyes can also be grown from root cuttings taken in the late winter just before new growth emerges. This is also a time to try stem cuttings, kept in moist potting soil and a humid environment.
INSIGHT: Most publications say that all parts of the plant are probably poisonous, but livestock will only graze on the young buds and foliage, generally ignoring the older growth, which is the most toxic. **Ohio buckeye** (*Aesculus glabra* var. *glabra*) is said to be not well-adapted for Texas, but there is a beautiful specimen growing in the Fort Worth Botanical Garden as you can see from the photo. It can be identified by its having fewer leaflets—usually 5. There are also some growing in east Texas.

Ohio buckeye at the Fort Worth Botanical Gardens.

Camphor tree in San Antonio.

Camphor tree.

Camphor Tree

COMMON NAMES: Camphor Tree, Camphor
BOTANICAL NAME: *Cinnamomum camphora*
PRONUNCIATION: sin-ah-MO-mum cam-FORE-rah
FAMILY: Lauraceae (Laurel Family)
TYPE: Evergreen shade tree
HEIGHT: 40–50 feet
SPREAD: 20–30 feet
FINAL SPACING: 20–40 feet
NATURAL HABITAT AND PREFERRED SITE: Native to Asia but thriving in California and the southern states, camphor tree does well in Texas from San Antonio and on south. It prefers deep, healthy soil. Camphor tree has naturalized in southeast Texas.
IDENTIFICATION: Camphor tree is a very beautiful, narrow, upright tree with shiny, fragrant leaves that smell of camphor.
FLOWERS AND FRUIT: Clusters of small, fragrant, white flowers bloom in the late spring, followed by small, black fruits.

FOLIAGE: The leaves are ficus tree-like and shiny. They have a drooping effect all the time but are very beautiful. The leaves are very fragrant and bright green.
BARK: The bark is smooth and gray, developing a heavier texture with age.
CULTURE: Camphor tree is easy to grow in the warm climates of Texas. When planted north of San Antonio, it needs protection in winter. It always needs excellent drainage.
PROBLEMS: It is susceptible to freeze damage in the northern two-thirds of Texas. Roots are very competitive. Root rot is also a possibility but not nearly as much of a problem when the plant is grown under an organic program.
PROPAGATION: It can be grown from seed or stem cuttings taken in the very late winter prior to bud break.
INSIGHT: The wood is used in cabinetwork in Asia. Camphor is produced by distilling the wood. Many of the camphor trees are multi-trunked and very interesting in the landscape.

Carolina buckthorn in the fall.

Carolina buckthorn in the late summer.

Carolina Buckthorn

COMMON NAMES: Carolina Buckthorn, Indian Cherry, Yellow Buckthorn, Yellow Wood

BOTANICAL NAME: *Rhamnus caroliniana*

PRONUNCIATION: RAM-nus care-oh-lin-ee-AN-ah

FAMILY: Rhamnaceae (Buckthorn Family)

TYPE: Deciduous large shrub or small tree

HEIGHT: 15–20 feet

SPREAD: 12–15 feet

FINAL SPACING: 4–10 feet

NATURAL HABITAT AND PREFERRED SITE: Carolina buckthorn likes growing in the bottomlands and lowlands of east, southeast, and south central Texas as far west as the Pecos River. It seems to do well in either acid or alkaline soil in full sun, partial shade, or even fairly heavy shade. Carolina buckthorn has been found in all of the woody areas of Texas. It adapts easily in the landscape to sandy or clay soils.

IDENTIFICATION: Carolina buckthorn is a bushy shrub or small tree with large, glossy leaves and yellow to orange fall color. It has decorative berries in the late summer through fall.

FLOWERS AND FRUIT: The flowers are small and inconspicuous, blooming in the late spring to early summer—usually May to June. The fruits are red berries that form in the late summer, ripening to blue-black in the fall and winter. Each fruit contains 2 seeds about ¼ inch long.

FOLIAGE: The large leaves are simple and alternate, scattered along the branches. Their length will vary from 2–6 inches. They are medium green in the summer. Fall color ranges from yellow to orange.

BARK: The bark is gray-brown, sometimes black. It is usually smooth but develops shallow furrows with age.

CULTURE: Carolina buckthorn is easy to grow and seems to adapt to most conditions except for extremely wet soils. It does very well in rocky calcarious soils and is quite drought tolerant. It needs very little fertilizer and responds well to the organic program.

PROBLEMS: Very few, if any, problems exist unless the plant is completely over watered or never watered when planted in full sun.

PROPAGATION: Carolina buckthorn can be grown from seed or cuttings. Fresh seed can be planted without any pretreatment. Stored seed should be kept at approximately 41°F for about 30 days. Germination normally happens in about 5 weeks. Seedlings are rapid-growing. Semi-hardwood cuttings taken in midsummer through the fall root fairly well. Cuttings should be 6–8 inches long and kept under a mist system or in a humid environment. As with all cuttings, the lower half of the leaves should be removed. Rooting will normally happen within 5 weeks. Another time to take the cuttings is in the late winter just before bud break.

INSIGHT: The fruit is attractive to several bird species. The leaves and bark are browsed by deer. Carolina buckthorn is an ornamental-sized tree that should be used considerably more.

Catalpa.

Catalpa in the winter with seed pods.

Catalpa

COMMON NAMES: Catalpa, Cigar-tree, Bean-Tree, Catawba, Indian-Bean, Western Catalpa, Shawnee-Wood, Hardy Catalpa, Smoking-Bean, Bois-Plant, Northern Catalpa

BOTANICAL NAME: *Catalpa speciosa*

PRONUNCIATION: kuh-TALL-puh spee-see-OH-suh

FAMILY: Bignoniaceae (Catalpa or Trumpet Vine Family)

TYPE: Deciduous shade tree

HEIGHT: 50–90 feet

SPREAD: 40–50 feet

FINAL SPACING: 30–40 feet

NATURAL HABITAT AND PREFERRED SITE: Catalpa is native to the deep, moist, rich soils of east Texas but grows easily in a wide range of soils from sand to clay. It needs moderate moisture. Catalpa is found in damp woods along the edges of swamps and streams and has been used quite extensively in landscaping. My recommendation for its best use is in parks and golf courses where it can be viewed from a distance.

IDENTIFICATION: Catalpa is a very stately tree with extremely large leaves, showy flowers in the early summer, and dramatic, long, cigar-like seed pods in the fall and winter.

FLOWERS AND FRUIT: Showy, orchid-like flowers bloom in the late spring, usually from May to June or sometimes starting earlier. The flowers are bell-shaped and about 2 inches in length. Their color is white to lavender on the outside with two yellow stripes inside the throat and sometimes pale, purplish blotches on the edges. The fruits are cylindrical, cigar-like capsules up to 18 inches in length containing papery-thin seeds that are $\frac{1}{6}$ inch long.

FOLIAGE: The leaves of catalpa are large, dramatic, papery thin, and heart-shaped. They get ragged looking by the end of the growing season from wind and/or insect damage. The leaves can be 6–12 inches long and 4–8 inches wide, and they have a yellow fall color.

BARK: The bark is smooth and dark gray to brown or sometimes reddish. The surface is broken into long, irregular fissures with flat top ridges.

CULTURE: Catalpa is easy to grow in most any soil. It needs moderate amounts of water and little fertilizer. It is a tree for full sun. Catalpa is a relatively fast-growing tree but has a relatively short life.

PROBLEMS: The plant is regularly attacked by the beautiful, black and white catalpa sphinx (catalpa worm), which is used for brim and/or perch fishing especially in east Texas. The ragged leaves in the late summer are somewhat of a cosmetic problem. Catalpa's biggest problem is that it is so maligned by horticultural educators. I was taught at Texas Tech that it is the most terrible, lousy, crummy, awful tree on earth and that all of them should be cut down. I don't agree with that. I very much enjoyed the catalpas that were in my parent's yard in Pittsburg, Texas, where I grew up. They are one

Catalpa with summer flowers.

Chitalpa.

Chitalpa foliage and flowers.

of the best climbing trees around because of the sparse limbs and smooth bark. Leaf blight can sometimes attack the tree, causing the leaves to suddenly blacken and die.

PROPAGATION: Collect the fruits after they have turned brown and begun to dry. Crush them inside a bag and retrieve the seed. Plant the seed outdoors in the spring after the last frost date. Good seed crops are borne only every 2–3 years after the tree is 20 years old. There is some indication that germination is increased by leaving the seed capsules on the tree until February. Seed can be stored for some period of time at 50°F. Catalpa can be rooted from hardwood cuttings taken in the late summer. Root cuttings can be successful when taken in December.

INSIGHT: **Southern catalpa** (*Catalpa bignonioides*) is often confused with the northern species. They are very similar plants. **Chitalpa** is a smaller deciduous hybrid that is a cross between the desert willow and catalpa. It has long narrow leaves, 6–8 inches long and 1–2 inches wide, and pink or white catalpa-like flowers that bloom all summer. It is somewhat susceptible to root rot, so extremely well-drained soil is important. Dr. Carl Whitcomb thinks that this tree is simply a sport of desert willow. He may be right.

Young eastern red cedar.

Mature eastern red cedar.

Cedar

COMMON NAMES: Mountain Cedar—Ashe Juniper, Mountain Cedar, Rock Cedar, Post Cedar, Mexican Juniper, Break Cedar, Texas Cedar, Sabino, Enebro

Eastern Red Cedar—Red Cedar, Pencil Cedar, Virginia Juniper, Red Juniper, Carolina Cedar, Baton Rouge (Red Stick), Red Savin, Virginia Red Cedar

Red Berry Juniper—Texas Juniper, Christmas Berry Juniper, Pinchot's Juniper, Redberry Cedar

BOTANICAL NAME: *Juniperus* spp.

Mountain cedar—*Juniperus ashei*

Eastern red cedar—*Juniperus virginiana*

Red berry juniper—*Juniperus pinchottii*

PRONUNCIATION: jew-NIP-er-is

FAMILY: Cupressaceae (Cypress or Redwood Family)

TYPE: Evergreen tree

HEIGHT: Eastern red cedar grows 40–60 feet. Red and ashe junipers grow to approximately 20 feet.

SPREAD: 15–20 feet

FINAL SPACING: 20–40 feet

NATURAL HABITAT AND PREFERRED SITE: All three of these native junipers prefer the rocky, alkaline limestone soils but adapt well to deeper, more healthy soils and landscape situations. They all need full sun and all three are able to take low water situations. Ashe juniper is thicket-forming and creates cedar "brakes."

IDENTIFICATION INFORMATION: Ashe juniper is more spreading than the other two junipers and usually has a candelabra-like or multi-trunked structure. It also has stiffer twigs and more fragrant foliage. Red berry juniper also has multiple trunks from the base. Eastern red cedar usually has one main trunk. Red berry and ashe juniper are more rounded and bushy from youth to maturity. The eastern red cedar tends to be Christmas tree-shaped when young and then spreads into a more typical shade tree structure with maturity. Red berry juniper tends to be more slender and erect than ashe juniper, although it is quite similar.

FLOWERS AND FRUIT: Cedars have small, unimpressive flowers in the spring, followed by small, blue/purple berries in the fall on female plants. Red berry juniper has reddish or coppery brown fruit. Eastern red cedar and ashe juniper have blue fruit. Male and female flowers are on different plants (dioecious). The catkins on male plants are small. The female cones are rounded and very tight. The fruit ripens in the fall. The cones are berry-like and

Eastern red cedar branching structure.

Male eastern red cedar.

Female eastern red cedar.

pale blue, sweet and resinous. Fruit from all the junipers is eaten by many species of wildlife.

FOLIAGE: All three have the same dense evergreen foliage. Leaves are scale-like.

BARK: The bark is light reddish brown and separates into long, fibrous, shaggy strips.

CULTURE: Native cedars are easy to grow in most well-drained soils, but they do best in the black and white soils. They need excellent drainage but little water and fertilizer.

PROBLEMS: Eastern red cedar is a host tree for cedar apple rust.

PROPAGATION: Cedar can be easily grown from seed. The small cones can be gathered in the fall. They don't need any special treatment and should be planted in the fall.

Red berry juniper. (Photo by Andy Wasowski.)

Ashe juniper branching.

Ashe juniper or mountain cedar

INSIGHT: Eastern red cedar does not resprout after cutting or burning. Ashe juniper is harder to eliminate by fire and cutting down. It has had a more significant negative impact on ranchland in Texas than the other two species. All the junipers, but especially ashe juniper, have occupied the steep hillsides in canyons where they are protected from fires. Wood from these trees is used to make cedar chests and cedar-lined closets because of its insect-repelling quality. The narrow strips of bark from ashe juniper are a primary nesting material for the golden-cheeked warbler. Eastern red cedar is excellent fence post material, and ashe juniper is resistant to the cedar apple rust. Ashe juniper, however, creates the biggest cedar allergy problem because of the pollen produced by male trees in the winter months. **Alligator juniper** (*Juniperus deppeana*) grows at high altitudes and is easily identified by its rough-textured, checkered bark. It is a very long-lived tree that resprouts from stumps like ashe juniper. **Drooping juniper** (*J. haccida*) is a graceful juniper with drooping branches that create an almost wilted appearance. It grows in Big Bend. **One-seed juniper** (*J. monosperma*) is a multi-trunked juniper that grows on the northern plains and in the Trans-Pecos. It is similar to ashe juniper but has smaller, blue-black to rust female cones or berries.

Incense cedar.

Incense cedar.

Cedar, Incense

COMMON NAMES: Incense Cedar, California Incense Cedar

BOTANICAL NAME: *Calocedrus decurrens*

PRONUNCIATION: cal-oh-SEED-rus day-KER-enz

FAMILY: Cupressaceae (Cypress or Redwood Family)

TYPE: Evergreen tree

HEIGHT: 70–90 feet

SPREAD: 20–30 feet

FINAL SPACING: 15–30 feet

NATURAL HABITAT AND PREFERRED SITE: Incense cedar is native to Asia but has been used extensively in California. The specimens I know of exist in the black soil of Garland and in east Dallas. The tree has also been planted on the Plano campus of Collin County Community College.

IDENTIFICATION: An upright evergreen tree with arborvitae-like foliage, it is tall-growing, symmetrical, and straight-trunked. The foliage is very dark green and dense.

FLOWERS AND FRUIT: Male and female cones form on the same tree (monoecious). There are two winged seeds per scale (the protruding piece of the cone). The larger wing is nearly as long as the scale. The small, brown cones look like ducks' bills when opened.

FOLIAGE: The leaves are very dark green and similar in appearance to arborvitae.

BARK: The reddish brown bark is relatively smooth on younger trees but develops very deep fissures—very redwood-like—with maturity.

CULTURE: Incense cedar seems to be adapted to a wide variety of soils, although very few plants have been attempted at this point in Texas.

PROBLEMS: Finding the tree in the nursery trade is difficult, and root rot diseases can develop during establishment when the plant is over watered and over fertilized.

PROPAGATION: It can be grown from seed and stem cuttings under mist.

INSIGHT: 'Compacta' is a dwarf compact form. Incense cedar gives off a very pleasant fragrance in the summer. It makes a beautiful single specimen or can be planted closely together to form a windbreak or tall screen. As soon as we can increase the availability of this plant, it should be used more often in Texas. *Libocedrus* is the old genus name. You can tell from these photographs that the plant does very well here in our alkaline soils.

Cherry, Black

COMMON NAMES: Black Cherry, Wild Cherry, Wild Black Cherry, Choke Cherry, Rum Cherry

BOTANICAL NAME: *Prunus serotina*

PRONUNCIATION: PROO-nus ser-oh-TEN-ah

FAMILY: Rosaceae (Rose Family)

TYPE: Deciduous tree

HEIGHT: 25–50 feet. It has been reported to grow to as much as 100 feet in the deep, acid sandy soils of east Texas.

SPREAD: 25–30 feet

FINAL SPACING: 25–30 feet

NATURAL HABITAT AND PREFERRED SITE: It grows in far east Texas, the Hill Country, and the Trans-Pecos in west Texas. It is commonly found in full sun in fence rows, thickets, and on the edges of woods. Black cherry can grow in sandy to rocky alkaline soils.

IDENTIFICATION: Black cherry is a medium-sized tree, capable of growing to a great height, but it normally stays under 50 feet. It develops a narrow crown with a single, slender trunk with open branching and has beautiful, shiny foliage.

FLOWERS AND FRUIT: Blooms form in the spring as the leaves emerge, usually around March. The flowers are pure white and about ¼ inch in diameter with 5 petals. The thick-skinned fruits (drupes) ripen from June to October. They are black when mature, but all shades of cherries will be present on the tree at the same time—black, red, and green—sometimes within the same cluster.

BARK: The bark is a reddish brown to gray, smooth when young but becoming more heavily textured with age.

FOLIAGE: The leaves are simple, alternate, and deciduous. It has yellow fall color—sometimes spectacular.

CULTURE: Black cherry can grow with minimal maintenance in a wide range of soils.

PROBLEMS: The thin bark is easily damaged by fire. Tent caterpillars sometimes attack, and black knot fungal galls sometimes disfigure limbs.

PROPAGATION: Seed germinates best after stratification at 41°F for 30–60 days (or even longer) prior to planting in the spring. The tree can also be grown from semi-hardwood and softwood cuttings taken in the summer. Another method is to soak the seed

Black cherry.

in vinegar for a short period of time (30 minutes to 1 hour) before planting. Seed will also germinate easier after passing through the digestive system of some animals.

INSIGHT: The **escarpment black cherry** (*Prunus serotina* var. *eximia*) is found primarily in the Hill Country area of central Texas. **Southwestern black cherry** (*P. s.* var. *rufula*) is found in the Trans-Pecos and far west Texas. It occurs in deep canyons and protected bottomlands. Black cherry makes a fine landscape tree and should be used more. Herbalists recommend cherries and cherry juice for intestinal cleaning. Black cherry is an important food source for wildlife.

Cherry laurel.

Cherry Laurel

COMMON NAMES: Cherry Laurel, Carolina Cherry Laurel, Carolina Cherry, Wild Peach

BOTANICAL NAME: *Prunus caroliniana*

PRONUNCIATION: PROO-nus ka-ro-lin-ee-AY-nah

FAMILY: Rosaceae (Rose Family)

TYPE: Evergreen tree

HEIGHT: 25–40 feet

SPREAD: 15–20 feet

FINAL SPACING: 8–20 feet

NATURAL HABITAT AND PREFERRED SITE: It likes the well-drained, moist soils of east Texas but will adapt to a wide range of soils in full sun to light shade. Cherry laurel prefers acid soil and will sometimes develop chlorosis in alkaline soils.

IDENTIFICATION: Cherry laurel is an evergreen tree with shiny, smooth evergreen leaves. Small, off-white flowers bloom in the spring followed by black fruit.

FLOWERS AND FRUIT: Fragrant, white flowers form in short racemes in the spring. Black fruit develops into the fall and lasts usually into the winter. The fruit is eaten by birds but is reported to be poisonous to livestock, especially during a drought or after the first frost of the year when the plant is stressed. The fruits (drupes) are oval and approximately ½ inch long.

FOLIAGE: The leaves are alternate, simple, and smooth, 2–4½ inches long.

BARK: The bark is gray, thin, and smooth when young but develops roughness and blotches with age.

CULTURE: Cherry laurel is relatively easy to grow in most soils, although it will tend to become chlorotic in alkaline soils. That problem can usually be eliminated with the use of Texas greensand or the overall Sick Tree Treatment (see Appendix 3). It needs moderate moisture with good drainage. It responds well to moderate fertilizing.

PROBLEMS: Cherry laurel is highly susceptible to cotton root rot and ice storm damage, so it is not a good idea to invest a lot of the landscape budget in this tree in the northern part of the state. Other occasional pests include borers and crown gall. It is a relatively short-lived tree and not highly recommended for use anywhere in Texas.

PROPAGATION: It can be grown from seed harvested in the late fall or from stem cuttings taken in the late winter and kept under mist.

INSIGHT: Improved hybrids on the market seem to perform fairly well here in Texas.

Chinaberry in bloom.

Chinaberry foliage and fruit in the late summer.

Chinaberry

COMMON NAMES: Chinaberry, Umbrella Tree, China Tree, Bead Tree, Pride-of-India, White Cedar, Ceylon Mahogany, Indian Lilac

BOTANICAL NAME: *Melia azedarach*

PRONUNCIATION: ME-lee-ah ah-ZED-ah-rak

FAMILY: Meliaceae (Mahogany Family)

TYPE: Deciduous tree

HEIGHT: 30–50 feet

SPREAD: 20–30 feet

FINAL SPACING: 15–30 feet

NATURAL HABITAT AND PREFERRED SITE: Chinaberry is a native of Asia and, after being introduced here, escaped to grow wild all over Texas. It has now naturalized in flood plains, forests, thickets, and forest margins.

IDENTIFICATION: Chinaberry is a fast-growing tree with delicate, dark green foliage and strongly fragrant, lilac flowers in the spring.

FLOWERS AND FRUIT: Clusters of fragrant, lavender flowers bloom in the late spring or early summer, generally from March to May. The fruit ripens in the fall, generally from September to October, to ¾ inch in diameter. The fruit is smooth, yellow, translucent, and fleshy. There are 3–5 smooth, black seeds in each fruit.

FOLIAGE: The leaves are large, deciduous, and twice compound. They have an overall lacy look with yellow fall color.

BARK: The thin, reddish brown bark tends to form strips and become more heavily textured with age.

CULTURE: Chinaberry is considered a fast-growing junk tree by many. I like it, although it does not live a long time. It should not be used as a major tree in the landscape. It needs moderate soil moisture.

PROBLEMS: Fast growth, short life, and brittle wood are the main problems. It sometimes produces suckers from the ground. Wind damage is also a concern.

PROPAGATION: It is easy to grow from seed. Fruit is collected in the fall, and the seed can be planted immediately after removing the pulp, or it can be dry stored for at least 1 year. Store in glass after treating with natural diatomaceous earth to remove moisture. Chinaberry can also be propagated by root suckers and stem cuttings.

INSIGHT: A rancher friend of mine reports that during a summer of heavy grasshopper infestation, he found beneath chinaberry trees large numbers of dead grasshoppers, which apparently had fed on the foliage. Chinaberry is very close kin to the **neem tree** (*Azadirachta indica*) and appears to have some of the same insecticidal and disease-control qualities.

Chittamwood.

Chittamwood foliage and blooms.

Chittamwood

COMMON NAMES: Chittamwood, Gum Elastic, Wooly Bumilia, Gum Bumilia, Woolybucket Bumilia, Woolybuckthorn, Gum Woolybucket, False Buckthorn, Ironwood, Coma

BOTANICAL NAME: *Sideroxylon langinosum* (syn. *Bumelia lanuginosa*)

PRONUNCIATION: sy-der-OX-eh-lon lan-gee-NO-sum

FAMILY: Sapotaceae (Chicle, Sapote, or Sapodilla Family)

TYPE: Semi-evergreen to deciduous tree

HEIGHT: 50–60 feet

SPREAD: 30–40 feet

FINAL SPACING: 20–40 feet

NATURAL HABITAT AND PREFERRED SITE: Chittamwood grows in full sun in all of Texas except for the High Plains and is tolerant of a wide range of soils.

IDENTIFICATION: Chittamwood is an upright tree that looks similar to a live oak. It has generally an irregular shape with stiff, spiny branches, clusters of leaves, and dark fruit in the fall. It sometimes forms thickets.

FLOWERS AND FRUIT: The flowers are fragrant, small, and off-white to yellow and bloom primarily from June to July. They are ¼–½ inch across. The fruit is a fleshy, black, lustrous drupe that matures from September through October. Each fruit contains 1 seed, which is brown and rounded.

FOLIAGE: The leaves are clustered, similar to live oak tree foliage. They are smooth on the top but hairy beneath, which gives a white, gray, or tan color to the underside of the leaf. The leaves are almost evergreen,

and they will sometimes stay on the tree for more than one season. Chittamwood is fully evergreen in the southern part of the state. But in the northern part of the state, the tree turns yellow in the fall.

BARK: The bark is dark brown to gray and fissured into narrow ridges. Heavy texture develops with age.

CULTURE: It is relatively easy to grow in most soils with normal amounts of water and fertilizer. Considered fairly drought tolerant, it is a relatively slow-growing tree with a deep taproot that provides the drought tolerance. It adapts well to most landscape conditions.

PROBLEMS: Borers will attack the tree when it is in stress from too much or too little water, compaction, or over fertilization. The Sick Tree Treatment (see Appendix 3) is the solution. Some people consider the thorns a problem.

PROPAGATION: Fruit can be gathered in the early fall at maturity and either air dried or macerated in water. Some recommend soaking the fruit in vinegar for 2 hours and then washing it with water to help speed up germination. Sometimes the seed is stratified in moist sand or peat at 41°F for 30–60 days in the fall prior to a spring planting. Chittamwood can also be propagated from softwood cuttings.

INSIGHT: The flowers are fragrant and are popular with honeybees. The fruit is edible, and birds are fond of it. The wood is used to make tool handles and in cabinetmaking. It is hard and heavy but brittle and sometimes weak. Children of early pioneers chewed the sap of the chittamwood.

Hardy or trifoliate orange.

Citrus

COMMON NAMES: Orange, Grapefruit, Lemon, Lime, Tangerine, Tangelo, Kumquat

BOTANICAL NAME: *Citrus* spp.

PRONUNCIATION: SIT-rus

FAMILY: Rutaceae (Citrus or Rue Family)

TYPE: Tropical evergreen tree

HEIGHT: 5–20 feet (varies greatly)

SPREAD: 5–20 feet (varies greatly)

FINAL SPACING: 8–20 feet (varies greatly)

NATURAL HABITAT AND PREFERRED SITE: Citrus is tropical, can only be grown in the Rio Grande Valley in the southern tip of Texas, and prefers deep sandy loam soil. Citrus grows best in a well-drained, slightly acidic sandy loam soil. It can tolerate sand or clay soils if the drainage is good. If grown anywhere other than the southern tip of Texas, citrus needs to be grown in containers or very carefully protected from winter freezes. Citrus will produce 4 or 5 blushes of new growth a season, but in Texas it will only flower and bear fruit on the spring bloom.

IDENTIFICATION: This small evergreen tree has glossy foliage, fragrant flowers, and colorful summer fruit.

FLOWERS AND FRUIT: Small, fragrant, white flowers bloom in the spring, followed by decorative and delicious fruit. The flowers are edible and can be used in herb teas.

FOLIAGE: The leaves are evergreen and glossy. They can be used in herb teas.

BARK: The bark is gray to brown and relatively smooth.

CULTURE: Except in the southern tip of the state, citrus needs to be grown in containers. Plant all citrus high in the soil with the graft union above the soil line. Citrus needs very little to no pruning. Citrus matures in 4–5 years. It is a tropical tree.

PROBLEMS: Citrus is susceptible to freeze damage in all but the southern tip of the state. Root knot nematodes can be easily controlled with orange rinds ground into a pulp and worked into the soil.

PROPAGATION: Citrus can be grown easily from seed, but the fruit will not necessarily come true. The best time for stem cuttings to be made is at the end of the winter just before the emergence of new leaves. Seed or stem cuttings can be planted anytime as long as they are protected from freezing weather. Best results come from planting in warm soil and warm weather in the spring.

Tangerine.

INSIGHT: All of the citrus species can be grown in the Rio Grande Valley and the most southern part of the state, but even there some winters can be damaging. **Satsuma orange** (a mandarin) is the most commonly recommended and supposedly the most cold tolerant of all the citrus, but even it still needs winter protection in most of the state. **Trifoliate** or **hardy orange** (*Poncirus trifoliata*) is a deciduous tree that will grow all over the state in full sun to a height of 15 feet. It has fragrant spring flowers and a hard, bitter, inedible, yellow-orange fruit. It can be propagated easily from cuttings or seed, and it is easy to grow to form an impenetrable hedge. It is often used as the root stock for citrus trees. Considered by some to be ugly, it is an interesting plant with a very good use as a barrier plant on property lines. *Citrus hystrix*, commonly called **kaffir lime** or lime leaf, has very interesting double leaves, which have a lemony taste. The leaves make an excellent ingredient for cooking and herb teas. **Orange** is *C. sinensis*, tangerine or **mandarin** is *C. reticulata*, **grapefruit** is *C. paradisi*, **lemon** is *C. limon*, **lime** is *C. aurantifolia*, **tangelo** is *C. reticulata x C. paradisi*, **clementines** are mutations, and **kumquats** are a completely different genus —*Fortunella* spp.

Cottonwood fall color.

Cottonwood

COMMON NAMES: Cottonwood, Eastern Cottonwood, Southern Cottonwood, Carolina Poplar, Eastern Poplar, Necklace Poplar, Alamo

BOTANICAL NAME: *Populus deltoides* var. *deltoides*

PRONUNCIATION: POP-you-lus del-TOID-ess

FAMILY: Salicaceae (Willow Family)

TYPE: Deciduous tree

HEIGHT: 80–100 feet

SPREAD: 40–50 feet

FINAL SPACING: Do not plant.

NATURAL HABITAT AND PREFERRED SITE: It grows in the eastern half of Texas and a wide variety of soils, especially lowlands. Cottonwood has been considered almost an aquatic plant because it likes moist soil so much, but it can adapt to fairly dry situations. Cottonwood is considered a pioneer species that quickly invades other areas, especially disturbed soil and new sandbars.

IDENTIFICATION: Cottonwood is a very fast-growing, upright, messy tree. It sends out cotton (seeds with a cotton-like wrapping) all over the place in the spring. It has brittle wood and large limbs. Its root system is extremely shallow, destructive, and ravenous, gobbling up water and nutrients from the soil. There will normally be quite a bit of deadwood in the tree as well.

FLOWERS AND FRUIT: The flowers are borne separately on male and female trees from February through May. Male flowers are about 2 inches long. Female flowers are up to 4 inches long. The fruit ripens from May to June in drooping racemes with many seeds in each pod. Each seed has a tuft of cottony hairs, which enables it to drift in the wind and which becomes a maintenance problem, especially around air conditioners.

FOLIAGE: The leaves are simple, alternate, and deciduous with so-so yellow fall color. The leaves are on 2–3-inch petioles. Triangular leaves can be 3–6 inches long and equally wide. They are shiny green on top and lighter green below.

BARK: The bark is thin and smooth on the young stems. It turns gray to almost black and becomes heavily fissured with maturity on the trunks. Some mature bark is still very light and ashy gray in color.

CULTURE: Cottonwood is easy to grow in almost any soil.

PROBLEMS: Cottonwood is short-lived and has a destructive root system, and the cottony seed from the female plant is a nuisance and damaging to electrical appliances. Stressed trees are commonly attacked by borers. The root system is susceptible to cotton root rot and other root diseases. This is a dangerous tree because large limbs or the entire tree can fall on cars, structures, and even people. This is one tree that should be removed from most residential property.

PROPAGATION: Cottonwood trees can be grown from seed easily and can be transplanted from seedlings

Cottonwood with lightning damage.

Lombardy poplar.

with almost no loss. In fact, rather large trees, up to 3 and 4 inches in caliper, can be ripped out of the ground and transplanted bare root with almost 100% success.

INSIGHT: A related tree, **silver poplar** (*Populus alba*), is a pretty tree but sprouts up everywhere and becomes a huge pest by spreading from the parent tree's root system. The leaves are green on top and very light to silvery on the bottom. The **lombardy poplar** (*P. nigra*) is a narrow, upright poplar that is short-lived, problematic, and considered another junk tree. Neither of these should be planted in Texas.

Although I strongly advise against using cottonwood on residential property, cottonwood trees are beautiful on ranches and larger properties in lowlands around creeks away from structures. The look, the sound of the leaves in the wind, and the size of these trees can be quite spectacular if they are grown in the proper place.

Cottonwood pulp is used for book and magazine paper, pallet lumber, and food containers. The bark, seed, and leaves are eaten by wildlife. The famous San Antonio mission Alamo is named for this tree.

Silver poplar foliage.

Crabapple in the spring.

Crabapple

COMMON NAMES: Crabapple
BOTANICAL NAME: *Malus* spp.
PRONUNCIATION: MAH-lus
FAMILY: Rosaceae (Rose Family)
TYPE: Small deciduous tree
HEIGHT: 15–25 feet
SPREAD: 20–25 feet
FINAL SPACING: 15–20 feet
NATURAL HABITAT AND PREFERRED SITE: Many of the various crabapple species will do well in a wide range of soils. Most of the crabapples on the market are introduced hybrids. **Common crabapple** (*Malus floribunda*) is one of the most common and easiest to grow across the state. Crabapple will grow in a range of soils, from sandy to clay, but needs well-drained soil in every case to avoid cotton root rot and other root diseases.

IDENTIFICATION: Crabapple is a wide-spreading ornamental tree with dramatic flowers in the spring, small fruits called crabapples, and fall color that ranges from yellow to red.

FLOWERS AND FRUIT: Dramatic spring flowers bloom in various colors including white, red, and pink. The fruit is ½ inch in diameter, maturing in the fall.

FOLIAGE: The leaves are simple, alternate, and deciduous. Fall color ranges from yellow to red.

BARK: The bark is smooth when young and ranges from reddish brown to gray. Fissures and deep ridges develop on older trees.

CULTURE: Crabapple is easy to grow in any well-drained soil, requiring only moderate amounts of moisture and fertilizer.

PROBLEMS: Crabapple is susceptible to aphids, scale, spider mites, webworms, rust, apple scab, fire blight, borers, and cotton root rot. It is also a fairly short-lived tree. All of these problems can be kept to a minimum with the use of the organic program. Sick trees can be revived with the Sick Tree Treatment (see Appendix 3).

PROPAGATION: Propagate from cuttings for the plant to come true to the parent plant. Crabapples can be grown very easily from seed, although the resulting plant might be a great surprise. The native crabapple fruit is collected in the fall when the pulp has turned fleshy but before it has fallen from the trees. Clean the seed before sowing or storage to avoid fermentation. Seed to be planted immediately does not need to be dried, but seed to be stored should be dried. Seed can be sown in the spring after being stratified at 41°F over the winter. Seedlings will benefit from light shade the first season. All crabapples will root from suckers and softwood cuttings in the growing season or in February.

INSIGHT: Native crabapples are in the genus *Pyrus* and are much more adapted to alkaline and drier soils. The native crabapples produce yellowish green apples about 1 inch in diameter that ripen in the fall. They are sour to eat but make excellent jelly, cider, and vinegar. **Blanco crabapple** (*Pyrus ioensis*) grows in Blanco, Kerr, and Kendal counties. *P. angustifolia* grows only in the southeastern part of the state. According to Tull's *Edible and Useful Plants of Texas and the Southwest,* the seeds and leaves of crabapples are toxic.

Flowering crabapple in the spring.

Crape myrtle with fall color.

Crape Myrtle

COMMON NAMES: Crape Myrtle, Common Crape Myrtle

BOTANICAL NAME: *Lagerstroemia indica*

PRONUNCIATION: lah-ger-STROH-me-ah IN-dik-kah

FAMILY: Lythraceae (Crape Myrtle or Loosestrife Family)

TYPE: Deciduous ornamental tree

HEIGHT: 20–30 feet

SPREAD: 12–15 feet

FINAL SPACING: 15–20 feet

NATURAL HABITAT AND PREFERRED SITE: Crape myrtle is native to the tropics from Asia to Australia but has adapted extensively in many parts of Texas, especially the southern two-thirds of the state. It needs full sun.

IDENTIFICATION: Crape myrtle is a beautiful ornamental tree that is upright to spreading with light, smooth bark and small, oval opposite leaves. It has showy color for most of the summer. The excellent fall color is red on all crape myrtles except the white-flowering varieties, which have yellow autumn leaves.

FLOWERS AND FRUIT: The flowers are lacy and showy and have a multitude of colors and shades. They are followed by decorative seed pods on the terminal growth. These fruits, or capsules, are oval and about ⅓ inch long. The seeds have a winged top.

FOLIAGE: The small, opposite, deciduous leaves are rounded at the base and generally ½–2 inches long.

BARK: The bark is even and smooth and ranges in color from pinkish to reddish to even some grays. It is thin and exfoliates to expose smooth and pale-colored new bark.

CULTURE: Crape myrtle is easy to grow in most any well-drained soil. Pruning can be done after the flowers fade to force a second burst of bloom. Pruning in the winter, which is often done, is not

Crape myrtle with summer color.

Crape myrtle in the winter.

recommended. I like to leave the decorative seed pods in the winter. I think they are part of the beauty of this ornamental tree.

PROBLEMS: Aphids, mildew, and suckers are the biggest pests, but they are more of an irritation than a serious problem. When planted in the full sun, in healthy soil, and under an organic program, crape myrtles have few problems.

PROPAGATION: It can be grown from seed or cuttings. Stem cuttings can be taken in the summer right after the first blooming period. The seed is saved dry and planted in the spring in moist, organic soil.

INSIGHT: It is a severe misconception that pruning back crape myrtles in the winter increases the flower production the next year. This hacking back actually creates less flower production because the plant tries to first make up the growth that has been cut away before setting new buds and flowers.

Dwarf crape myrtle in summer color.

Arizona cypress foliage.

Cypress, Arizona

COMMON NAMES: Arizona Cypress
BOTANICAL NAME: *Cupressus arizonica*
PRONUNCIATION: koo-PRESS-us air-ah-ZON-ih-ca
FAMILY: Pinaceae (Pine Family)
TYPE: Evergreen tree
HEIGHT: 40–50 feet, up to 90 feet
SPREAD: 30–40 feet
FINAL SPACING: 20–30 feet
NATURAL HABITAT AND PREFERRED SITE: Well-drained soil at altitudes of 3,000–8,000 feet is the native habitat of this plant. Arizona cypress grows wild in the Chisos Mountains of the Big Bend National Park in Brewster County but adapts to a wide range of soils in other parts of the state.
IDENTIFICATION: Arizona cypress is an evergreen tree that reaches an ultimate height of 90 feet. It has stout, horizontal branches and a conical or rounded crown or sometimes an irregular shape. It tends to be more upright when young and more spreading with age and has aromatic, blue-green evergreen foliage.
FLOWERS AND FRUIT: The flowers are inconspicuous, small, and borne in the spring. The fruits are cones, ¾–1 inch long and dark reddish brown, maturing at the end of the second year. There are numerous dark reddish brown seeds that are compressed and winged.
FOLIAGE: The aromatic blue-green evergreen foliage has leaves that are minute and scale-like, about ¹⁄₁₆ inch long.
BARK: The bark is colorful and flaky, becoming dark reddish brown with age. A sticky sap will often be present.
CULTURE: Arizona cypress is relatively easy to grow in most soils that drain well. It likes west Texas, a dry climate, or at least a well-drained site. It is drought tolerant and needs little fertilizer.
PROBLEMS: Over fertilizing can cause various root fungal diseases and other problems. The heat and humidity of the eastern part of the state are tough on this tree.

Arizona cypress.

Leyland cypress.

Italian cypress.

PROPAGATION: Arizona cypress can be grown easily from seed. Germination occurs in 2–3 weeks. Cones can be opened by sun drying prior to planting. Propagation by cuttings is also possible.

INSIGHT: Arizona cypress is an excellent Christmas tree when young. It is a good tree to plant in the western part of the state and should be used more. It should be avoided in the eastern part of the state (east of the Trinity River) unless excellent soil conditions exist.

　　Italian cypress (*Cupressus sempervirens*) is the extremely vertical evergreen tree that is used in formal gardens. It has very dark green, juniper-like foliage and grows well in any well-drained soil in full sun. It is used as a background plant, a tall border, a screen, or a specimen tree for formal gardens. It can also be used as a windbreak. Problems include spider mites and bagworms. It has other disease problems, and it is relatively short-lived.

　　Leyland cypress (*C. ocyparis leylandii*) is another introduced cypress that doesn't grow quite as tall as Italian cypress but is wider and often used as an evergreen Christmas tree. It is relatively well-adapted in Texas in very well-drained soils. It can be used as background or an evergreen specimen. Its problems include root rot and poorly drained soils.

Bald cypress.

Bald cypress foliage and fruit.

Cypress, Bald

COMMON NAMES: Common Bald Cypress, Montezuma Bald Cypress, Pond Bald Cypress

BOTANICAL NAME: *Taxodium* spp.

Common Bald Cypress—*Taxodium distichum*

Montezuma Bald Cypress—*Taxodium mucronatum* or *Taxodium distichum* var. *mexicanum* (per *Shinners & Mahler*)

Pond Bald Cypress—*Taxodium distichum* var. *nutans* (syn. *Taxodium ascendens*)

PRONUNCIATION: tax-OH-dee-um

FAMILY: Cupressaceae (Cypress or Redwood Family)

TYPE: Deciduous conifer tree

HEIGHT: 70 feet, up to well over 100 feet

SPREAD: 20–30 feet

FINAL SPACING: 20–30 feet

NATURAL HABITAT AND PREFERRED SITE: Bald cypress is native to the Piney Woods, Gulf prairies and marshes, Post Oak Savannah, Rio Grande Plains, and Edwards Plateau. It will adapt to a wide range of soils from sandy to heavy clays. Depending on the seed, it may not grow in black and white soils.

IDENTIFICATION: Bald cypress is a deciduous conifer that grows in a dramatic, upright form, usually with a strong central stem. It is pyramidal when young but spreads with age. The foliage is light green and lacy in texture and has reddish brown fall color. The branching structure is layered and distinctive. Root "knees" appear in wet soil.

FLOWERS AND FRUIT: It produces 3–5-inch male cones from March through April in drooping clusters.

Pond cypress.

Pond cypress with new foliage in the spring.

Mature pond cypress foliage and fruit.

Montezuma bald cypress.

Mystery bald cypress at Frito-Lay's national headquarters in Plano—may be a montezuma.

Bald cypress "knees."

A few female cones appear from at the branch tips in the spring. The fruits are wrinkled, rounded cones about 1 inch long, maturing in the fall.

FOLIAGE: The leaves are alternate, small (½–¾ inch), and pointed at the tip. Light green in summer, they have reddish brown fall color. The leaves of pond cypress don't open but stay folded to form a filament effect.

BARK: The bark is gray to light reddish brown. It is fibrous with shallow furrows and broad, flat ridges.

CULTURE: All of the bald cypress trees are easy to grow in a wide range of soils. They can grow in wet soil or in water but can also do well in normal garden soil and moisture. Some growers have found bald cypress to be quite drought tolerant. It has a medium growth rate under moderate to little fertilization.

PROBLEMS: It is susceptible to chlorosis when grown on top of white limestone rock in shallow soils. Crown gall will attack stressed trees, as will spider mites and bagworms. The Basic Organic Program (see Appendix 5) will prevent these pests.

PROPAGATION: It is grown primarily by seed. Collect the seed in late September when the cones have turned brown but haven't shattered. Before sowing, soak the seed in a 10% vinegar solution or in water that has been heated to just under the boiling point. Some books recommend using a 1% lye solution instead.

INSIGHT: Montezuma bald cypress comes out earlier in the spring and holds its foliage longer in the fall than bald cypress. It also seems to be more salt tolerant.

Bald cypress in native east Texas setting.

Bald cypress in fall color.

Flowering dogwood flowers.

Dogwood, Flowering

COMMON NAMES: Dogwood, Flowering Dogwood, Virginia Dogwood, Florida Dogwood, Arrowwood, Boxwood, False Box, White Cornel
BOTANICAL NAME: *Cornus florida*
PRONUNCIATION: KOR-nus FLOR-eh-duh
FAMILY: Cornaceae (Dogwood Family)
TYPE: Small to medium-sized, flowering, deciduous tree
HEIGHT: 20–40 feet
SPREAD: 20–30 feet
FINAL SPACING: 15–30 feet
NATURAL HABITAT AND PREFERRED SITE: Flowering dogwood grows primarily in the deep, sandy, acid soils of deep east Texas, the Piney Woods, and the Post Oak Savannah, in sun to part shade. It can be grown around the state in landscape gardens that have had very intense bed preparation that includes high levels of compost and other organic amendments.
IDENTIFICATION: Flowering dogwood is a much-loved, easily identified ornamental tree good for use in formal or natural gardens. It has a graceful, layered structure, striking, pink or white spring flowers, attractive foliage, and showy fall color. Red berries and fat flower buds form prominently on the ends of the twigs throughout the winter.
FLOWERS AND FRUIT: The flowers are on display before most other trees have leafed out. Tiny, greenish yellow flowers are surrounded by 4 white (sometimes pink), showy bracts up to 2⅜ inches in length. The fruit ripens in the fall and persists over the winter as tight clusters of shiny, red, oval drupes about ⅜

Flowering dogwood in full flower in the spring.

inch long, which contain 1 or 2 seeds. The fruit is inedible and somewhat toxic.
FOLIAGE: The leaves are 2–5 inches in length, opposite, simple, and deciduous. They have smooth margins, are dark green above and paler to almost silvery

on the bottom, and have curving leaf veins that parallel the margins. Fall color is red.

BARK: The bark is reddish brown to gray, becoming darker and almost black on older trunks. The bark has a distinctive checkerboard texture of square blocks and shallow furrows. The wood is very hard and close-grained and is used to make spindles, pulleys, tool handles, and jewelry boxes.

Young flowering dogwood in flower.

CULTURE: Flowering dogwood is fairly easy to grow as long as the bed preparation is good and the soil remains moist. In the black and white soils and other alkaline soil areas, the beds require double the normal bed preparation that I usually recommend. This includes adding 8 inches of compost, 1 inch of Texas greensand, 2 inches of lava sand, and ½ inch of earthworm castings. The beds should be mounded so that the drainage is positive. Flowering dogwood responds well to the gentle organic fertilizers. It needs moist soil but also very positive drainage.

PROBLEMS: Borers and cotton root rot can be problems. Soil alkalinity, dry soil, and improper bed preparation and planting can also cause problems.

PROPAGATION: Flowering dogwood is grown from seed, which should be hand-picked in the fall. Remove the hulls by maceration or by washing away the pulp. Seed should be stratified in sand or peat for at least 30–90 days at 41°F and planted in April or early May. One-year-old seedlings can be transplanted to final sites. The tree can also be propagated by layering, root cuttings, and divisions. Dogwoods will root from softwood or semi-hardwood cuttings taken in the late summer, from hardwood cuttings taken in the winter, and by suckers, divisions, and layers taken in the early spring.

INSIGHT: Pioneers realized they had good soil for growing crops if dogwood was found growing wild. Many species of birds and other wildlife feed on the fruits.

Flowering dogwood fruit in the late summer.

Rough-leaf dogwood in early stages of bloom.

Rough-leaf dogwood foliage and fruit.

Dogwood, Rough-Leaf

COMMON NAMES: Rough-Leaf Dogwood, Native Dogwood

BOTANICAL NAME: *Cornus drummondii*

PRONUNCIATION: KOR-nus druh-MUN-dee-eye

FAMILY: Cornaceae (Dogwood Family)

TYPE: Deciduous large shrub or small tree

HEIGHT: 10–15 feet

SPREAD: It continually spreads by root suckers.

FINAL SPACING: 6–12 feet

NATURAL HABITAT AND PREFERRED SITE: Its natural habitat is the edges of thickets, streams, creeks, and fence rows. Rough-leaf dogwood will grow well in a range of soils from sand to clay.

IDENTIFICATION: The tree is thicket-forming and bushy. Its stems are reddish and very decorative in the winter.

FLOWERS AND FRUIT: Small, white flowers bloom in clusters in the late spring. White fruits in the fall disappear quickly because the birds love them.

FOLIAGE: The rough, hairy leaves are simple, opposite, and deciduous. The leaves are 1–5 inches long, olive green on top and paler beneath. Fall color ranges from red to deep purple.

BARK: The young stems are reddish, becoming gray with age.

CULTURE: Rough-leaf dogwood is very easy to grow in most any soils, but it does spread easily by seeds and suckers and can become a pest. It is a drought tolerant plant.

PROBLEMS: Fairly common leaf fungus can be controlled with the Sick Tree Treatment (see Appendix 3) and a spray of Garrett Juice (see Appendix 2) plus garlic or potassium bicarbonate for serious problems. It can become a very invasive plant, so be careful where it is planted.

PROPAGATION: Growth is extremely easy from stem cuttings, root division, or seed (which can be planted immediately after harvest).

INSIGHT: The wood is used to make woodenware products and charcoal. The fruit is eaten by several species of wildlife.

American elm in fall color.

Elm, American

American elm foliage.

COMMON NAMES: American Elm, Rock Elm, Common Elm, Soft Elm, White Elm, Water Elm

BOTANICAL NAME: *Ulmus americana*

PRONUNCIATION: ULL-mus uh-mer-ee-KAHN-ah

FAMILY: Ulmaceae (Elm Family)

TYPE: Deciduous shade tree

HEIGHT: 70–90 feet

SPREAD: 70–90 feet

FINAL SPACING: 40–50 feet

NATURAL HABITAT AND PREFERRED SITE: American elm is found in all areas of Texas except the High Plains in the Trans-Pecos. It is also absent from the Rio Grande Plains. It primarily inhabits the eastern half of Texas. American elm adapts fairly well to a wide range of well-drained soils but likes moist soils such as bottomlands, flats, and river and creek bottoms. It is also found in deep forests, including those that receive very heavy rainfall.

IDENTIFICATION: American elm is a wide-growing, graceful shade tree with large leaves and yellow fall color. It will usually be wider than tall.

FLOWERS AND FRUIT: The flowers are small and green and form on hanging stalks in the early spring. The fruit is a winged nut that ripens in the late spring to early summer.

FOLIAGE: The leaves are simple, alternate, and deciduous with yellow fall color. They are large, 4–6 inches in length and 2–3 inches wide, with serrated edges.

BARK: The bark is light to dark gray with long, flattened ridges and scaly, deep fissures on older tree trunks.

CULTURE: American elm is relatively easy to grow except for the problem of Dutch elm disease and other soil fungal diseases. Planted in healthy well-drained soil, the tree needs moderate water and low amounts of fertilizer.

PROBLEMS: American elm is susceptible to Dutch elm disease, which can be prevented with the Sick Tree Treatment (see Appendix 3). Over planting and creating monocultures is the primary cause of the spread of this root fungal disease.

PROPAGATION: Propagation is easily done from seed. Sow the seed immediately after collection. American and most other elms can also be propagated from softwood cuttings and cuttings taken in the late winter just prior to bud break.

INSIGHT: I don't recommend planting this tree, but I would recommend saving existing specimens and applying the Basic Organic Program (see Appendix 5) and the Sick Tree Treatment (see Appendix 3) if necessary. When healthy, American elm is a graceful tree that in some years has fall color that is quite spectacular.

Elm, Cedar

COMMON NAMES: Cedar Elm, Shrub Elm, Lime Elm, Texas Elm, Basket Elm, Red Elm, Southern Rock Elm

BOTANICAL NAME: *Ulmus crassifolia*

PRONUNCIATION: ULL-mus krass-ee-FOLE-ee-ah

FAMILY: Ulmaceae (Elm Family)

TYPE: Deciduous shade tree

HEIGHT: 70–90 feet

SPREAD: 50–60 feet

FINAL SPACING: 20–40 feet

NATURAL HABITAT AND PREFERRED SITE: Cedar elm exists in the bulk of the eastern half of the state. It grows well in a wide range of soils including rocky limestone soils. It is drought tolerant but can stand a fair amount of moisture as well. Cedar elm is native to all areas of Texas except the Trans-Pecos High Plains and the rolling plains of the Panhandle.

IDENTIFICATION: It is an upright-growing tree with small leaves that are sandpaper-like in texture. It has yellow fall color and produces its seed in the fall, which is unusual for the native elms.

FLOWERS AND FRUIT: The flowers form in the late spring or early summer. They are small and unattractive. The fruit (samara) that forms in the late summer and fall is composed of a single seed surrounded by a wing.

FOLIAGE: The simple, alternate, and small (1–2 inches long) leaves are oval and sandpapery to the touch. It has yellow fall color.

BARK: The bark is brown to reddish or gray. Its ridges are flat and then broken into narrow, loose scales. It is a fairly smooth and fine-textured bark.

CULTURE: Cedar elm is easy to grow in a wide range of soils. It needs moderate amounts of water and has low fertilizer requirements. It has moderate growth and in some years rather spectacular golden yellow fall color. Although drought tolerant, it is a tree that can stand fairly wet soil.

PROBLEMS: Cedar elm will occasionally have insect pests, such as aphids, as well as some minor elm leaf beetle damage. Mildew in the late summer has become its main imperfection, but it can be controlled to some degree with the Sick Tree Treatment (see Appendix 3). Mistletoe will attack cedar elms that are in stress and poor health.

PROPAGATION: Cedar elm can be grown easily from seed. Collect the seed immediately after it matures in the late summer or fall and store over the winter at 41°F before planting in the spring.

INSIGHT: Cedar elm has been referred to as poor man's live oak and has been over planted in the landscapes

Cedar elm.

Cedar elm fall color.

Winged elm in the fall.

during the last three decades. In recent years it has become more susceptible to mildew, which discolors the foliage to a brown color in the late summer. This malady may have something to do with the decline of air quality. A similar tree that is often confused with cedar elm is **winged elm** (*Ulmus alata*), which has larger and very obvious corky wings on the young branches. It flowers in the spring with its fruit maturing in the early summer. **Slippery elm** (*U. rubra*) has rough leaves as large as American elm leaves and a slimy or slippery, white inner bark that has been used medicinally. It is also called **red elm** because of its reddish brown heartwood. It is faster-growing than American elm and a little easier to transplant. Its overall size is smaller, but it has the same vase-like shape.

Young lacebark elm trunk.

Mature lacebark elm trunk.

Elm, Lacebark

COMMON NAMES: Lacebark Elm, Chinese Elm, Drake Elm, Evergreen Elm

BOTANICAL NAME: *Ulmus parvifolia*

PRONUNCIATION: ULL-mus par-vah-FOAL-ee-ah

FAMILY: Ulmaceae (Elm Family)

TYPE: Deciduous shade tree

HEIGHT: 40–60 feet

SPREAD: 30–40 feet

FINAL SPACING: 20–30 feet

NATURAL HABITAT AND PREFERRED SITE: Lacebark elm is native to China but has adapted well to various soils except those where cotton root rot is a problem.

IDENTIFICATION: Lacebark elm is a medium-sized tree with an overall rounded or oval crown. It generally does not have a central stem. It has small, typical elm leaves, limber stems, and a distinctively mottled trunk bark. The fall color is weak at best.

FLOWERS AND FRUIT: The flowers are not showy and are borne in clusters in October. The fruit forms in clusters among the leaves in the fall, usually October through November. The fruit is green when young. It turns a somewhat showy maroon when the seeds are exposed to full sun.

FOLIAGE: The leaves are alternate, simple, and ovate. They are about 1–1½ inches long and have sawtooth margins that taper to a point at the tip. Like most elms the leaves are rather lopsided at the base. They are medium to dark green above and a lighter color beneath. Fall color is generally weak yellow.

BARK: The bark is smooth when young. It develops a general flakiness with age. It also turns a reddish tan color. The outer bark peels away to reveal a salmon-colored inner bark. The bark is the most interesting feature on the tree.

CULTURE: Lacebark elm is a very fast-growing tree. Its structure can range from upright to spreading to even drooping. It has delicate foliage for an elm. In the past I have said this tree is extremely easy to grow, which it is, except for one fatal flaw. It is susceptible to cotton root rot and should not be planted in the black soils where cotton crops have grown in the past. The Sick Tree Treatment (see Appendix 3) can prevent this problem in most cases but not all. It is cold and wind tolerant as well as relatively drought tolerant. It requires only moderate fertilization and

Lacebark elm with fruit.

can tolerate extremely poor soils and restricted root growth areas—even soil compaction. It is also resistant to the elm diseases and typical elm insect pests.

PROBLEMS: Although highly resistant to Dutch elm disease, lacebark elm is susceptible to minor elm leaf beetle attack and is very susceptible to cotton root rot.

PROPAGATION: It can be grown easily from seed, softwood cuttings, or cuttings taken in the late winter just prior to spring bud break.

INSIGHT: Lacebark elm is often confused with **Siberian elm** (*Ulmus pumila*), which is incorrectly called **Chinese elm**. Siberian elm is devastated every year by the elm leaf beetle. It is one of the few trees I recommend removing if it exists on-site, and you should certainly never consider planting one. Siberian elm is one of the poorest tree choices. It has larger leaves than other elms as well as more deeply furrowed bark, and it does not develop a flaky pattern on the trunk. Also it flowers and bears fruit in the spring rather than the fall. Only cedar elm and lacebark elm produce fruit that matures in the fall.

Siberian elm showing elm leaf beetle damage.

Eve's Necklace

Eve's necklace.

COMMON NAMES: Eve's Necklace, Texas Sophora, Pink Sophora, Necklace Tree

BOTANICAL NAME: *Sophora affinis*

PRONUNCIATION: so-FORE-ah af-FIN-is

FAMILY: Fabaceae (Legume, Bean, or Pulse Family)

TYPE: Small to medium-sized deciduous tree

HEIGHT: 25–35 feet

SPREAD: 20 feet

FINAL SPACING: 10–15 feet

NATURAL HABITAT AND PREFERRED SITE: It grows from north Texas down through central Texas (particularly in the Blackland Prairies and Cross Timbers) as well as in the Edwards Plateau. Often seen in small groves on hillsides or along streams, it will grow in full sun or as an understory tree. Eve's Necklace will grow well in rocky limestone slopes and ravines.

IDENTIFICATION: This delicate, lacy tree has spreading branches, a rounded head, pink flowers in the spring, and bead-like seed pods in the fall. New stem growth and young branches have a distinctive green color that turns dark with age.

FLOWERS AND FRUIT: The fragrant flowers are 2–4 inches long, pink, and wisteria-like. Seed pods form a necklace-like appearance in the fall and turn a dark gray to black color. They are reported to be poisonous.

Eve's necklace in bloom in the spring.

FOLIAGE: The leaves are alternate, compound, and delicate in appearance. The upper surface of the leaves is dark green while the lower surface is paler and fuzzy. The leaves are ¾–1½ inch long and ½ inch wide.

BARK: The bark is very light green on the young twigs, turning dark green to gray and reddish brown with age. The bark is broken into small, thin, oblong scales.

CULTURE: Eve's necklace is easy to grow in a wide range of soils. Moderately fast-growing, it needs very little fertilizer and is drought tolerant.

PROBLEMS: With few, if any, problems, it should be used more.

PROPAGATION: Eve's necklace can be grown from seed or cuttings. The seeds are very hard. Germination can be helped by mechanically scarring, or damaging, the seed coat with a knife or file. Some people soak the seed in a mild solution of sulfuric acid for 30–90 minutes. A solution of acetic acid or vinegar would be safer and probably work as well. Seedlings don't transplant well from flats and are fairly sensitive to overhead watering. Seedlings should be placed in full sun as early as possible to encourage upright growth. Stem cuttings should be taken in the late winter before the new growth emerges. They should be kept under a mist system if at all possible.

INSIGHT: The dense, hard wood is light reddish brown. Its yellow sapwood is used to make a yellow dye.

Eve's necklace with seed pods in the fall.

Fringe Tree

COMMON NAMES: Fringe Tree, Old Man's Beard, White Fringe Tree, Flowering Ash, Snow Flower Tree, Grandfather Graybeard, Grancy Graybeard, Poison Ash

BOTANICAL NAME: *Chionanthus virginicus*

PRONUNCIATION: key-oh-NAN-thus ver-JIN-eh-kus

FAMILY: Oleaceae (Olive Family)

TYPE: Small deciduous to semi-evergreen tree

HEIGHT: 15–30 feet

SPREAD: 15–20 feet

FINAL SPACING: 15–35 feet

NATURAL HABITAT AND PREFERRED SITE: Fringe tree likes the deep, rich, sandy, acid soil conditions of east Texas but will grow fairly well in soil with a neutral pH such as is found in Houston. It prefers dappled shade and is often seen growing on the edges of forests.

IDENTIFICATION: A beautiful ornamental tree with a slender trunk and an irregular, rounded crown, it has delicate, showy, white flowers in the spring.

FLOWERS AND FRUIT: The flowers of fringe tree are spectacular. They are lacy, white, fragrant clusters that appear in the spring from March to June in delicate, drooping panicles, 5–10 inches long. The flowers last for two weeks or more if a hard rain doesn't knock them off. Both male and female flowers are beautiful but are usually on separate plants. The female plants have dark blue or purple clusters of berries, or drupes, that ripen in the late summer to fall. The fruit is eaten by many species of wildlife.

BARK: The bark is brown to gray, usually thin, and finely textured even as it matures. Old stems will tend to get a silvery gray color.

FOLIAGE: The leaves are opposite, simple, and about 4–8 inches long and 2–4 inches wide. The tops are very dark blue-green and the undersides are a lighter color with fuzz. The leaves have a smooth margin. The base is a distinctive purple color. Fall color is pure yellow.

CULTURE: Fringe tree is only adapted to sandy, acid soils like those in east Texas and will not adapt to the alkaline soils well at all. It likes moist soil and relatively high fertility.

PROBLEMS: Pest problems are minimal. It is not adapted to alkaline soils. In such soils it will be in stress and have insect and disease problems. Few, if any, problems occur if the tree is planted in the proper locations. It will occasionally have spider mites due to stress.

Fringe tree in full bloom.

PROPAGATION: Natural germination of the fringe tree happens in the second spring following seed fall. Collect the fruits from July to September after they have turned purple but before they have fallen from the tree. Clean the seed of pulp and keep it in cold, moist storage until planting. Seedlings require light shade until well-established. Fringe tree can also be propagated by cuttings, layering, grafting, and budding; however, it is slow to root from cuttings. Stratification at 41°F in sand or peat for a year is recommended before spring planting.

INSIGHT: The fringe tree is considered deciduous, but the leaves are persistent in the winter in the Gulf coast area. In most of the state, the foliage turns a bright yellow and falls.

The author's famous ginkgo.

Ginkgo fall color.

Ginkgo

COMMON NAMES: Ginkgo, Maidenhair Tree
BOTANICAL NAME: *Ginkgo biloba*
PRONUNCIATION: GINK-oh bye-LOBE-ah
FAMILY: Ginkgoaceae (Ginkgo Family)
TYPE: Deciduous shade tree
HEIGHT: 50–70 feet. Trees have been identified as growing to as much as 100 feet.
SPREAD: 30 feet
FINAL SPACING: 20–40 feet
NATURAL HABITAT AND PREFERRED SITE: Ginkgo is native to China but adapts to a wide range of soils as long as there is ample moisture and decent drainage. The only place in Texas I have seen the plant not grow well is in solid white rock or in soils that are too dry. Ginkgo tolerates a wide range of rough conditions such as downtown urban sites, smoky areas, air pollution, and confined root system spaces. I have discovered from working with my ginkgo at home that the tree responds dramatically to the organic program and grows as much as 24 inches a year in ideal conditions—in soil that has lots of organic matter, has lots of life and moisture, and is fairly well drained. It is a classic example of how trees respond to the organic program and how beneficial fungi can grow on the roots of healthy plants.

IDENTIFICATION: Ginkgo is an unusual shade tree in that it has light-colored and smooth bark and grows wide open, generally with a central leader, or stem. The flowers are not showy, but the bright yellow color on the fan-shaped leaves is spectacular for a very short period of time in the fall.

FLOWERS AND FRUIT: The flowers are puny and waxy. The small, disagreeable smelling, fleshy fruit forms on mature female trees only. The fruits are oval and 1 inch in diameter—acid but sweet. The seeds are large, single, oval, cream-colored, thin-shelled, sweet, and edible. It is not a true fruit but a seed with a fleshy outer layer bearing a silvery fuzz. Ginkgo seeds are considered to have medicinal value; they benefit the lungs, enrich the blood, stimulate menstrual flow, ease the excretion of urine, and alleviate high blood pressure. After removing the fleshy layer, seeds are marketed internationally as an important export from China. They are sold as ginkgo nuts and are roasted before eaten. Many people do not like the flavor, which is resinously sweetish, but the nuts are highly esteemed as food in China and Japan. The flesh of the seed is baked and eaten between meals to aid digestion.

FOLIAGE: The leaves are medium green in the summer, fan-shaped, and beautiful. The tree has spectacular yellow fall color that doesn't last very long. The

Ginkgo fall color.

leaves tend to fall all at one time. Green leaves are where the medicinal properties lie for aid in increasing the circulation to the brain. *Ginkgo biloba* capsules are the best source of the proper concentration of the medicinal herb.

BARK: The color is light tan to a medium brown. The bark is smooth when young but darkens and becomes roughened by fissures with age.

CULTURE: Ginkgo grows well in most well-drained soils but does not like solid white rock, especially the limestone rock of north Texas. It has moderate water needs and fertilizer requirements. It responds beautifully to the organic program.

PROBLEMS: Ginkgo has few problems. I have never seen any insect or disease damage. Everything bad relates to dry or rocky soil or fertilizing with high nitrogen, synthetic fertilizers. Another problem is that the female trees have a fruit that is stinky. It is difficult to know for sure whether you have a female because the fruit normally does not start to form until the tree is about 14 years old.

PROPAGATION: Ginkgo can be grown easily from seed or by grafting the male cultivars.

INSIGHT: Ginkgo has been called a "living fossil" and also the "tree of life." Buddhist monks believed the ginkgo could restore youth and vitality. I think they were right. It is one of the oldest trees on earth and can be found on every continent in the world. Ginkgo can ultimately reach a height of more than 100 feet. It was first identified from fossil records in China and has a reputation for being an extremely slow grower. The tree's root system, when it has the natural beneficial fungi, is the key. Ginkgos are believed to have been around for approximately 200 million years. There is indication in some Chinese publications that some ginkgo trees may be as old as 2,000 years. "The King of Trees" is the imperial title given to the tree by the emperor of Quianlong in the 18th century in Beijing. The name *ginkgo* is from the Chinese word meaning silver fruit. The species name *biloba* refers to the two-lobed leaves.

Ginkgo open branching and good climbing structure.

Golden raintree in full bloom.

Golden Raintree

COMMON NAMES: Golden Raintree, Panicled Raintree

BOTANICAL NAME: *Koelreuteria paniculata*

PRONUNCIATION: cole-roo-TEH-ree-ah pa-nik-ew-LAH-ta

FAMILY: Sapindaceae (Soapberry Family)

TYPE: Deciduous shade tree

HEIGHT: 20–35 feet

SPREAD: 15–20 feet

FINAL SPACING: 15–20 feet

NATURAL HABITAT AND PREFERRED SITE: Native to China, Korea, and Japan, it adapts well in Texas to a variety of soils if they are well-drained. It needs full sun.

IDENTIFICATION: This upright, open-branching shade tree has beautiful, yellow flowers in the early summer and distinctive seed pods in the fall. It is deciduous with yellow fall color. It typically has a compact, rounded head.

FLOWERS AND FRUIT: Bright yellow flowers bloom in large terminal clusters in the late spring to early summer, from May to June, covering the entire tree. Each flower is about ½ inch in diameter with orange markings at the base. The flowers are followed by decorative and distinctive seed pods. The pods are paper-walled, bladder-like (or lantern-like) capsules, 1–2 inches long. The seed pods are light yellow-brown at first, changing to reddish brown and persisting into the winter. Each pod contains 3 round, black seeds about ¼ inch in diameter.

Golden raintree flowers and foliage.

Golden raintree fruit capsules.

FOLIAGE: The leaves are alternate, compound, 8–14 inches long, and composed of 7–17 leaflets. They are medium green to almost blue-green on top, with a lighter green below. The leaves drop early in the fall after turning a moderately interesting yellow to yellow-orange fall color.

BARK: The bark ranges from a silvery gray color to a grayish brown. It is fairly smooth when young, but the texture becomes more coarse with age.

CULTURE: Golden raintree is easy to grow in moderately moist and well-drained soil. It does not need heavy fertilization. It is susceptible to some root diseases, but those can be easily overcome with the Basic Organic Program (see Appendix 5), and problems that pop up can be cured with the Sick Tree Treatment (see Appendix 3).

PROBLEMS: Few exist, other than the relatively short life. Also, diseases can be a problem if the tree is not growing in healthy soil.

PROPAGATION: Golden raintree is grown by seed primarily. Collect the seed from the mature, brown seed capsules in the fall and plant in containers immediately. Protect the plants through the winter and move containers out of doors in the spring. Seed can be saved if stored at 44°F and planted directly into beds outdoors in the spring.

INSIGHT: Chinese flame tree (*Koelreuteria bipinnata*) is a close kin, but it is not as cold hardy as *K. paniculata* and is not recommended for the northern half of the state. It grows much larger at 40–60 feet in height, has twice-compound leaves, and blooms in August with a salmon-pink to orange-pink fruit that is somewhat larger than that of *K. paniculata*. When in bloom, these beautiful trees strongly attract honeybees.

Goldenball lead tree.

Goldenball Lead Tree

COMMON NAMES: Goldenball Lead Tree, Wahootree, Wahoo-Tree, Little Leaf Lead Tree, Lemonball, Little Leucaena, Golden Lead Ball, Mimosa

BOTANICAL NAME: *Leucaena retusa*

PRONUNCIATION: loo-SEE-nah reh-TOO-sah

FAMILY: Fabaceae (Legume, Bean, or Pulse Family)

TYPE: Deciduous ornamental tree

HEIGHT: 12–25 feet

SPREAD: 8–15 feet

FINAL SPACING: 12–15 feet

NATURAL HABITAT AND PREFERRED SITE: Native to the dry canyons of west Texas, it grows in the Trans-Pecos in the far west and central Texas areas. It is primarily found in hard-to-reach areas such as ditches, fence rows, and craggy niches where the grazing animals can't get to it and eat it. It likes dry, well-drained, rocky limestone soils as well as igneous rock and sandier soils. It will grow in sun to partial shade.

IDENTIFICATION: This shrub or small tree has delicate foliage and distinctive, round, golden yellow flowers in the spring and summer. It has open branching with lacy foliage and is naturally multi-trunked.

FLOWERS AND FRUIT: The flowers bloom from April to October. They are the most showy in spring but also flower again after every rain throughout the summer. They are bright yellow and compact with round heads and bloom at the ends of the branches. The fruit is a woody legume. When ripe, the pod twists open to disperse the seeds. The long pods, 3–10 inches long, ⅓–½ inch wide, mature in the late summer. The seeds are thin, brown, and lustrous.

FOLIAGE: The leaves are alternate, compound, bright green, and lacy in appearance. The leaflets are small, rounded, and bluish green.

BARK: The young branches are smooth and often bright brown. Otherwise, the bark is light gray to brown, becoming scaly with age. Mature bark is flaky, cinnamon-colored, and interesting-looking.

CULTURE: Goldenball lead tree needs well-drained soils and does well in extremely rocky, infertile soils. It will grow in sand or clay as long as drainage is good. It has very low water and fertilizer requirements. Under good conditions, it will have moderate growth. It does need some protection from winds because the wood is extremely brittle, and high winds and ice storms can cause frequent breakage.

PROBLEMS: It is susceptible to wind damage, root rot if over watered, freeze damage in the northern part of the state, and destruction by browsing animals.

PROPAGATION: Gather the pods in the late summer when they are brown and beginning to dry but before splitting open and falling to the ground. Spread seed to dry for a few days and dust with cornmeal and diatomaceous earth prior to storing in glass containers at room temperature. Goldenball lead tree is easy to grow from seed. Fresh, untreated seed will germinate in 2–3 weeks. Although germinating quickly, the tree tends to grow slowly and becomes spindly if not placed in strong sunlight and fertilized with mild organic fertilizers. Semi-hardwood cuttings can be taken in the summer and root fairly well if kept under mist. Transplanting is rather difficult because of the long taproot and less-than-dense root system.

INSIGHT: Goldenball lead tree is highly palatable to grazing animals and can be wiped out of its native habitat easily if the animals have access to the plants. That goes for your landscaping, too, if you live in central Texas. Goldenball lead tree is questionably cold tolerant north of Dallas/Fort Worth.

Hackberry engulfed in mistletoe.

Hackberry showing its always present leaf galls.

Hackberry

COMMON NAMES: Sugar Hackberry, Texas Hackberry, Sugar Berry, False Elm, Nepaltree, Common Hackberry, American Hackberry, Northern Hackberry, Beaver Wood, Bastard-Elm, Juniper-Tree, Hoop-Ash, One-Berry, Palo Blanco

BOTANICAL NAME: *Celtis laevigata*

PRONUNCIATION: SEL-tis lie-vee-GAT-tah

FAMILY: Ulmaceae (Elm Family)

TYPE: Deciduous tree

HEIGHT: 40–60 feet

SPREAD: 40 feet

FINAL SPACING: Do not plant.

NATURAL HABITAT AND PREFERRED SITE: Texas hackberry grows across the eastern two-thirds of the state. It grows in almost any type of soil but cannot stand to grow in wet soil.

IDENTIFICATION: Hackberry is a scruffy-looking shade tree with medium green foliage and berries in the fall. It has smooth bark when young, adding warts with age. It tends to always have some portion of the tree turning brown, dying, or falling apart.

FLOWERS AND FRUIT: Inconspicuous flowers appear with the new leaves in the spring. The fruit is a round red to black drupe that ripens in the fall and that the birds love to eat.

FOLIAGE: The leaves are green, simple, alternate, and darker on top than on the bottom. The leaves tend to have hackberry galls or nipple galls as a common feature. Fall color is a weak yellow.

BARK: Pale gray, thin, and smooth when young, the bark develops wart-like growths with age.

CULTURE: Hackberry is a fast-growing, short-lived tree. It self-propagates easily from every seed that falls and does not need a lot of water or fertilizer. Nevertheless, it appears to be slowly declining across the country. The source of the problem is unknown. It could be the declining quality of the air.

PROBLEMS: It is short-lived and prone to twig dieback, root fungal problems, leaf galls, generally untidy appearance, brittle wood, falling limbs, and so on.

PROPAGATION: It is easy to grow from seed. The fruit can be picked by hand in the late summer to early winter and planted right away. Seed may be sown outdoors in the fall in prepared beds. Natural germination occurs in the spring. Hackberry is also easily rooted from juvenile cuttings and from root sprouts and suckers.

INSIGHT: Hackberry wood is used in furniture making and also in sporting and athletic goods. The dry, sweet fruit is eaten by a large number of birds. Hackberry's most important values are its use as a fence row plant, its drought tolerance, and in providing habitat for wildlife and shade for livestock. **Common hackberry** (*Celtis occidentalis*) has a much more limited distribution in Texas than the other species. The biggest difference between the different species of hackberry is the size—especially the height to which they grow.

Downy hawthorn.

Cockspur hawthorn.

Hawthorn, Downy

COMMON NAMES: Downy Hawthorn, Common Hawthorn, Red Haw, Summerhaw, Downyhaw, Downy Thorn

BOTANICAL NAME: *Crataegus mollis*

PRONUNCIATION: krah-TEEG-us MAH-las

FAMILY: Rosaceae (Rose Family)

TYPE: Small deciduous tree

HEIGHT: 25–40 feet

SPREAD: 20–30 feet

FINAL SPACING: 15–20 feet

NATURAL HABITAT AND PREFERRED SITE: Downy and other Texas hawthorns grow primarily in the eastern third of the state in open woods, along fence rows, in stream banks, in meadows, and on the edges of fields. They are also found in higher, well-drained, rocky soils.

IDENTIFICATION: Hawthorns are a complex and confusing group of small trees and multi-stemmed shrubs—mainly because they crossbreed so readily. Their leaves are deciduous, simple, and serrated, but some are lobed. The branches in general are crooked and thorny.

FLOWERS AND FRUIT: Hawthorn has gorgeous, white spring flowers and bright red fruit that ripens from August to October. Fruits from some of the other species of hawthorn turn blue or yellow when ripe. The summer-flowering fruits usually have a soft, pulpy flesh that decomposes quickly.

FOLIAGE: The leaves are deciduous, simple, and serrated (toothed) or lobed.

BARK: The bark is generally smooth and gray, getting a heavier, even flaky, texture with age.

CULTURE: Hawthorns are easy to grow in any well-drained soil. They can grow from sand to pretty heavy clays and are drought tolerant. Most hawthorns are intolerant of shade.

PROBLEMS: Damage comes from cedar apple rust, aphids, and other minor insect infestations.

PROPAGATION: Fruits can be hand-picked from the plants from midsummer until frost, depending on the species. Clean the seed of the pulp to avoid mold and fermentation, and air dry for 2 or 3 days before storing. Store at 45°F in sealed glass containers. Seed is a little bit hard to germinate and requires scarification and stratification prior to germination. Scarify for about 5 hours in concentrated vinegar, then place in warm, moist storage for up to 120 days or plant outside in the early fall. Or expose the seed to cold temperatures for 100–300 days. Some species require

Texas hawthorn.

Gregg hawthorn—a rare native tree.

no scarification and can be planted straight away with a high rate of germination. Hawthorns are difficult and slow to root from cuttings, but it is possible.

INSIGHT: According to Simpson's *A Field Guide to Texas Trees*, there have been many species listed as synonyms for *Crataegus mollis* such as *C. berlandieri, C. brachyphylla, C. invisa,* and *C. limaria.* Other authors believe that several other species should be merged together. In other words, there is not a lot of agreement, and there seems to be quite a bit of crossbreeding. The botanists at the Botanical Research Institute of Texas (BRIT) in Fort Worth say that the species are more clear-cut and that little crossbreeding exists.

Texas hawthorn (*Crataegus texana*) is similar to the common, native, or downy hawthorn. **Parsley hawthorn** is *C. marshallii,* **reverchon hawthorn** is *C. reverchonii,* **greenhaw hawthorn** is *C. viridis,* **cockspur hawthorn** is *C. crusgalli,* **Washington hawthorn** is *C. phaenopyrum,* and **little-hip hawthorn** is *C. spathulata.*

Greenhaw hawthorn.

Washington hawthorn.

Hawthorn, Washington

COMMON NAMES: Washington Hawthorn
BOTANICAL NAME: *Crataegus phaenopyrum*
PRONUNCIATION: krah-TEEG-us file-no-PIE-rum
FAMILY: Rosaceae (Rose Family)
TYPE: Deciduous ornamental tree
HEIGHT: 15–25 feet
SPREAD: 10–15 feet
FINAL SPACING: 10–15 feet
NATURAL HABITAT AND PREFERRED SITE: Growing in the United States, Europe, and North Africa, Washington hawthorn adapts well to a wide variety of soils in Texas as long as they are well-drained. It needs full sun.
IDENTIFICATION: This upright, oval, small to medium-sized ornamental tree has typical hawthorn foliage and long thorns. A very dense plant, it has red berries in the fall and winter and yellow fall color.
FLOWERS AND FRUIT: The flowers are white to white-pink and generally grow in clusters in the mid to late spring. The fruits are small, red to red-orange, apple-like berries that form in the fall.

FOLIAGE: The leaves are alternate and simple on slender petals, yellow to yellowish orange in the fall.
BARK: The bark is gray to light brown and smooth when young but develops heavier texture with age.
CULTURE: Washington hawthorn needs moderate water and fertilization and tolerates a wide range of soils and growing conditions. It is moderately drought resistant. Because it has a strong taproot, it is not easy to transplant.
PROBLEMS: Cedar apple rust is the most severe problem, but the Sick Tree Treatment (see Appendix 3) and the overall organic program help considerably. Most books recommend keeping the hawthorns away from eastern red cedars, which are the alternate hosts for cedar apple rust. Fire blight can also be a problem.
PROPAGATION: This is the same as for the native hawthorns.
INSIGHT: This is a good tree, although thorny. It has been my experience that the Washington hawthorn is less susceptible to rust on its foliage than the native trees—quite interesting.

Hickory.

Hickory foliage and fruit.

Hickory

COMMON NAMES: Hickory, Bitter Pecan, Water Pig Nut, Bitter Walnut, Bitternut

BOTANICAL NAME: *Carya* spp.

PRONUNCIATION: CARE-ee-ah

FAMILY: Juglandaceae (Walnut Family)

TYPE: Deciduous tree

HEIGHT: 50–100 feet

SPREAD: 40–50 feet

FINAL SPACING: 20–40 feet

NATURAL HABITAT AND PREFERRED SITE: Hickory grows in the moist, acid soils of east Texas and other similar areas, primarily in full sun. Several species of hickory prefer moist soil near the edges of swamps and streams.

IDENTIFICATION: Hickory tends to be upright in growth with usually a narrow crown and sometimes open branching with crooked branches. Some trees have a more rounded crown. There are about eight species of hickory in Texas. It is very difficult to tell them apart. They have similar characteristics and hybridize freely between the species.

FLOWERS AND FRUIT: The flowers are male and female on different plants (dioecious) from March to April. They are catkins. The fruit is a very hard nut that is not very tasty in most species. The nuts are generally round to pear-shaped and often have a neck-like base.

FOLIAGE: The compound leaves are alternate and deciduous with so-so yellow fall color. The leaves can range from 8–14 inches long. They usually have 5–7 leaflets, and the terminal leaflets are normally larger than those closer to the tree. Its foliage looks similar to that of pecan, but its leaflets are bigger.

BARK: The bark ranges from a very smooth texture to a very shaggy, coarse texture with age, especially on certain species. The color will be anywhere from brown to gray to almost black. The bark has irregular ridges, and in some species it is broken into deep fissures.

CULTURE: Hickory is not an easy plant to transplant or grow. It is sensitive to activity around the root system, as is the case with the native post oak and blackjack oak. If hickories exist on a construction site, the trees should be physically fenced off to prevent compaction of the root system.

PROBLEMS: Hickory won't grow well in alkaline soils, and is subject to root diseases and very sensitive to compaction and other disturbances due to construction or human activity.

PROPAGATION: Hickory is grown from seed, which should be planted immediately after collection in the fall. You never know for sure what you will get because the trees crossbreed readily.

INSIGHT: These are beautiful trees but not easy to grow in a landscape situation. The **pig nut hickory** (*Carya glabra*) likes well-drained higher soils. **Black hickory** (*C. texana*) likes dry, granite, rocky hillsides. The **shagbark hickory** (*C. ovata*) has the sweetest nuts of all.

East palatka holly.

East palatka holly foliage and fall berries.

Holly, East Palatka

COMMON NAMES: East Palatka Holly
BOTANICAL NAME: *Ilex attenuata* 'East Palatka'
PRONUNCIATION: EYE-lex ah-ten-you-AH-tah
FAMILY: Aquifoliaceae (Holly Family)
TYPE: Evergreen ornamental tree
HEIGHT: 15–30 feet
SPREAD: 10–15 feet
FINAL SPACING: 8–10 feet
NATURAL HABITAT AND PREFERRED SITE: This hybrid is adapted to a fairly wide range of soils with the exception of solid white rock in poorly drained soils. It can grow in full sun to fairly heavy shade.
IDENTIFICATION: An upright, evergreen holly with smooth-edged leaves and red berries in the fall and winter, it is normally a single-trunked and stately tree. Depending on whether lower limbs are removed, it resembles either a large bush or a small tree with upright, moderate growth, open branching, and smooth, light bark.
FLOWERS AND FRUIT: Small, white flowers appear in the spring and attract bees and other pollinators. The fruit is red berries in the fall and winter and is quite showy.

FOLIAGE: The smooth-edged, oval leaves tend to be slightly cupped downward. There is a single spine on ends of the leaves.
BARK: The bark is very smooth, light to medium gray, darkening with age.
CULTURE: It grows well in most soils except highly rocky, alkaline, or poorly drained soils. It needs moderate water and fertilization and excellent drainage.
PROBLEMS: East palatka holly, when in stress, can be attacked by scale insects, mealybugs, and other pests. It develops iron deficiency in white rock or if fertilized heavily with synthetic fertilizers. This problem can be overcome with the Sick Tree Treatment (see Appendix 3) and the Basic Organic Program (see Appendix 5).
PROPAGATION: East palatka holly can be grown from seed collected when mature in the fall and early winter, but who knows what the resulting plant will be since this is a hybrid tree?
INSIGHT: One of the prettiest holly trees, it is distinguished by one spine on the end of the leaf rather than several as with savannah and Foster hollies. These are hybrids of the **American holly** (*Ilex opaca*).

Foster holly.

Holly, Foster

COMMON NAMES: Foster Holly
BOTANICAL NAME: *Ilex attenuata* 'Foster'
PRONUNCIATION: EYE-lex ah-ten-you-AH-tah
FAMILY: Aquifoliaceae (Holly Family)
TYPE: Evergreen ornamental tree
HEIGHT: 20–25 feet
SPREAD: 8–10 feet
FINAL SPACING: 3–10 feet
NATURAL HABITAT AND PREFERRED SITE: This hybrid holly is adapted to a fairly wide range of soils with the exception of solid white rock in poorly drained soils. It can grow in full sun to fairly heavy shade.
IDENTIFICATION: The upright, pyramid-shaped evergreen has small, spiny, dark green leaves and many small, red berries in the winter.
FLOWERS AND FRUIT: Small, white flowers in the spring are followed by small, showy, red berries in the fall and winter.
FOLIAGE: The small, dark green leaves have mini-spines that are fairly soft compared to the spines of the Chinese holly.

BARK: The bark is smooth, light to medium gray.
CULTURE: Foster holly is relatively easy to grow in any well-drained soil. It prefers slightly acid conditions but adapts well to alkaline clays, especially when the soil is maintained under an organic program. Chlorosis sometimes shows up when the tree is grown in alkaline clay soils but can be corrected with Texas greensand and the other amendments of the organic program. Severe conditions can be corrected by using the Sick Tree Treatment (see Appendix 3).
PROBLEMS: It is susceptible to leaf miners occasionally and chlorosis due to poor soil conditions including bad drainage.
PROPAGATION: Foster holly can be grown from seed collected in the winter before the birds get it, but the resulting tree will be a mystery because this is a hybrid tree. To reproduce the same plant, use stem cuttings.
INSIGHT: An excellent plant for dark evergreen color, it can be used as a screening hedge or specimen plant—even in pots.

Holly, Savannah

COMMON NAMES: Savannah Holly
BOTANICAL NAME: *Ilex opaca x attenuata* 'Savannah'
PRONUNCIATION: EYE-lex o-pay-kuh
FAMILY: Aquifoliaceae (Holly Family)
TYPE: Evergreen ornamental tree
HEIGHT: 15–30 feet
SPREAD: 10–15 feet
FINAL SPACING: 8–12 feet
NATURAL HABITAT AND PREFERRED SITE: It prefers garden settings with well-prepared soil and excellent drainage. Savannah holly can adapt to both sandy and clay soils that have been made healthy with the amendments of compost and rock powders.
IDENTIFICATION: Savannah holly is a distinctive, upright, moderate-growing, pyramidal-shaped ornamental tree with medium green, shiny leaves and lots of red berries in the winter.
FLOWERS AND FRUIT: Small, white flowers in the spring are followed by red berries in the fall and winter.
FOLIAGE: The medium green foliage has multiple soft spines.
BARK: The bark is smooth, light to medium gray.
CULTURE: Much larger and more open-growing than Foster holly, savannah holly has an overall character similar to east palatka holly.
PROBLEMS: Leaf miners will occasionally hit stressed trees grown in lousy soil conditions or under artificial, high nitrogen, salt-based fertilizers. Some trees will have chlorosis in some situations.

Savannah holly.

PROPAGATION: Savannah holly, like all the hybrid hollies, can be grown from berries, but good luck on what the seedlings end up being since this is a hybrid tree.
INSIGHT: One of the best places to see this excellent tree in north Texas is the State Fairgrounds in Dallas at the horticultural center. They line the formal gardens designed by Naud Burnett.

Savannah holly foliage and winter berries.

Female yaupon holly foliage and winter berries.

Holly, Yaupon

COMMON NAMES: Yaupon Holly, Yaupon, Cassine, Evergreen Cassena, Emetic Holly, Evergreen Holly, Indian Blackdrink, Cassio Berry, Bush Tree

BOTANICAL NAME: *Ilex vomitoria*

PRONUNCIATION: EYE-lex vom-ee-TORE-ee-ah

FAMILY: Aquifoliaceae (Holly Family)

TYPE: Evergreen ornamental tree

HEIGHT: 15–25 feet

SPREAD: 15–20 feet

FINAL SPACING: 10–15 feet

NATURAL HABITAT AND PREFERRED SITE: Yaupon holly grows in the moist, acid woods of the pinelands as well as on the prairies throughout southeastern Texas. It is a tree well-adapted to a variety of soils from sand to clays. It can take fairly moist soil but is, on the other hand, also quite drought tolerant. Common in low woods and thickets along streams, it is the most abundant native holly in Texas, although its kin, the **possumhaw** (*Ilex decidua*), has a wider range. Both can grow in sun or shade.

IDENTIFICATION: Bushy unless trimmed into a tree shape, it has light-colored bark, interesting branching, and small evergreen leaves without spines. Female plants have red berries in the winter.

FLOWERS AND FRUIT: Small, white to greenish white flowers bloom in the spring and attract honeybees as

Yaupon holly.

Possumhaw.

pollinators. The fruit is a round, mealy berry. Each fruit contains 4–8 seeds. The fruit is eaten by many birds and other wildlife.

BARK: The bark is smooth, light to medium gray.

FOLIAGE: The small, round, spineless evergreen leaves are simple, alternate, thick, and smooth or mildly toothed.

CULTURE: Yaupon holly is easy to grow in most any soils and is fairly drought tolerant, although it can stand quite moist soil as well. It grows faster when under irrigation and with regular fertilizer applications.

PROBLEMS: Leaf miners occasionally damage it, but nothing very serious.

PROPAGATION: Yaupon hollies can be grown from seed or stem cuttings.

INSIGHT: The biggest problem I've ever seen with yaupon holly relates to the plant's being dug in the wild from large mottes or masses of trees. When trees are cut out of these masses, each individual tree has little root system left, and the transplant-shock death rate is extremely high. It is best to buy container-grown or at least nursery-grown yaupon hollies for best results. If you buy transplanted yaupon hollies, be sure to choose those that have been in the nursery for some period of time and have hardened off.

Weeping yaupon holly.

Honey locust.

Honey locust foliage and fruit.

Honey Locust

COMMON NAMES: Honey Locust, Sweet Locust, Thorny Locust, Sweet Bean Tree, Sweet Locust, Honey Shucks Locust, Common Honey Locust

BOTANICAL NAME: *Gleditsia triacanthos*

PRONUNCIATION: glad-IT-see-ah try-ah-CAN-thos

FAMILY: Fabaceae (Legume, Bean, or Pulse Family)

TYPE: Deciduous shade tree

HEIGHT: 50–70 feet

SPREAD: 30–40 feet

FINAL SPACING: 20–30 feet, although I don't recommend planting.

NATURAL HABITAT AND PREFERRED SITE: It grows in the eastern third of Texas in a variety of soils.

IDENTIFICATION: Honey locust is an upright, spreading, lacy-textured shade tree that has huge thorns on the limbs with clusters of thorns on the trunks. Large brown beans develop in the fall or winter.

FLOWERS AND FRUIT: The flowers are green racemes that bloom from May through June. They are not showy. The fruit ripens from September to October. The bean pods are ½–1½ feet long and ½–1½ inches wide.

FOLIAGE: The leaves are alternate, compound, and deciduous with yellow fall color. They have an overall lacy look. The leaflets are small.

BARK: The bark is grayish brown to black on the older trees. Fissures are narrow and get deeper with age, separating into scaly ridges.

CULTURE: Honey locust grows pretty much in any soil, is drought tolerant and tough, but is not recommended due to the incredibly large and vicious thorns.

PROBLEMS: Its problems include big nasty thorns, borers, and root diseases. Honey locust also tends to throw off limbs when in stress, especially during drought in the summer.

PROPAGATION: If you really want to, you can grow honey locust from seed. Pods should be gathered from the ground or picked when brown and dry and planted in the fall or kept at about 41°F over the winter and planted in the spring.

INSIGHT: If decent specimens are growing on your property, it is okay to keep them unless the thorns present a serious problem. I do not recommend planting new ones. Thornless hybrids do exist, but they don't seem nearly as healthy. The pods are eaten by cattle, deer, and other wildlife.

Huisache.

Huisache in full bloom in the spring.

Huisache

COMMON NAMES: Huisache, Sweet Acacia

BOTANICAL NAME: *Acacia farnesiana*

PRONUNCIATION: Ah-KAY-shuh far-nes-ee-AYN-ah

FAMILY: Fabaceae (Legume, Bean, or Pulse Family)

TYPE: Small, semi-evergreen, deciduous tree

HEIGHT: 20–30 feet

SPREAD: 15–20 feet

FINAL SPACING: 15–20 feet

NATURAL HABITAT AND PREFERRED SITE: Growing throughout south and south central Texas, it likes sandy or silty soil but can also take well-drained clays. It is adapted as far north as Austin and seems to be quite comfortable in landscape gardens.

IDENTIFICATION: The small, spreading tree has a rounded or flattened crown and feather-like foliage. It is armed with 1–3-inch spines at the base of each leaf.

FLOWERS AND FRUIT: Spring flowers are round, yellow, and fragrant. The fruit forms in midsummer through the early fall as black to brown woody pods, 1–2 inches long. Each pod contains two rows of shiny, hard, gray seeds.

FOLIAGE: The leaves are compound and feathery-looking with tiny leaflets and yellow fall color.

BARK: The bark is reddish brown when young, becoming furrowed and ridged with age.

CULTURE: Huisache is a fast-growing, pioneer-type plant. It grows easily in lousy soils and needs almost no care.

PROBLEMS: Freeze damage in the northern half of the state and poorly drained soil are the only two problems the plant seems to have. Weevils will sometimes attack the seed if it is left on the tree too long.

PROPAGATION: It is very easy to propagate from seed. Because the seed is covered with a very hard seed coat, mechanical or acid scarification is sometimes necessary. Seed will then germinate in 7–12 days with proper conditions and warm soil temperatures. Without scarification, germination may take as long as 1 month. Cuttings can be taken from softwood or semi-hardwood in the late spring or early summer. Transplanting is difficult on all but very small seedlings.

INSIGHT: It is sometimes confused with mesquite, but its wood is not good to use for barbeque because of the unpleasant flavor it can give food. It is said that cattle given too much of the young foliage can produce bad-tasting meat. Nevertheless, its flowers are used to produce perfume and honey. Huisache is a good tree for xeriscape (or desert) landscaping.

Jujube zigzag branches.

Jujube

COMMON NAMES: Jujube, Japanese-Apple, Common Jujube, Chinese Jujube, Chinese-Date, False Date

BOTANICAL NAME: *Ziziphus jujuba*

PRONUNCIATION: ziz-ah-FUSE jew-JEW-ba

FAMILY: Rhamnaceae (Buckthorn Family)

TYPE: Deciduous tree

HEIGHT: 25–50 feet

SPREAD: 15–30 feet

FINAL SPACING: 20–30 feet

NATURAL HABITAT AND PREFERRED SITE: Native to Syria and adjacent areas of the Middle East as well as to the warmer parts of Europe, Asia, Africa, and Australia, it is cultivated here and grows well on most soils except heavy, non-draining clay soils. It needs full sun.

IDENTIFICATION: Jujube is an interesting tree that grows to a height of 50 feet and generally has a rounded head. Its twigs grow in an unusual zigzag shape. The fruit develops in the late summer, and the leaves have yellow fall color.

FLOWERS AND FRUIT: Clusters of small, yellow flowers appear from March to May. Shiny, edible, brown fruit starts developing in the late summer and matures in the fall. The date-like fruit starts out green and turns yellowish and reddish brown to black at maturity. The pulp is sweet, like dried apples, and is eaten fresh or made into preserves. Young trees will bear fruit when they are about 2 years old.

FOLIAGE: The leaves are alternate on zigzagging twigs. Fall color is yellow.

BARK: The mottled gray or black bark tends to be very smooth on younger growth but gets rougher with age.

CULTURE: Jujube is easy to grow in most well-drained soils. It has slow to moderate growth and requires minimum amounts of water and fertilization (although it will do better with moderate amounts).

PROBLEMS: It can spread by roots, ground sprouts, and seeds to become a rather severe pest, but I still recommend it.

PROPAGATION: It is easy to grow by seed. Collect the seed as it matures in the fall and plant straight away or clean the pulp from the seed and store at 41°F through the winter to plant in the spring. It can also be grown from suckers or by grafting selected cultivars.

INSIGHT: Jujube is a unique shade tree that should be used more. Its fruit tastes like dried apples and is used medicinally, especially by Asian gardeners. In fact, you will rarely see mature fruit on jujube trees in public gardens because it is sought after. 'Enermis' is a thornless variety.

Jujube foliage and fruit.

Katsura tree.

Katsura tree foliage.

Katsura Tree

COMMON NAMES: Katsura Tree, Katsuratree, Katsura
BOTANICAL NAME: *Cercidiphyllum japonicum*
PRONUNCIATION: ker-ki-dee-FILE-um jah-PON-ih-come
FAMILY: Cercidiophyllaceae (Katsuratree Family)
TYPE: Deciduous ornamental tree
HEIGHT: 40–70 feet
SPREAD: 30–40 feet
FINAL SPACING: 10–15 feet
NATURAL HABITAT AND PREFERRED SITE: Native to China and Japan, katsura tree adapts very well here in Texas to a variety of soils, given some moisture and moderate fertility. It grows well in full sun but would benefit from afternoon shade.
IDENTIFICATION: The neat, upright tree has a delicate branching and leaf pattern and beautiful blue-green foliage that has tints of red through the growing season.
FLOWERS AND FRUIT: The non-showy male and female flowers are on separate trees (dioecious). The fruit is a small, non-showy pod.
FOLIAGE: The foliage is blue-green with distinctively heart-shaped leaves from 2–4 inches in length. The leaves are purplish when young. As they mature, they are bluish green above, lighter-colored below. Fall color is usually yellow. The leaves resemble redbud leaves except katsura leaves are opposite instead of alternate and their margins are wavy.
BARK: The young bark and stems are light brown and smooth. Older bark is shallowly furrowed and darker in color.
CULTURE: Relatively easy to grow, it does need moisture. It does not handle drought and drying winds very well and tends to get leaf scorch in the heat of the summer in full sun, especially in the afternoon.
PROBLEMS: Few problems are serious. It suffers occasional insects and burning from the heat of summer if the beds aren't healthy and mulched.
PROPAGATION: It is grown by seed primarily because cuttings are hard to establish. Remove seed from mature fruit and plant immediately or store at 41°F.
INSIGHT: This is a good tree for people to use around swimming pools and in other areas where neatness is a factor. The Katsura tree has no messy flowers, fruits, or large leaves to create a maintenance problem. The best specimen for you to see in north Texas is on the east side of the main building at the Collin County Community College in Plano, Texas. This is a tree that can stand some fairly moist soil.

Kidneywood.

Kidneywood

COMMON NAMES: Kidneywood, Texas Kidneywood, Bee Brush, Vara Dulce

BOTANICAL NAME: *Eysenhardtia texana*

PRONUNCIATION: eye-zen-HAR-dee-ah tex-AN-ah

FAMILY: Fabaceae (Legume, Bean, or Pulse Family)

TYPE: Small deciduous tree

HEIGHT: 8–15 feet

SPREAD: 6–8 feet

FINAL SPACING: 6–8 feet

NATURAL HABITAT AND PREFERRED SITE: Common in the calcarious soils of central and west Texas, it prefers full sun or light shade. It likes the dry hills and canyons of central and southwestern Texas.

IDENTIFICATION: This irregularly shaped, shrubby tree, usually less than 8 feet tall, grows in calcarious soils. It is wonderfully fragrant when in flower, and the foliage is tangerine scented when bruised.

FLOWERS AND FRUIT: The flowers are fragrant, white to pale yellow. The blooming period begins in the summer, especially after rains. Sometimes the blooming begins in May and goes through late August or September. The fruit is a small legume, ¼–⅝ inches long, containing 1 seed.

FOLIAGE: The leaves are compound with tiny, delicate leaflets that have an odor when crushed.

BARK: The stems are very smooth and become more heavily textured with age.

CULTURE: Kidneywood is fairly easy to grow in most soils as long as it is well-drained. It is drought tolerant but grows better with adequate moisture. It needs very little fertilizer.

PROBLEMS: It suffers freeze damage from very harsh winters in the northern part of the state, but it usually freezes to the ground only and returns the following spring.

PROPAGATION: Kidneywood is easily grown from fresh untreated seed and is easily rooted from softwood or hardwood cuttings taken in the summer or early fall.

INSIGHT: Dyes have been made from the wood and the wood is fluorescent in water. It is a beautiful and fragrant little tree that should be used more. It attracts bees and butterflies.

Linden

COMMON NAMES: Linden, Carolina Basswood, Basswood, Lime Tree, Whitewood, Bee Basswood, Florida Linden, Florida Basswood, Kendel Basswood, Lime Blossom Tree

BOTANICAL NAME: *Tilia americana* var. *caroliniana*

PRONUNCIATION: TILL-ee-ah ah-mer-ah-CON-ah, care-ah-len-ee-AYN-ah

FAMILY: Tiliaceae (Linden Family)

TYPE: Deciduous shade tree

HEIGHT: 40–90 feet

SPREAD: 25–35 feet

FINAL SPACING: 20–30 feet

NATURAL HABITAT AND PREFERRED SITE: Linden is native to east Texas and a small area in central Texas, but it seems to grow well in a wide variety of soils. It grows natively north and west of San Antonio.

IDENTIFICATION: Linden is a large tree with an irregular, rounded top; large, heart-shaped leaves; and a pleasant fragrance in the spring. The introduced lindens are straight-trunked and symmetrical and neat in appearance in most cases. The native linden tends to be more irregular in form. It also tends to be multi-trunked and to sucker from the base.

FLOWERS AND FRUIT: The flowers are suspended from papery bracts that look like leaves. The flowers

Little leaf linden.

Little leaf linden in full bloom.

are small, fragrant, and off-white, with 5 petals in drooping clusters. The fruit is a winged, hard capsule with 1 or 2 seeds called nutlets.

FOLIAGE: The alternate, simple, deciduous, heart-shaped leaves have yellow fall color. The leaves have a lopsided or flattened base, pointed tip, and toothed margins. They are similar to those of red mulberry (*Morus rubra*), but mulberry leaves are often lobed and symmetrical at the base.

BARK: The bark is gray with shallow fissures and flat ridges.

CULTURE: Linden is easy to grow in most soils given moderate to average moisture and requires very little fertilization. It is fairly rapid-growing.

PROBLEMS: Pests include aphids sometimes and some leaf-eating insects when the plant is in any kind of stress at all.

PROPAGATION: Linden can be grown from seed or stem cuttings taken in the late winter.

INSIGHT: Linden wood is used for interior woodwork and is great for whittling. It is an excellent tree for providing nectar for bees to make a wonderful honey. Unfortunately, there aren't enough lindens in Texas anymore to have a significant effect. We need to plant more. **Little leaf linden** (*Tilia cordata*) is a European tree but well-adapted to most of the soils in Texas as long as it is not solid white rock. Its leaves are smaller and silvery on the underside, and it generally has a more compact, symmetrical growth. There are some beautiful specimens of little leaf linden at the Collin County Community College in Plano, Texas. Teas made from the flowers are good for digestive problems, insomnia, nervous attention, and even hyperactivity in children.

Carolina basswood.

Florida basswood shown with yellow fall color.

Madrone foliage.

Madrone

COMMON NAMES: Madrone, Texas Madrone, Naked Indian, Lady's Leg, Texas Arbutus, Madrono

BOTANICAL NAME: *Arbutus xalapensis* (syn. *A. xalapensis*)

PRONUNCIATION: ar-BYOO-tus zal-ah-PEN-sis

FAMILY: Ericaceae (Heath or Blueberry Family)

TYPE: Small, evergreen ornamental tree

HEIGHT: 20–40 feet

SPREAD: 20–30 feet

FINAL SPACING: 15–25 feet

NATURAL HABITAT AND PREFERRED SITE: Madrone grows in the Chisos, Davis, Del Norte, Vieja, and Guadalupe mountains of the Trans-Pecos and parts of the Edwards Plateau. It grows well in rocky, limestone, or igneous soils in canyons and occasionally open areas in the mountainous regions of Texas. It can grow in slightly acid to alkaline soils but needs excellent drainage in either case. It can grow in full sun or light shade.

IDENTIFICATION: Madrone is usually a multi-trunked tree with beautiful bark that is reddish brown and thin and peels in sheets to reveal various colors of underbark. It usually has crooked, stout trunks and dark green evergreen leaves.

FLOWERS AND FRUIT: The flowers are creamy white to pale pink, urn- or lantern-shaped, blooming from February through April. The fruit is a round, ¼–⅓-inch in diameter, dark red (sometimes orange or golden), fleshy, edible berry that contains up to 10 seeds. It has been referred to as growing in "raspberry-like" clusters. It forms from October to December.

FOLIAGE: New leaves are reddish, maturing to glossy green, with red tinges on the undersides of the edges.

BARK: The bark is exfoliating and beautiful. When the older layers slough off, the newer bark is smooth and shows a range of colors from white to orange to shades of apricot and tan and even dark brick reds. In the Hill Country the plant is called naked Indian or lady's leg because of its smooth, red bark.

CULTURE: Madrone is easier to grow than is reported, if it isn't over watered. The Basic Organic Program (see Appendix 5) helps to eliminate typical damping off and other root fungal diseases that can plague madrone. It grows best in full sun but can take some light shade. The critical cultural factor on madrone is, don't over water and make sure the plant has excellent drainage. Horticultural cornmeal and the Basic Organic Program are quite important to this plant.

PROBLEMS: It can be damaged by root fungal diseases from soil that doesn't drain properly and other problems related to poor drainage. Madrone is also hard to transplant from the wild.

PROPAGATION: The collection of fruit can start in September, but usually the berries aren't fully ripe until October or November. You have to move fast because the birds often get the best berries, which are the heaviest and most fertile. The seed does not store well and should be planted immediately. If it can't be, place seed in cold, moist storage at 35–40°F. If the seed is gathered from November to December, it usually needs no pretreatment. Seed collected earlier may require about 30 days of cold treatment for uniform germination. Seedlings are extremely sensitive to excessive moisture, environmental stress, and damping off. Damping off can be prevented with horticultural cornmeal. Elimination of high nitrogen, synthetic, soluble fertilizers will help greatly. Garrett Juice (see Appendix 2) in a diluted form is the best fertilizer for the young seedlings. Young seedlings do benefit from partial shade during the first growing season. Madrone in the wild will germinate and start to grow under native junipers. Add shredded cedar or cedar flakes to the potting soil (or planting medium) and success rates dramatically increase.

INSIGHT: Madrone has the reputation of being cold sensitive but that is simply not true. Madrone survived the winters of 1983 and 1984 in Texas at the A&M Research Center and other sites without any problem.

Madrone.

Southern magnolia.

Southern magnolia foliage and flower.

Magnolia

COMMON NAMES: Magnolia, Southern Magnolia, Bull-Bay, Great Laurel Magnolia

BOTANICAL NAME: *Magnolia grandiflora*

PRONUNCIATION: mag-NOLE-ee-ah gran-dee-FLORE-ah

FAMILY: Magnoliaceae (Magnolia Family)

TYPE: Large evergreen tree

HEIGHT: 60 to over 100 feet

SPREAD: 30–50 feet

FINAL SPACING: 30–50 feet

NATURAL HABITAT AND PREFERRED SITE: It prefers the rich, moist soils of eastern Texas. It can grow in any moist soil if well-drained. Magnolia likes the rich bottomlands and the gentle hills of the Piney Woods. Magnolias can adapt to a wide range of soils in landscape situations. The evergreen magnolias can be grown as far north as Lubbock and Amarillo. The deciduous ones can take even colder weather.

IDENTIFICATION: Magnolia is a large-growing ornamental tree that is regal and stately with large, dark green leaves and dramatic, white flowers that appear randomly on the tree in the summer. It generally has a

Bay magnolia.

Saucer magnolia.

Star magnolia spring bloom.

Bay magnolia foliage.

straight stem and foliage to the ground unless pruned up. It has a dense, fibrous, shallow root system.

FLOWERS AND FRUIT: The off-white, fragrant flowers appear from April to August. They are solitary, 6–9 inches across. Each flower opens by midmorning and closes at night. The next day it opens much wider, but it generally starts shedding its petals at that point. The seed pods that follow are tan to rust in color and contain bright red seeds that hang by thin threads. Seeds are eaten by birds, squirrels, and other animals. The fruit ripens from July to October.

FOLIAGE: The leaves are simple, alternate, evergreen, thick, and waxy.

BARK: The aromatic, bitter, grayish brown bark breaks into thin, small scales with age.

CULTURE: Magnolia is easy to grow in any well-drained soil. It can stand a wide range of soils except for shallow white rock or soil that stays too wet. It needs lots of room and cannot grow in the shade. It needs moist soil and moderate fertilizer applications.

PROBLEMS: Magnolia can develop chlorosis from a lack of trace minerals if the soil if not healthy. This condition can be helped with the Basic Organic Program (see Appendix 5), and severe cases can be

Little gem magnolia.

helped with the Sick Tree Treatment (see Appendix 3). The evergreen magnolias are also a little messy because of their continuous leaf drop. It is difficult to grow anything beneath the trees because of the dense root systems and the heavy shade.

PROPAGATION: Gather the red seeds as soon as they are ripe and clean them before storage. They should be placed in sand or peat moss in the refrigerator after cleaning. Cold, moist stratification at 41°F for about 60 days before sowing in the spring helps. Seedlings grow slowly. Cuttings can be propagated from semi-hardwood cuttings taken in the summer. Magnolias are difficult to transplant from the wild.

INSIGHT: The deciduous **saucer** or **tulip magnolia** (*Magnolia soulangiana*) has pink flowers in the spring. It grows to about 20 feet in height. Another deciduous species is **star magnolia** (*M. stellata*). It has white spring flowers and grows to about 12 feet high. These deciduous magnolias will do better with

some shade—a plot with morning sun and afternoon shade is the ideal location. Soil conditions, water, and fertilizer requirements are about the same for all. There are also cultivars of the evergreen magnolia. One is called **little gem** (*M. grandiflora*). It has the reputation of being a dwarf, but it actually isn't. It is just a slower-growing plant with smaller leaves. The original mother plant of little gem is about 50 feet tall now and still growing. The beautiful **bay magnolia** or **sweet bay** (*M. virginiana*), which is deciduous or semi-evergreen, has fragrant, creamy white flowers from the summer to fall. It grows to as tall as 50 feet. The leaves are grayish green above and almost white underneath. This tree is suited primarily to deep east Texas but adapts to various garden soils fairly well. I've grown the plant as far north as the Dallas/Fort Worth area. It should not be used in shallow soils over white limestone rock. It is also called **swamp bay** or **beaver tree.**

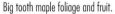
Big tooth maple foliage and fruit.

Big tooth maple fall color.

Maple, Big Tooth

COMMON NAMES: Big Tooth Maple, Sabinal Maple, Western Sugar Maple, Uvalde Big Tooth Maple, Canyon Maple, Southwestern Big Tooth Maple, Plateau Big Tooth Maple, Limerock Maple

BOTANICAL NAME: *Acer grandidentatum*

PRONUNCIATION: A-sir gran-dee-den-TA-tum

FAMILY: Aceraceae (Maple Family)

TYPE: Deciduous shade tree

HEIGHT: 40–50 feet

SPREAD: 20–30 feet

FINAL SPACING: 20–30 feet

NATURAL HABITAT AND PREFERRED SITE: It prefers valleys, canyons, and the banks of mountain streams primarily at higher elevations such as the sheltered canyons of the Edwards Plateau, the Lampasas cut plains, and the high country of the Trans-Pecos. Big tooth maples like growing in limestone soils but can adapt to a wide range of soils.

IDENTIFICATION: Big tooth maple is a beautiful, upright to spreading tree, growing to 50 feet, with yellow to golden fall color.

FLOWERS AND FRUIT: Small, yellow flowers appear with the leaves in April and May. The fruit is a green or rose color, a double samara (winged seed) maturing in September.

FOLIAGE: The leaves are simple, alternate, and deciduous and have golden yellow to red fall color. The leaves (on the same tree even) can be 3–5 lobes.

BARK: The dark brown to gray bark has narrow fissures and flat ridges creating plate-like scales. The bark is thin and easily damaged.

CULTURE: Big tooth maple can be easily grown in a variety of well-drained soils from sand to clays to even white limestone areas. It is drought tolerant and does not need heavy fertilization.

PROBLEMS: It does not have many pests. The only problem with it that I have ever heard about is that it is slow-growing when young and the foliage can sometimes burn on the tips in extremely hot summers.

PROPAGATION: Propagation is primarily done by seed collected in the fall and given cold stratification at 41°F for 30–160 days before planting. Seed from higher elevations requires longer cold stratification.

INSIGHT: This is a wonderful tree that should be planted more. It is becoming more available in the nursery trade but has been scarce in the past. **Uvalde big tooth maple** (*Acer grandidentatum* var. *sinuosum*) differs somewhat by its having leaves with 3 lobes and smooth margins.

Big tooth maples.

Caddo maple foliage in the fall.

Shantung maple.

Maple, Caddo

COMMON NAMES: Caddo Maple
BOTANICAL NAME: *Acer saccharum* 'Caddo'
PRONUNCIATION: A-sir sah-KAR-um CAD-oh
FAMILY: Aceraceae (Maple Family)
TYPE: Deciduous tree
HEIGHT: 50–60 feet
SPREAD: 25–35 feet
FINAL SPACING: 20–30 feet
NATURAL HABITAT AND PREFERRED SITE: Caddo maple is native to parts of Oklahoma and Arkansas. It has been called a native Texas plant, but no one seems to be able to confirm that.
IDENTIFICATION: It is an upright, rounded shade tree with attractive foliage in the summer, beautiful, golden yellow fall color, and a neat, clean appearance.
FLOWERS AND FRUIT: Fairly showy flowers bloom in the spring, followed by samaras (winged seeds) in the fall.
FOLIAGE: It has dark green summer foliage. The leaves are thick and sturdy with golden yellow to salmon shades in the fall—beautiful fall color.

BARK: Caddo maple has a thin, light gray to tan bark that darkens with age.
CULTURE: It is easy to grow in almost any soil including rocky, alkaline soils as long as the drainage is good. Caddo maple is a drought tolerant plant that grows in full sun and needs very little fertilization.
PROBLEMS: Finding the plant in the nursery industry is the biggest problem, but it is getting easier every year.
PROPAGATION: Like all maples, it is best propagated by seed. There is not much information available on growing it from stem cuttings, but most maples are hard to propagate from stem cuttings.
INSIGHT: Caddo maple is one of the best of the large-growing maple trees for the alkaline soils of Texas. It really should be used quite a bit more as soon as the availability increases. Shantung maple (*Acer truncatum*) is a Chinese immigrant that looks similar to Caddo maple but grows over twice as fast. It is definitely worth a try. I am very impressed with this tree. Best specimens in Texas so far are at the Fort Worth Botanical Gardens.

Caddo maple.

Chalk maple.

Maple, Chalk

COMMON NAMES: Chalk Maple, White Bark Maple
BOTANICAL NAME: *Acer leucoderme*
PRONUNCIATION: A-sir loo-co-DER-me
FAMILY: Aceraceae (Maple Family)
TYPE: Deciduous shade tree
HEIGHT: 15–30 feet
SPREAD: 10–15 feet
FINAL SPACING: 10–15 feet
NATURAL HABITAT AND PREFERRED SITE: Very rare in Texas, it does occur in Jasper, Sabine, San Augustine, and Newton counties in southeast Texas. It is the predominant maple in the Sabine National Forest but is being planted in many other areas of Texas now. It is commonly found in moist soil along riverbanks and streams.
IDENTIFICATION: Chalk maple is a small tree with a rounded top. The branches are slender, and it has beautiful foliage and fall color.
FLOWERS AND FRUIT: Small, yellow flowers bloom in the spring—usually in April. The fruit, which is a samara (winged seed), matures in September and is usually heavy and showy on the tree.

FOLIAGE: The foliage appears at the same time that the flowers emerge. The young foliage has pale hairs, which give a velvety feel to the underside of the leaves. The mature foliage usually droops. Fall color is golden or red and sometimes a combination of colors at one time on the tree.
BARK: The bark is smooth, pale gray to almost white when young. With age the bark develops narrow ridges separated by deep fissures.
CULTURE: Chalk maple is easy to grow in any moist soil but adapts to drier situations. It needs very little fertilizer but does respond to good conditions.
PROBLEMS: Few problems exist other than environmental stresses. Under the Basic Organic Program (see Appendix 5), it should be virtually pest-free. Lack of availability in the nursery trade is currently a common problem.
PROPAGATION: Like all maples, chalk maple is best grown from seed. Growing most *Acer* species from cuttings is difficult.
INSIGHT: This is one of those well-adapted Texas maples that should be used quite a bit more. At the moment, availability at the nurseries is not great. As more people request the tree, availability will increase.

Fan leaf Japanese maple.

Fan leaf Japanese maple in the fall.

Maple, Japanese

COMMON NAMES: Japanese Maple
BOTANICAL NAME: *Acer palmatum*
PRONUNCIATION: A-sir pal-MAY-tum
FAMILY: Aceraceae (Maple Family)
TYPE: Small deciduous tree
HEIGHT: 6–20 feet
SPREAD: 10–20 feet
FINAL SPACING: 10–15 feet
NATURAL HABITAT AND PREFERRED SITE: Japanese maple is native to Japan and China but adapts well to typical garden soils in Texas. It needs moisture and good drainage. Most of these trees prefer filtered light or morning sun with afternoon shade. The green *Acer palmatum* tends to be able to stand the most direct sun.
IDENTIFICATION: Japanese maples vary tremendously in size, appearance, leaf texture, and color. They range from dwarf, lacy-leafed varieties to very tall, wide-leafed varieties and cultivars. Fall color can range from yellows and gold to deep reds and maroons.

FLOWERS AND FRUIT: The flowers of most Japanese maples are insignificant, and the bloom effect comes from the unfolding of the colorful new foliage growth in the spring. The fruit is a typical maple samara (winged seed) appearing in the late summer and fall.
BARK: The bark ranges tremendously from green through various shades of gray and brown. On the *Acer palmatum*, 'Coralbark,' the bark is even red.
FOLIAGE: Japanese maple foliage is fascinating. The leaves vary tremendously in size, shape, and color. Some species have delicate, lacy, deeply cut leaves, and others have leaves that are almost rounded, while some leaves resemble elm leaves. The color varies as much, ranging from green to various shades of reds, pinks and oranges. Some varieties have string-like leaves and some have all-variegated leaves with dramatic color combinations.
CULTURE: Most varieties of Japanese maple are easy to grow in Texas as long as they are given ample moisture and some protection from the hot afternoon sun. The red-leafed varieties are the most susceptible to their foliage edges' burning. When this happens, there

Coralbark Japanese maple in the early spring.

Green Japanese maple in the fall.

is really not much that can be done other than change the location of the plant. Japanese maples can be grown in pots. One of the best for pots is the **Dwarf Japanese maple** (*A. palmatum disectum*). Japanese maple needs a moderate amount of fertilizer.

PROBLEMS: Few problems exist other than the scorch of the leaves during the summer. In most cases cold damage is not a worry unless an extremely hard freeze follows a long warm spell and the plant has not had time to harden off.

PROPAGATION: This is done primarily from seed and grafting but also budding and layering. An excellent way to get exactly the Japanese maple you want is to do air layering.

INSIGHT: Yes, it is an introduced plant but it adapts well into Texas gardens.

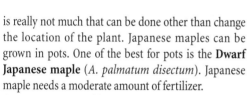

Coralbark Japanese maple in the fall.

Green Japanese maple in the summer.

Red maple.

Maple, Red

COMMON NAMES: Red Maple, Drummond Red Maple, Trident Red Maple, Swamp Maple, Water Maple, Scarlet Maple, Soft Maple

BOTANICAL NAME: *Acer rubrum* var. *drummondii*

PRONUNCIATION: A-sir ROO-brum

FAMILY: Aceraceae (Maple Family)

TYPE: Deciduous shade tree

HEIGHT: 60–90 feet

SPREAD: 30–40 feet

FINAL SPACING: 20–40 feet

NATURAL HABITAT AND PREFERRED SITE: Red maples occur primarily in the wetter areas in the Piney Woods of east Texas. For best results, plant them in full sun.

IDENTIFICATION: They are an upright-growing tree with dramatic and colorful buds, fruit, and fall color.

FLOWERS AND FRUIT: During the winter the buds become large and bright red and showy. In February before the leaves unfold, the pink to bright red stamens of the male flowers appear. Then the trees produce the clusters of brightly colored pink and red samaras (winged seed). The fruits are paired samaras with yellow or red wings.

FOLIAGE: The foliage is medium green in the summer but turns dramatic shades of crimson and scarlet in the fall.

BARK: The bark is smooth and gray when young but grows coarser in texture and color with age.

CULTURE: Red maple is easy to grow in deep soils, preferring sandy, acid conditions, but it can adapt to clay soils as long as white rock is not near the surface. Success will be fair to moderate in the clay soils. The easiest of the red maples to grow is **trident red maple** or **trident maple** (*Acer rubrum* var. *tridens* or *trilobum*). This tree has 3-lobed leaves instead of the typical maple leaf, and it also turns golden yellow in the fall rather than red. This tree is very easy to grow in a wider range of soils. It should be used more.

PROBLEMS: Scorching and chlorosis in the heavy clay soils and white rock are problems. The tree is not highly drought tolerant and does better in moist soil. Stress from these environmental problems can lead to various insect and disease infestations. The Sick Tree Treatment (see Appendix 3) will always help.

PROPAGATION: Like all maples, propagation is primarily done from seed. Best results come from stratification after collection in the fall. Place seed in moist sand or organic matter and store at 41°F for 30–160 days.

INSIGHT: This tree is a great choice for the sandy soils of east Texas as well as the sandy bands of soil that run throughout the other parts of Texas.

Red maple foliage.

Fruit in the early spring.

Trident maple.

Silver maple.

Maple, Silver

COMMON NAMES: Silver Maple
BOTANICAL NAME: *Acer saccharinum*
PRONUNCIATION: A-sir sah-kar-RINE-um
FAMILY: Aceraceae (Maple Family)
TYPE: Deciduous shade tree
HEIGHT: 40–80 feet
SPREAD: 20–30 feet
FINAL SPACING: Do not plant.
NATURAL HABITAT AND PREFERRED SITE: Its most common habitat is the nurseries that sell junk trees.
IDENTIFICATION: This upright to spreading tree tends to have slender, drooping branches and a relatively open overall character.
FLOWERS AND FRUIT: The flowers show before the leaves in the spring, are greenish yellow, and are not very pretty. The fruit (samara or winged seed) ripens when the leaves are almost mature.

FOLIAGE: The leaves are opposite, simple, deciduous, and weak yellow in fall color.
BARK: The bark is smooth when young but with age turns gray and breaks into loose flakes.
CULTURE: This is an easy tree to plant and grow for a few years, before the problems start.
PROBLEMS: Silver maple is an extremely short-lived tree, has weak wood, and is subject to many insect and disease problems, including chlorosis, borers, and cotton root rot. The fact is, this tree is an unhealthy, lousy tree. I get more calls about problems with this tree than probably any other. Close seconds would include Siberian elm, fruitless mulberry, mimosa, and poplars.
PROPAGATION: Not a good idea.
INSIGHT: Try to pick a better quality tree.

Mesquite

COMMON NAMES: Mesquite, Honey Mesquite, Algaroba
BOTANICAL NAME: *Prosopis glandulosa*
PRONUNCIATION: pruh-SO-pis glan-due-LO-suh
FAMILY: Fabaceae (Legume, Bean, or Pulse Family)
TYPE: Deciduous tree
HEIGHT: 25–30 feet
SPREAD: 20–30 feet
FINAL SPACING: 20–40 feet
NATURAL HABITAT AND PREFERRED SITE:
Mesquite is very common throughout the state and occupies all but the far eastern side of the state and the top of the Panhandle. It grows in all soils. It is a native plant but functions like an introduced weed, especially if there is an attempt to control it.
IDENTIFICATION: Mesquite is an open-growing, airy, lacy, quite attractive tree. Its leaves emerge late in the spring, usually after the last frost, and are shed early in the fall. It has subtle, yellow flowers in the spring and hard, beadlike seed pods in the fall. The fall color is yellow but unexciting. It has large thorns and begins to spread wider with age. The lacy airiness of the tree creates dapple shade on the ground, allowing grass to grow right up to the base of the trunk.
FLOWERS AND FRUIT: The flowers are creamy white or yellowish and have a nice fragrance in the late spring or early summer, especially after heavy rains. These flowers are an excellent source of pollen, which bees use to create a wonderful, light, and clear honey. The fruit is a tough, leathery, bean-like seed pod that does not open at maturity.
FOLIAGE: The foliage is lacy, compound leaves with tiny leaflets, light green in color through the summer.
BARK: The rough, reddish brown to gray bark has shallow fissures and thick scales.
CULTURE: Mesquite is an easy-to-grow native tree. Mesquite is drought tolerant and does not need any fertilizer to do well.
PROBLEMS: Insect problems are few. In fact, most of the ranchers in Texas are looking for a pest to control this tree. Mesquite actually does get borer infestations from time to time, which are usually related to getting too much water. The spread of, and problem with, mesquite trees has been primarily from mismanagement of the land. The large, single-trunk trees not only

help to improve the soil and allow grass to grow under them for livestock, but have evolved to keep other mesquite trees and brush away. It is only when the trees are killed to the ground that they become a problem. Then the trees grow back as multi-trunked, bushier trees that are a much bigger problem.
PROPAGATION: Mesquite is grown by seed, cuttings, and transplants. Even though the pods stay on the tree all winter, they should be gathered in the late summer or early fall as soon as they are firm, filled out, and brown. This will minimize loss due to insect infestations. Mesquite is easily grown from fresh untreated seed, but seed will germinate faster if scarified first with a physical injury from a knife or file. Some people recommend soaking the seed in sulfuric acid for 15–30 minutes. Using strong vinegar would be a more organic and equally effective approach. Cuttings will root from juvenile wood and from suckers or root sprouts. Transplanting is fairly difficult except for nursery-grown trees, which grow and transplant easily. Some books recommend cutting the treetop back when transplanting. That is incorrect advice. All limbs and twigs should be left on the tree.
INSIGHT: Mesquite is considered a junk tree and an aggressive pest, except by ranchers. It now covers over 60 million acres of Texas rangeland. Early in my career, I was asked how to control mesquite organically. I told the caller I didn't know but would find out. When I checked with one of my rancher friends, the rancher told me that once ranchers stopped throwing money at trying to control the mesquites, they realized that they were a benefit on the property. Because they are a legume, the grass under the trees is preferred by the livestock, plus the animals like the shade from the big trees. The real problem from mesquite comes from futile attempts to destroy it, especially by cutting it down and poisoning it with toxic chemicals. The tree, rather than growing back as a single-trunked tree as it originally was, grows back in multiple trunks in bushy form and becomes a much bigger problem. This happens because dormant buds sprout from below the ground line once the top of the plant is killed. Indians once used mesquite beans as food. The beans are still used as food by livestock.

Mesquite.

Mexican elder in El Paso.

Mexican Elder

COMMON NAMES: Mexican Elder, Mexican Elderberry, Tapiro, Sauco

BOTANICAL NAME: *Sambucus mexicana*

PRONUNCIATION: sam-BOO-kus mex-eh-KAH-nah

FAMILY: Caprifoliaceae (Honeysuckle Family)

TYPE: Mostly evergreen ornamental tree

HEIGHT: 10–15 feet, but known to reach 35 feet

SPREAD: 10–15 feet

FINAL SPACING: 10–15 feet

NATURAL HABITAT AND PREFERRED SITE: It grows primarily from El Paso to Del Rio and likes moist soils. It's a tree that could probably be used in much more of Texas except for the most northern parts.

IDENTIFICATION: Mexican elder is a beautiful, small tree that is usually evergreen but sometimes drops its leaves during hot summers if not watered regularly. If you don't mind the partial defoliation, the tree is relatively drought tolerant. It has a nice flower display primarily in the early summer and in the fall. It also has berries that are attractive and eaten by birds.

FLOWERS AND FRUIT: The flowers are clusters of white to pale yellow and bloom primarily in the early summer and in the fall. The small fruits look like clusters of dark blue or black berries, and they attract several species of birds. When the fruit is fully ripe, the tree is covered with a dense, white bloom.

FOLIAGE: The leaves are primarily evergreen except when the summer drought causes partial defoliation. The leaves have 3–7 leaflets that are serrated (toothed) except at the base and point. Both sides are green and the texture ranges from smooth to fuzzy.

BARK: The young bark is smooth but the main trunk becomes furrowed with age.

CULTURE: This is a tree that can be grown in the warm half of the state and responds well to soil moisture even though it is a drought tolerant tree. It has few pest problems and needs little fertilizer. It's a perfect tree for the organic program. It's a fairly fast grower, too.

PROBLEMS: Few, if any, problems exist other than freeze damage in the northern part of the state.

PROPAGATION: I have to be honest; I have never propagated this plant. But I think it would be easy to grow from the seed in the blue-black fruit. Give it a try and let me know what you see. Other books have reported that it can be started from softwood cuttings.

INSIGHT: As with all elders, this tree likes plenty of water, and given that moisture, it will grow quite fast. The tree will have brittle branches that can be frozen back. This is just a cosmetic problem.

Mimosa foliage.

Mimosa seed pods.

Mimosa

COMMON NAMES: Mimosa, Catclaw, Sensitive-Briar
BOTANICAL NAME: *Albizia julibrissin*
PRONUNCIATION: al-BIZ-ee-ah jul-leh-BRY-sin
FAMILY: Fabaceae (Legume, Bean, or Pulse Family)
TYPE: Deciduous tree
HEIGHT: 15–20 feet
SPREAD: 25–40 feet
FINAL SPACING: Do not plant.
NATURAL HABITAT AND PREFERRED SITE: The plant is actually native to India and Nepal—and it should have stayed there. It now grows all over the place but poorly.
IDENTIFICATION: It is a wide-spreading tree with long stems and branches. It has fluffy, pink flowers in the summer, followed by bean-like pods in the fall.
FLOWERS AND FRUIT: Fluffy, pink, attractive flowers bloom in the summer. The bean pods are typical legume bean pods, 5–8 inches long. The flowers bloom from May to August.
FOLIAGE: This deciduous tree has pretty lousy yellow fall color. The leaves are alternate, lacy, typical legume foliage.

BARK: The bark is very smooth and gray. Mimosa trees do make excellent climbing trees for kids. The bark is nice and smooth, and since the limbs are wide-spreading, the fall is not great.
CULTURE: It will grow basically anywhere, but the tree doesn't last long in any soil. It is dying out across the United States, which is unfortunate because it is really pretty when it's healthy. It needs normal water and normal fertilization. The Sick Tree Treatment (see Appendix 3) might be able to keep the tree healthy and alive for a longer period of time, but nothing can change the fact that it is a very short-lived tree.
PROBLEMS: Mimosa suffers from a short life, a destructive root system, and various insect and disease infestations.
PROPAGATION: It is grown easily from seed or cuttings, but who would want to? They will break your heart with their short lives.
INSIGHT: I have said it before and I'll say it again—it may be the ultimate junk tree, but it is in a close race with Siberian elm, fruitless mulberry, and silver maple.

Red mulberry foliage and fruit.

Mulberry, Red

COMMON NAMES: Red Mulberry, Mulberry, Moral, Lampasas Mulberry

BOTANICAL NAME: *Morus rubra*

PRONUNCIATION: MORE-us ROO-bra

FAMILY: Moraceae (Mulberry Family)

TYPE: Deciduous shade tree

HEIGHT: 30–50 feet

SPREAD: 40–50 feet

FINAL SPACING: 20–40 feet

NATURAL HABITAT AND PREFERRED SITE: It grows in the eastern two-thirds of Texas, primarily in river bottoms and deep, rich soils. Fruiting mulberries can adapt to a wide range of soils from sand to clays, as long as there is ample moisture and drainage.

IDENTIFICATION: It is a large, spreading tree with big leaves, edible fruit, and yellow fall color.

FLOWERS AND FRUIT: The flowers are inconspicuous drupes in the early spring, followed by blackberry-like fruit, which ripens and drops from the tree from May through August. The fruit is sweet, edible, and attractive to wildlife, especially birds. The flowers are perfect, or unisexual.

FOLIAGE: The leaves are simple, alternate, deciduous, and 3–9 inches long. They can be oval or lobed and with serrated edges.

BARK: The bark is smooth when young, becoming scaly with age.

CULTURE: Red mulberry is easy to grow in any soil that is well-drained.

PROBLEMS: Mulberries can have several pest problems, even cotton root rot, if growing in unhealthy soil, but the Basic Organic Program (see Appendix 5) usually eliminates these troubles. The most common problem is the mess that is made from birds after they eat the ripe fruit, so be very careful where you plant these trees.

PROPAGATION: Mulberries are grown easily from seed. Sow directly after collection or stratify for 60–90 days at 41°F and then plant in the spring (or earlier in a greenhouse). The fruit should be collected after it has turned red or dark purple. Seed should be thoroughly air dried and stored at the cold temperature in sealed containers.

INSIGHT: Hybrid **fruitless mulberry** is a fast-growing junk tree with large various-shaped leaves and shallow, destructive root systems. The plant uses large quantities of water, is a worthless weed, and should never be planted. Other varieties of mulberry include **mountain mulberry** (*Morus microphylla*), which is a more bushy, drought tolerant form that grows to 20 feet in height and may be multi-trunked. Its fruit, like other mulberries, is edible when ripe. It grows in the canyons, in limestone or igneous rock soils, in the western two-thirds of the state. The famous **white mulberry** (*M. alba*) from China grows leaves used to feed silkworms. Small weeping forms of mulberry are available and are effective for use in Oriental gardens.

Fruitless mulberry—a big weed.

Oak, Blackjack

COMMON NAMES: Blackjack Oak, Blackjack, Barron Oak, Jack Oak, Black Oak

BOTANICAL NAME: *Quercus marilandica*

PRONUNCIATION: KWEAR-cus mar-ah-LAN-di-cah

FAMILY: Fagaceae (Beech Family)

TYPE: Deciduous shade tree

HEIGHT: 50–60 feet

SPREAD: 30–40 feet

FINAL SPACING: 30–40 feet

NATURAL HABITAT AND PREFERRED SITE: It grows in the eastern half of Texas, especially in the sandy, acid soils. There is a western form of blackjack oak that grows to only 30 feet and can grow in sand, gravel, or clay soils that are only slightly acidic.

IDENTIFICATION: This rounded, symmetrical tree has club-like leaves and very dark, heavily textured bark. It is stiff in overall appearance.

FLOWERS AND FRUIT: The flowers appear with the leaves in the spring as slender, hairy, yellowish green catkins, 2–4 inches long. The fruit is an acorn, growing either alone or in pairs, that ripens in 2 years.

FOLIAGE: The leaves are simple, alternate, deciduous, and club-shaped. Fall color is yellow but not a knockout.

BARK: The bark is dark brown to almost solid black, broken into rough, block-like plates with a heavy texture.

CULTURE: For the most part, blackjack oak needs sandy, acid soil to survive. It does not do well in the black and white soils of north Texas. It is drought tolerant and needs very little fertilization.

Blackjack oak.

PROBLEMS: It does not do well in the alkaline clay soils.

PROPAGATION: It is grown from acorns planted in the soil immediately after they fall from the tree in the fall.

INSIGHT: Blackjack oak is said to indicate poor soil areas. The tree is rarely cultivated because it is difficult to transplant.

Blackjack oak foliage and fruit.

Bur oak.

Bur oak foliage and fruit.

Oak, Bur

COMMON NAMES: Bur Oak, Mossycup Oak, Mossy
Overcup Oak, Prairie Oak

BOTANICAL NAME: *Quercus macrocarpa*

PRONUNCIATION: KWER-cus mack-row-CAR-puh

FAMILY: Fagaceae (Beech Family)

TYPE: Deciduous shade tree

HEIGHT: 60–80 feet

SPREAD: 60–80 feet

FINAL SPACING: 30–50 feet

NATURAL HABITAT AND PREFERRED SITE: Bur
oak is a resident of the tall grass prairie from north
central Texas to central Texas. It will adapt to a wide
range of garden and landscape conditions.

IDENTIFICATION: Bur oak is a stately, tall, rounded
tree with huge leaves and golf ball-sized acorns. The
yellow fall color is so-so at best.

FLOWERS AND FRUIT: Rust-colored male flowers
hang from the terminal growth in the spring. Female
flowers bloom singly or in small clusters. The fruits
are very large acorns—some are as large as golf balls.

FOLIAGE: The leaves are alternate, simple, and very
large—6–10 inches long and sometimes 4–5 inches
wide—with rounded lobes. The fall color is yellow to
brown and usually nothing to write home about. If
this tree had good fall color, it would be the perfect
tree, unless you don't like big acorns.

BARK: The bark is medium textured, light to medium
gray. It sometimes develops a rough texture in spots,
even on some of the young branches. The terminal
stems are quite large. The buds are also large and
egg-shaped. Stems and twigs occasionally have
wings or ribs.

CULTURE: It is probably the easiest to grow of all the
oaks. Bur oak is drought tolerant and does well in

many different soil types from sand to heavy clays. It grows well in the black and white soils of north Texas. It is susceptible to very few diseases or insect pests and is the fastest-growing and probably the longest living of all the oaks of Texas. It can grow up to 150 feet in height in deep soil.

PROBLEMS: Bur oak is occasionally attacked by lacebugs, which turn the leaves a brownish color in the summer, but such attacks are always due to stressful conditions: too much or too little water, too much high nitrogen fertilizer, not using the organic program, etc.

PROPAGATION: Plant the large acorns as soon as they fall from the tree. If they lie on the ground any length of time at all, the insects realize how tasty they are and eat them before you can get them. After you put the large acorns in the potting soil or in the ground, your only worries will be to keep the soil from drying out and to keep the squirrels from getting your little treasures.

INSIGHT: It is probably my favorite shade tree and should be planted on any site where there is enough room. **Overcup oak** (*Quercus lyrata*) is often confused with bur oak but grows only in acid sandy loam and wet soils, as opposed to the calcarious and limestone soils of the bur oak. Overcup oak is almost always confined to swamps and other wet soil areas. Its other common names are **swamp post oak, swamp white oak,** and **water white oak.**

Bur oak acorns showing relative size.

Chinkapin oak.

Oak, Chinkapin

COMMON NAMES: Chinkapin Oak, Chestnut Oak, Yellow Chestnut Oak, Rock Chestnut Oak, Rock Oak, Yellow Oak, Chinquapin Oak

BOTANICAL NAME: *Quercus muehlenbergii*

PRONUNCIATION: KWER-cus mule-len-BERG-ee-eye

FAMILY: Fagaceae (Beech Family)

TYPE: Deciduous shade tree

HEIGHT: 70–90 feet

SPREAD: 70–80 feet

FINAL SPACING: 20–50 feet

NATURAL HABITAT AND PREFERRED SITE: From northeast Texas through central Texas as well as spots in the Trans-Pecos, chinkapin oak is seen often in deeper, well-drained soils along rivers and in creek bottoms. It likes moist and swampy soil but can also grow in drier, rocky soils.

IDENTIFICATION: Chinkapin oak is a large-growing, dramatic tree with true chinquapin-type leaves, large acorns, and a light gray-colored, flaky bark. Fall color is yellowish brown and not spectacular.

FLOWERS AND FRUIT: Male flowers are rust-colored and hang from the terminal growth in the early spring. Female flowers bloom singly or in small clusters. Male and female flowers are catkins, and they appear on the same tree after the leaves are about a third grown. The fruits are dark purple to black acorns that mature in the fall, from September through October, in clusters or singly—usually two on single, dark stems that are about as long as the leaf.

FOLIAGE: The pretty foliage has yellow to brownish fall color that is not spectacular. The leaves are toothed, not lobed, alternate, simple, and deciduous.

BARK: The bark is light gray-colored and flaky.

Chinkapin oak.

Chinkapin oak foliage and fruit.

CULTURE: The common name for this tree comes from the fact that its leaves are similar to those of the true **chinquapin**, *(Castanea pumila)*, which is native to the eastern United States, though it has been seen growing in deep east Texas. It needs deep, sandy, acid soil.

PROBLEMS: Chinkapin oak can't stand wet feet or poor drainage. Larger specimens are hard to transplant. It is best to buy this tree as a nursery-grown plant in order to start with a bigger tree. Container-grown plants are the best buy.

PROPAGATION: Chinkapin oak is easy to propagate from the acorns. Plant them as soon as possible after they release from the tree. Plant them in the same kind of soil the tree will eventually be growing in. Air root pruning of the seedlings is recommended by Dr. Carl Whitcomb in his books.

INSIGHT: This tree is easily confused with **swamp chestnut oak** *(Quercus michauxii)*, which does not grow well in alkaline soils. The swamp chestnut oak leaves have more rounded lobes in contrast to the chinkapin oak's sharp, pointed edges.

Oak, Durand

COMMON NAMES: Durand Oak, Durand White Oak, White Oak, Bluff Oak

BOTANICAL NAME: *Quercus sinuata* var. *sinuata*

PRONUNCIATION: KWER-kus sin-you-AH-taw

FAMILY: Fagaceae (Beech Family)

TYPE: Deciduous shade tree

HEIGHT: 60–90 feet

SPREAD: 30–40 feet

FINAL SPACING: 20–50 feet

NATURAL HABITAT AND PREFERRED SITE: It likes neutral to acidic, deep, rich, and moist soils, and the limestone flats and grasslands of the eastern third of the state. Durand oak will adapt well in a landscape situation to a wide range of soil types from sand to clay. It seems to grow well in most parts of Texas. Durand oak is found growing primarily in deeper soils such as those found in the east Texas Piney Woods. It is native to the Waco area.

IDENTIFICATION: This tall, rather irregularly shaped tree has open branching, smallish leaves with rounded lobes, and yellow to reddish fall color. Sometimes confused with the much shorter-growing bigelow oak that grows in the rocky limestone soils.

FLOWERS AND FRUIT: The male and female catkins are separate. They are ¾–1 inch long and fuzzy. Male flowers are rust-colored and hang from the terminal twig growth in the early spring. Female flowers

Durand oak.

Durand oak foliage and fall color.

Bigelow oak foliage.

Bigelow oak in the winter.

bloom singly or in small clusters. The fruits are one-seeded acorns as are all oaks. It matures in the fall, from October through November, and is borne on short stems close to the main stem.

FOLIAGE: The leaves are simple, alternate, and deciduous with yellow to reddish fall color.

BARK: The bark is pale gray to brown, smooth on young trees but developing heavier texture with maturity.

CULTURE: Durand oak is easy to grow in well-drained soils, from sandy to fairly heavy clays, with a minimum amount of water and fertilizer.

PROBLEMS: Few problems, if any, are encountered other than the fact that the tree is not widely available in the nursery trade at this time. It is a plant that should be used more.

PROPAGATION: It is grown from acorns planted immediately after they have released from the tree.

INSIGHT: A close relative, **bigelow oak** (*Quercus sinuata* var. *breviloba*), is a smaller-growing (12–15 feet) tree. It has pale, flaky bark, orange fall color, and very interesting, crooked branching. It is one of the trees considered a **shin oak** and is native to the north central part of Texas.

Graceful or evergreen oak.

Oak, Graceful

COMMON NAMES: Graceful Oak, Evergreen Oak, Slender Oak, Chisos Oak

BOTANICAL NAME: *Quercus graciliformis*

PRONUNCIATION: KWER-cus grace-ah-li-FORM-iss

FAMILY: Fagaceae (Beech Family)

TYPE: Semi-evergreen tree

HEIGHT: 20–40 feet

SPREAD: 20–25 feet

FINAL SPACING: 15–30 feet

NATURAL HABITAT AND PREFERRED SITE: It grows primarily in the Chisos Mountains in Brewster County.

IDENTIFICATION: It is an attractive, shiny-leafed plant that resembles the Chisos oak. Graceful oak or evergreen oak is a small to medium-sized tree that will grow in a wide range of soils.

FLOWERS AND FRUIT: It is a typical oak with separate male and female flowers or catkins. The fruits are acorns.

BARK: The bark is smooth on young trees, developing heavier texture with maturity.

FOLIAGE: The beautiful, shiny leaves look like a narrower and more deeply cut version of chinkapin oak leaves.

CULTURE: Graceful oak typically is seen growing above 5,000 feet but does seem to adapt to regular garden settings in most of Texas. Nevertheless, it needs excellent drainage because it is sensitive to too much soil moisture. It is a tree that should be used more. It needs a minimum amount of fertilizer.

PROBLEMS: The biggest problem with the graceful oak is finding it in the nursery trade, but it is hoped that will change in the near future.

PROPAGATION: Like all oaks, it is grown from seed or acorns collected immediately after they release from the tree.

INSIGHT: These trees are true evergreens but not as evergreen as the live oaks. They should be used much more in the landscape when they become available in the nursery trade.

Lacey oak.

Oak, Lacey

COMMON NAMES: Lacey Oak, Smoky Oak, Canyon Oak, Rock Oak, Blue Oak

BOTANICAL NAME: *Quercus laceyi* (syn. *Q. glaucoides*)

PRONUNCIATION: KWER-kus LACE-ee-eye

FAMILY: Fagaceae (Beech Family)

TYPE: Medium-sized deciduous shade tree

HEIGHT: 25–35 feet

SPREAD: 15–20 feet

FINAL SPACING: 15–20 feet

NATURAL HABITAT AND PREFERRED SITE: It grows in south central Texas to the Trans-Pecos in thin alkaline or rocky limestone soils up into the Chisos Mountains of Big Bend National Park.

IDENTIFICATION: Lacey oak is a beautiful, small to medium-sized tree with blue-green mature foliage and peach-colored new growth and fall color.

FLOWERS AND FRUIT: It produces separate male and female catkins in the early spring. Brown acorns grow in clusters of 2 or 3.

FOLIAGE: The leaves are leathery, dusky blue to blue-gray to grayish green. Fall color ranges from pink or peach to gold. The new growth in the spring is a similar color.

BARK: The bark is light gray to dark brown, flaky to deeply fissured.

CULTURE: Lacey oak is easy to grow and adapts to many soils from sand to heavy clays. It can be found growing natively in the rocky white limestone soils, so this is an excellent choice for the black and white soils of a large portion of Texas. It is drought tolerant and needs little fertilizer.

PROBLEMS: It lacks availability in the trade. It will become more available as people ask for it. The tree also would not be able to stand wet soil continuously.

PROPAGATION: All oaks are grown from seed (acorns) planted as soon as they are released from the trees in the fall.

INSIGHT: The leaves are quite small in comparison to other oaks. Lacey oak is a trouble-free tree that should be used much more in the landscape.

Lacey oak.

Coastal live oak.

Oak, Live (Coastal)

COMMON NAMES: Live Oak, Coastal Live Oak
BOTANICAL NAME: *Quercus virginiana*
PRONUNCIATION: KWER-cus vir-gin-ee-AYN-ah
FAMILY: Fagaceae (Beech Family)
TYPE: Evergreen shade tree
HEIGHT: 40–50 feet
SPREAD: 40–50 feet
FINAL SPACING: 25–40 feet
NATURAL HABITAT AND PREFERRED SITE: It grows only from central Texas south to the Gulf coast. It likes more rainfall and soil moisture than the escarpment live oak.
IDENTIFICATION: Coastal live oak is an extremely dramatic and beautiful tree with a wide and graceful head. Large limbs tend to dip and sweep to the ground. On some of the most beautiful coastal live oaks in the state, the limbs actually rest on the ground. It is an arborilogical crime to prune away these wonderful limbs.
FLOWERS AND FRUIT: Rust-colored male flowers hang from the terminal growth in the early spring, along with female flowers that bloom singly or in clusters. The fruits are acorns.
BARK: The bark is smooth and gray or off-white when young, becoming more heavily textured and very dark with age.
FOLIAGE: It has slightly larger foliage than the escarpment live oak. It has small, glossy, thick evergreen leaves that vary greatly in size and shape.
CULTURE: Coastal live oak is easy to establish and easy to grow but is a relatively high-maintenance tree because it is dropping something year round—leaves, flowers, or acorns. Most people have the misconception that it is a clean tree because it is evergreen. It responds well to ample moisture and fertilizer, but over fertilization can bring on various pest problems including root fungal diseases.
PROBLEMS: Oak wilt disease can be controlled by using the Sick Tree Treatment (see Appendix 3) and improving the immune system of the tree, the health of the soil, and the root system.
PROPAGATION: All oaks are grown from seed as soon as the acorns are released from the trees in the fall.

INSIGHT: Coastal live oak is much more sensitive to extreme cold temperatures than escarpment live oak, and it was the one tree primarily destroyed during the freezing weather of the winter of 1983 and 1984 when the northern part of the state had over 12 straight days of freezing weather. Coastal live oaks grow the best in well-drained soils but can tolerate moist soils as well. They are curiously tolerant of construction activity around their root systems.

Coastal live oak foliage.

Escarpment live oak foliage.

Oak wilt symptoms showing the typical veinal necrosis. (Texas Forest Service.)

Oak, Live (Escarpment)

COMMON NAMES: Escarpment Live Oak, Plateau Live Oak, Scrub Live Oak, West Texas Live Oak, Live Oak

BOTANICAL NAME: *Quercus fusiformis*

PRONUNCIATION: KWER-kus fuse-ah-FORM-iss

FAMILY: Fagaceae (Beech Family)

TYPE: Evergreen shade tree

HEIGHT: 40–50 feet

SPREAD: 40–50 feet

FINAL SPACING: 25–40 feet

NATURAL HABITAT AND PREFERRED SITE: Escarpment live oak grows in the same area where coastal live oak grows, but it also grows further inland and north in more rocky, alkaline, droughty areas.

IDENTIFICATION: Escarpment live oak is a dramatically beautiful evergreen tree with a wide, rounded head. Limbs tend to sweep out and dip all the way to the ground unless trimmed away. Single- and multi-trunked trees exist.

FLOWERS AND FRUIT: Rust-colored male flowers hang from the terminal growth in the early spring. Female flowers bloom singly or in clusters. Both are on the same tree. The fruits are one-seeded, black acorns.

FOLIAGE: The small, glossy, thick evergreen leaves vary considerably in shape and size. They range from 1–3 inches long and from ½–1 inch wide.

BARK: The bark is smooth and gray or off-white when young, becoming heavily textured and very dark with age. Live oaks and blackjack oaks probably have the darkest bark of all the oaks.

CULTURE: Escarpment live oak is easy to establish and easy to grow. It is a relatively high-maintenance tree because it is dropping something year round— leaves, flowers, or acorns. Most people have the misconception that it is a clean tree because it is evergreen. It responds well to ample moisture and fertilizer, but over fertilization can bring on various pest problems, including root fungal diseases.

PROBLEMS: Escarpment live oak is susceptible to aphids, ice damage, galls, and oak wilt. It also has an almost continuous flower, leaf, or acorn drop. It has to be considered a high-maintenance plant on most urban sites, although it is a very important tree for Texas. Another possible problem is freeze damage. During the winters of 1983 and 1984, hundreds of thousands of escarpment live oaks were killed or severely damaged from the prolonged below-freezing temperatures. Oak wilt is also killing out many thousands of escarpment live oaks. The disease is primarily a result of large monoculture plantings, synthetic fertilizers, and toxic pesticides, especially herbicides.

PROPAGATION: All oaks are grown from seed as soon as the acorns are released from the trees in the fall.

INSIGHT: The escarpment live oak does seem to be considerably more drought tolerant and cold hearty than the coastal live oak. Both live oaks lose their foliage in the spring when the swelling buds push the leaves off. Live oaks often look bad at this time, and homeowners worry that their trees are in trouble. The new leaves emerge quickly and everyone calms down again.

Mohr oak.

Oak, Mohr

COMMON NAMES: Mohr Oak, Shrub Oak, Shin Oak
BOTANICAL NAME: *Quercus mohriana*
PRONUNCIATION: KWER-cus MORE-ee-ann-ah
FAMILY: Fagaceae (Beech Family)
TYPE: Small evergreen to semi-evergreen tree
HEIGHT: 15–20 feet
SPREAD: 20 feet or greater
FINAL SPACING: 12–20 feet
NATURAL HABITAT AND PREFERRED SITE: It grows in west Texas in rocky limestone soils, dry areas, and well-drained situations, preferring areas that receive 25 inches or less annual rainfall. It will grow in full sun in a variety of soils in Texas landscapes.
IDENTIFICATION: This beautiful, small or shrubby oak (shin oak) grows to a maximum height of about 40 feet. The leaves are shiny green on top and fuzzy white underneath.
FLOWERS AND FRUIT: Male and female flowers (catkins) are ¾–1½ inch long and are on the same tree (monoecious). Acorns are borne annually. Young acorns are hairy. Mature acorns are oval, brown, and lustrous.
BARK: The bark is light gray and smooth when young, becoming darker and more heavily textured with age.
FOLIAGE: The leaves are alternate, persistent to semi-evergreen, shiny, smooth on top, and fuzzy white underneath. This beautiful foliage has an overall blue-gray-green look.
CULTURE: This drought tolerant plant is easy to grow in a wide range of well-drained soils. It tends to sucker into groves, which can become somewhat of a problem if you only wanted single-trunked trees.
PROBLEMS: It experiences few problems, although this tree must have good drainage. It cannot stand wet feet.
PROPAGATION: Mohr oak is grown from acorns like all oaks. Plant them just after the acorns release in the fall.
INSIGHT: Gray oak (*Quercus grisea*) is a similar tree that also grows in the dry gravel soils of the west Texas mountains, but its leaves are different. They are gray-green as well but are hairy on both sides.

Monterrey oak.

Monterrey oak foliage.

Oak, Monterrey

COMMON NAMES: Monterrey Oak

BOTANICAL NAME: *Quercus polymorpha*

PRONUNCIATION: KWER-kus poly-MORF-ah

FAMILY: Fagaceae (Beech Family)

TYPE: Deciduous to semi-deciduous shade tree in most of the state; evergreen in the southern tip and in Mexico

HEIGHT: 40–60 feet

SPREAD: 30–40 feet

FINAL SPACING: 20–30 feet

NATURAL HABITAT AND PREFERRED SITE: Monterrey oak is a native of eastern Mexico and Guatemala. It grows up to far south Texas. There is a grove growing near the Devils River in Val Verde County near Del Rio.

IDENTIFICATION: Monterrey oak is a deciduous-to-evergreen, medium-sized shade tree that has thick, rounded, dark green leaves. It has little to no fall color.

FLOWERS AND FRUIT: Male and female flowers (catkins) are on the same tree. The fruits are acorns that produce annually.

FOLIAGE: The leathery, blue-green leaves are 3–4½ inches long, untoothed, rounded, and smooth-surfaced.

BARK: The bark is smoothly textured and light gray when young, developing a heavier texture with age.

CULTURE: It is easy to grow in well-drained soil with one exception—freeze damage is a possibility in the northern part of the state. It has done very well, however, in the Dallas/Fort Worth area through several severe winters.

PROBLEMS: It has few problems other than possible freeze damage in the far northern part of the state.

PROPAGATION: Propagation is done by planting the acorns.

INSIGHT: Beavers seem to love chewing on this tree—I learned that the hard way. Monterrey oak is said to be a trademarked name owned by Lone Star Growers of San Antonio.

Top leaves are red oak. Bottom leaves are pin oak.

Pin oak showing chlorosis due to alkaline soil.

Oak, Pin

COMMON NAMES: Pin Oak, Swamp Oak, Spanish Oak, Northern Pin Oak

BOTANICAL NAME: *Quercus palustris*

PRONUNCIATION: KWER-kus pah-LUS-trus

FAMILY: Fagaceae (Beech Family)

TYPE: Deciduous shade tree

HEIGHT: 50 to over 100 feet

SPREAD: 40–50 feet

FINAL SPACING: 30–40 feet

NATURAL HABITAT AND PREFERRED SITE: It grows in the deep, rich soils of Oklahoma and Arkansas and small parts of deep east Texas.

IDENTIFICATION: It has an upright to pyramidal shape, especially when young, spreading with age. It has red oak-type leaves and usually a weeping nature, especially on the lower limbs. It has a stiff overall appearance.

FLOWERS AND FRUIT: The flowers form in the early spring, from April through May. Separate male and female flowers form on the same tree. The fruits are small acorns that form from September through October every other year.

FOLIAGE: The leaves are simple, alternate, and deciduous, 4–6 inches long. Fall color is usually red but can also be yellow and other color variations. The fall color display is usually quite good.

BARK: The bark is light brown to gray, smooth and lustrous when young. It gets darker and roughened with age.

CULTURE: Nuttall oak (*Quercus nuttallii*), which is also known by other common names such as **red oak, river red oak, red pin oak,** and **striped oak,** is a similar tree and one of the most rare in Texas. It grows in poorly drained soils and does well in areas where there is winter flooding and year-round moisture. Pin oak will not grow in such situations. Neither tree will grow in the calcarious soils of north and central Texas.

PROBLEMS: Pin oak develops chlorosis quickly in alkaline soils. This trace mineral deficiency leads to attack by other insect and disease pests.

PROPAGATION: Propagation is done by planting the acorns immediately after they release from the tree in the fall.

INSIGHT: Oaks crossbreed readily and pin oak's crossing with **Texas red oak** or **shumard red oak** (*Quercus shumardii*) is a major problem in Texas. Red oaks that have much pin oak "blood" will not grow in the black and white soils of north Texas.

Post oak.

Oak, Post

COMMON NAMES: Post Oak, Iron Oak, Cross Oak
BOTANICAL NAME: *Quercus stellata*
PRONUNCIATION: KWER-kus sta-LOT-ah
FAMILY: Fagaceae (Beech Family)
TYPE: Deciduous shade tree
HEIGHT: 30–80 feet
SPREAD: 20–20 feet

FINAL SPACING: 20–40 feet

NATURAL HABITAT AND PREFERRED SITE: Post oak occurs in all areas of Texas except the High Plains and the Trans-Pecos. It grows in sandy loam soils that range from neutral to acid, but it can also grow in acidic or neutral clay soils. It does not grow in the black and white alkaline or calcarious soils.

IDENTIFICATION: It is a rounded tree with stout, interestingly branched limbs, gnarly growth, and

Post oak foliage and fruit.

rounded, lobed leaves. Fall color is less than spectacular—yellow to brown.

FLOWERS AND FRUIT: The flowers appear with the leaves in March through May, male and female catkins on the same tree. The fruit ripens in the fall, from September through October. Small acorns mature in the first season.

FOLIAGE: The leaves are simple, alternate, and deciduous with yellow, unspectacular fall color. They are 4–7 inches long, 3–5 inches wide, with rounded lobes. The side lobes of the leaves are almost perpendicular to the midvein, creating a cross-like effect.

BARK: The gray-brown, fairly thick bark is heavily textured even when young. It develops a medium to dark color with age.

CULTURE: This is a slow-growing native oak that hates human activities. It is very difficult to transplant, fairly difficult to grow from seed, and hard to work around without damaging. Post oak needs extremely well-drained soil and neutral to acid soil conditioning. It does not like much fertilizer and needs adequate soil moisture. It is fairly drought tolerant but has been damaged in some of the extreme drought years. Compaction, construction, and application of herbicides and synthetic fertilizers have killed many thousands of post oaks and other native oaks in Texas.

PROBLEMS: Post oak suffers from wet feet, human impact, and secondary attack by insect pests and diseases. The cure is leaving the trees in their native state as much as possible and applying the Sick Tree Treatment (see Appendix 3) to those trees in stress.

PROPAGATION: It is grown from acorns planted as soon as they fall from the tree or acorns stored cool and moist at 32°–36°F prior to planting them the following spring.

INSIGHT: This is the most common native oak in north Texas. Many thousands of these trees die every year from damage during construction of new developments because contractors scrape away the topsoil and the native understory, compact the soil, and change the environment of the feeder roots. To keep post oak alive, water moderately, do not use fertilizer at all (or very little), do not thin out, do not change the soil grade, and do not remove the native understory growth. Other post oaks are as follows: **sand post oak** (*Quercus margaretta*), **drummond post oak** (*Q. drummondii*), and **boynton post oak** (*Q. boyntonii*), which grows near Lufkin and is a spreading, dwarf oak.

Sandpaper oak foliage.

Oak, Sandpaper

COMMON NAMES: Sandpaper Oak, Scrub Oak, Shin Oak, Encino Oak

BOTANICAL NAME: *Quercus pungens* var. *pungens*

PRONUNCIATION: KWER-kus PUN-gens

FAMILY: Fagaceae (Beech Family)

TYPE: Small deciduous tree, considered one of the shin oaks

HEIGHT: 15–20 feet

SPREAD: 10–15 feet

FINAL SPACING: 10–15 feet

NATURAL HABITAT AND PREFERRED SITE: One of the most widespread species of the Trans-Pecos area, sandpaper oak grows in dry creeks and on limestone hillsides.

IDENTIFICATION: This beautiful, small tree is similar in appearance to the vasey oak. It has gray-green, sandpapery leaves that are slightly larger than those of vasey oak.

FLOWERS AND FRUIT: Male and female catkins grow on the same tree. The fruits mature as acorns in the fall.

FOLIAGE: The leaves are small, rolled on the edge, and sandpapery to the touch.

BARK: The bark is light to medium gray when young. It darkens and gains a more heavy texture with age.

CULTURE: This drought tolerant tree needs little fertilizer. It's easy to grow but hard to find in nurseries at this time.

PROBLEMS: This interesting little tree is hard to find in the nursery industry.

PROPAGATION: It is grown from acorns planted soon after collection in the fall.

INSIGHT: The name comes from the sandpaper-like feel of its leaves. Sandpaper oak closely resembles **vasey oak**, (*Quercus pungens* var. *vaseyana*).

Sawtooth oak foliage.

Oak, Sawtooth

COMMON NAMES: Sawtooth Oak, Chinese Oak
BOTANICAL NAME: *Quercus acutissima*
PRONUNCIATION: KWER-kus ah-cue-TISS-eh-mah
FAMILY: Fagaceae (Beech Family)
TYPE: Deciduous shade tree
HEIGHT: 50–60 feet
SPREAD: 30–40 feet
FINAL SPACING: 20–40 feet
NATURAL HABITAT AND PREFERRED SITE:
Native to Korea, China, and Japan, it will grow well in Texas in deep, sandy soils with neutral to acid pH.
IDENTIFICATION: Sawtooth oak is an upright-growing, deciduous tree. It has a pyramidal form when young that becomes more rounded with maturity.
FLOWERS AND FRUIT: Male and female flowers are separate but grow on the same plant (monoecious). The male flowers are rust-colored and hang from the terminal growth in the early spring. Female flowers bloom singly or in small clusters. The fruits, or acorns, are about 1 inch in diameter and mature in two seasons.
FOLIAGE: The leaves are simple, alternate, serrated, 3–7 inches long, 1½–2 inches wide, and medium to deep green. They are yellow to dull brown in the fall. Brown foliage remains on the tree throughout the winter and only falls after the buds begin to expand and push the new foliage out in the spring. The leaves of the sawtooth oak can be confused with those of the Chinese chestnut, which are broader and have longer teeth at the leaf margin.
BARK: The bark is light gray to brown and smooth when young. It develops an irregular, almost diamond-shaped pattern with shallow furrows as the tree matures. The bark texture never becomes extremely rough.
CULTURE: Sawtooth oak is an extremely fast-growing oak when it is planted in deep, moist soils. It responds well to fertilization and moisture but is fairly drought tolerant. It is not tolerant of the alkaline soils, especially when white rock is near the surface.
PROBLEMS: Chlorosis is caused by nutrient deficiency in alkaline soils.
PROPAGATION: It is grown from acorns planted immediately after they are released from the tree in the fall.
INSIGHT: I have also seen this tree mistakenly sold as **chinkapin oak** (*Quercus muehlenbergii*). Chinkapin oak can grow in a wide range of soils. This tree cannot.

Oak, Shin

This is a generic term for all the small-scale oaks such as vasey, lacey, Mohr, and sandpaper oak.

Shumard red oak.

Texas red oak fall color.

Oak, Shumard Red

COMMON NAMES: Red Oak, Shumard Red Oak, Shumard Oak, Swamp Red Oak, Spotted Oak, Spanish Oak, Texas Red Oak
BOTANICAL NAME: *Quercus shumardii* (syn. *Q. buckleyi* [syn. *Q. texana*])
PRONUNCIATION: KWER-kus shoe-MARD-ee
FAMILY: Fagaceae (Beech Family)

Shumard red oak summer foliage.

TYPE: Deciduous shade tree
HEIGHT: 60–100 feet
SPREAD: 60–80 feet
FINAL SPACING: 30–50 feet
NATURAL HABITAT AND PREFERRED SITE: Shumard red oak grows in the eastern third of the state in a wide range of soils, from sandy to heavy clays to solid, white rock outcropping areas. It adapts to most any soil that is well-drained.

IDENTIFICATION: Shumard red oak is a graceful, majestic, tall-growing, and wide-spreading shade tree with beautiful fall color and lovely, deeply cut leaves. Fall color can range from yellowish browns to yellows and reds to deep maroons. Typically it has no central trunk, although I have seen some true shumard red oaks with central trunks.

FLOWERS AND FRUIT: Male and female flowers (catkins) grow on the same plant (monoecious). Rust-colored male flowers hang from the terminal growth in the early spring, and female flowers bloom singly or in small clusters. The fruits are medium to large acorns, generally ¾–1 inch long and ½–1 inch wide. Acorns mature in the fall of the second season, singly or in pairs.

FOLIAGE: The leaves are simple, alternate, and deciduous with fall color ranging from yellows to reds to even deep maroons. The only way to be sure to get the bright red fall colors is to buy plants in the fall. Even then the fall color will vary depending on the soil and weather conditions. The leaves are deeply and gracefully cut with pointed tips.

BARK: Young trees have light to medium gray, very smooth bark. It darkens with age and develops a heavy texture.

CULTURE: Shumard red oak is fast-growing, especially for such a high quality tree. It requires a minimum amount of fertilizer and moderate moisture. It is sometimes hard to establish from transplanting and can be easily over or under watered. Once established it is an easy-to-maintain and drought tolerant tree.

PROBLEMS: Shumard red oaks can't stand wet feet. Poorly drained soil causes root disease, illness, or death. It is highly susceptible to oak wilt. Occasionally shumard red oaks are bothered by scale, borers, and other insect pests, but that is always a symptom of a bigger problem of an environmental nature. Oak sawflies are fairly common, annoying pests that attack and skeletonize the leaves. Their damage is normally isolated in spots no larger than basketballs. They can be controlled by the Basic Organic Program (see Appendix 5) and occasional spraying of Garrett Juice (see Appendix 2) plus garlic. Another problem is when pin oaks or crossbred trees are bought by mistake.

PROPAGATION: Propagation is by planting acorns in the fall just after they have fallen from the trees.

INSIGHT: Shumard red oaks are magnificent and graceful trees. They have always been one of my favorites, but they are the subject of a large, confusing tree

Texas red oak in flower in the spring.

Oak wilt symptoms on Texas red oak. (Texas Forest Service).

Canby oak at the San Antonio Botanical Gardens.

Canby oak.

problem. Buying the right plant is not always easy. There are three red oaks that are very similar and will all work in the alkaline soils: shumard red oak (*Quercus shumardii* [syn. *Q. texana*]), **chisos oak** (*Q. gravesii*), and the very similar **canby oak** (*Q. canbyi*). Simpson's *A Field Guide to Texas Trees* explains the differences among them best by saying that the Chisos oak grows primarily west of the Pecos, the shumard red oak grows west and north of the Balcones escarpment and the White Rock escarpment just west of Dallas, and the canby oak simply grows east of that line.

Pin oak and crossbreeds of other oak trees such as **southern red oak** (*Q. falcata*) and **northern red oak** (*Q. rubra*) crossbreed readily with red oaks. If trees not adapted in Texas dominate the "blood" of the offspring, these trees, when growing in alkaline soil, will be sickly with nutrient deficiencies, appear chlorotic, and eventually die. The northern red oak doesn't do very well anywhere in Texas. The southern red oak grows very well over in the deep east Texas acid, sandy soils, and the same goes for pin oak.

Some folks still recommend wrapping tree trunks with paper, gauze, or other materials to allegedly protect the trees from various problems, from sunburn to insect attack, particularly borers. Wrapping tree trunks not only doesn't help the tree, it actually encourages weak bark, disease, and insect attack, and of course it wastes your money. See the first part of this book for the proper planting instructions, which apply for all trees but especially for red oaks, since these trees are usually wrapped the most.

Chisos oak.

Southern red oak in Pittsburg, Texas.

Oak, Southern Red

COMMON NAMES: Southern Red Oak, Spanish Oak, Swamp Red Oak, Swamp Spanish Oak, Cherry Bark Oak, Bottomland Red Oak, Three-Lobe Red Oak

BOTANICAL NAME: *Quercus falcata*

PRONUNCIATION: KWER-kus fal-KA-tah

FAMILY: Fagaceae (Beech Family)

TYPE: Deciduous tree

HEIGHT: 60 to over 100 feet

SPREAD: 50–60 feet

FINAL SPACING: 30–50 feet

NATURAL HABITAT AND PREFERRED SITE: It grows primarily in east Texas and the deep, acid, sandy soils.

IDENTIFICATION: This large-growing, graceful tree has a rather open top, droopy leaves, and so-so yellow fall color. It can only be successfully introduced and grown in the acid soils of the state.

FLOWERS AND FRUIT: Rust-colored male flowers hang from the terminal growth in the early spring. Female flowers appear at the same time on the same tree but are separate and will be either single or in small clusters. The fruits are acorns that form in the fall singly or in pairs. They are small, ½ inch long, and mature during the second season.

FOLIAGE: The foliage is simple, alternate, and deciduous with unimpressive yellow fall color most years. The leaves are variable in shape and lobed, and they tend to appear droopy and even have a wilted look. The leaves of the southern red oak will vary from 4–10 inches in length and from 2–7 inches in width. The upper and lower leaf surfaces can be either hairy or hairless. All of these leaf variations can be found on the same tree.

BARK: Young trunks can be reddish brown to gray. The bark turns grayish black and breaks into deep fissures and scales with age.

CULTURE: Southern red oak is moderately fast-growing.

PROBLEMS: It is relatively pest-free in sandy, acid soils. It will not grow in alkaline soils.

PROPAGATION: Southern red oak is grown from acorns collected immediately after falling from the tree in the fall. They should be planted quickly or stored in sealed containers for up to 2 years at just above freezing temperatures. Like all acorns, they should not be allowed to dry out and should be planted about ½ inch deep in the soil.

Southern red oak foliage.

INSIGHT: Other similar trees include **cherry bark red oak** (*Quercus falcata* var. *leucophylla*), **swamp red oak** (*Q. falcata* var. *pagodifolia*), and **three-lobe red oak** (*Q. falcata* var. *triloba*). There is much confusion among tree experts about the differences among all of these trees and their correct scientific names.

According to Simpson, cherry bark red oak usually occurs as a single tree rather than in groves. It is thought that is because the tree is allelopathic, which means it suppresses other seedlings from getting started within its root system.

Vasey oak foliage.

Oak, Vasey

COMMON NAMES: Vasey Oak, Scrub Oak, Shin Oak

BOTANICAL NAME: *Quercus pungens* var. *vaseyana*

PRONUNCIATION: KWER-cus PUN-gens, Vase-ee-ANN-ah

FAMILY: Fagaceae (Beech Family)

TYPE: Semi-evergreen tree

HEIGHT: 20–40 feet

SPREAD: 20–30 feet

FINAL SPACING: 15–20 feet

NATURAL HABITAT AND PREFERRED SITE: Vasey oak is native to far west Texas, and seems to do the best in dry canyons and creeks. It grows well in the limestone soils but will adapt to a wide range of soils, including normal landscape situations.

IDENTIFICATION: This small, compact, native tree has small leaves that are gently lobed and wavy-edged with short tips on the edges. It is almost evergreen and has the smallest leaves of all the shin oaks. It looks like a small live oak but has a lighter-colored, almost silvery bark.

FLOWERS AND FRUIT: The flowers are monoecious—separate but on the same trees. The male flowers are longer than the female flowers, as is the case with all the oaks. The fruits are annually produced acorns that grow singly or in pairs.

BARK: The bark is light gray to silvery and scaly.

FOLIAGE: The leaves are semi-evergreen, alternate, and small (usually ¾–2½ inches long and ½–¾ inch wide). The upper surface is grayish green to dark green and shiny. The lower surface is generally paler and hairy. It has the smallest leaves of all the shin oaks.

CULTURE: Vasey oak is an easy-to-grow tree that needs minimum amounts of fertilizer and water. It can grow in alkaline soils but adapts to deeper, sandier, more acid soils as well.

PROBLEMS: The main problem with vasey oak is finding specimens in the nursery industry to buy. It is hoped that availability will increase. Over watering can also be a problem. It needs positive drainage.

PROPAGATION: Vasey oak is grown from acorns planted immediately after they have released from the tree in the fall.

INSIGHT: This excellent small tree should be used for landscaping considerably more than it currently is. The species name *pungens* means "prickly" and refers to the short, abrupt points on the leaf edges.

Water oak in Houston.

Water oak foliage.

Oak, Water

COMMON NAMES: Water Oak, Possum Oak, Spotted Oak, Duck Oak, Punk Oak, Diamondleaf Oak, Swamp Laurel Oak, Laurel Leaf Oak, Obtusa Oak

BOTANICAL NAME: *Quercus nigra*

PRONUNCIATION: KWER-kus NI-gra

FAMILY: Fagaceae (Beech Family)

TYPE: Deciduous to evergreen shade tree

HEIGHT: 50–80 feet

SPREAD: 30–50 feet

FINAL SPACING: 20–50 feet

NATURAL HABITAT AND PREFERRED SITE: It lives in north and southeast Texas in moist to wet soils.

IDENTIFICATION: Water oak is a large-growing and spreading shade tree. It has a broad, oval-to-rounded overall shape. The leaves are spoon-shaped, persistent, and sometimes evergreen.

FLOWERS AND FRUIT: Male and female flowers are separate but on the same tree (monoecious). As with all oaks, the flowers are not very showy. The fruit ripens as ½-inch acorns in the fall, from September through October. The flowers emerge with the leaves in the spring.

FOLIAGE: The leaves are simple, alternate, and persistent. They come in various shapes but are often spoon-shaped. Some trees will be completely deciduous and others almost totally evergreen. Weak fall color varies from yellow to brown. Summer color is deep green.

BARK: The bark is light brown to grayish black, smooth in youth but developing heavier texture with age. Water oak will have irregular patches of smooth bark and slightly furrowed, heavily textured bark on both young and mature trees.

CULTURE: Water oak grows well in east Texas, the Houston area, and other similar soil locations. It likes moist, neutral-to-acid soils and can be even grown in waterlogged, oxygen-deficient soils where other trees would have a great problem. It responds well to fertilizer and grows well under the Basic Organic Program (see Appendix 5).

PROBLEMS: This tree needs plenty of moisture and neutral-to-acid soils. It will not grow well in the alkaline black and white soils of north and central Texas. It is occasionally attacked by scale insects and various chewing insects, but the appearance of these pests is always related to environmental stress.

PROPAGATION: It is grown from acorns by planting them immediately after they have released from the tree in the fall. They can also be kept stratified at 30°–35°F in the winter and planted in the spring.

INSIGHT: Laurel oak (*Quercus laurifolia*) is similar in appearance and adaptability and is often found growing near water oak. Laurel oak has longer and more slender leaves, similar to those of willow oak. Laurel oak is also sold as **Darlington oak**. This tree is basically evergreen and does best in the same moist soils as willow and water oaks, but it likes soils that are better drained.

White oak foliage.

White oak fall foliage.

Oak, White

COMMON NAMES: White Oak, Stave Oak, Ridge White Oak, Forked-Leaf White Oak

BOTANICAL NAME: *Quercus alba*

PRONUNCIATION: KWER-kus ALL-ba

FAMILY: Fagaceae (Beech Family)

TYPE: Large, deciduous shade tree

HEIGHT: 80 to over 100 feet

SPREAD: 50–60 feet

FINAL SPACING: 30–50 feet

NATURAL HABITAT AND PREFERRED SITE: It grows in far east Texas and other deep, sandy, acid soil areas.

IDENTIFICATION: White oak is a large, gorgeous tree with beautiful summer foliage and excellent red fall color.

FLOWERS AND FRUIT: It's a typical oak with male and female flowers separate but on the same tree (monoecious). The male flowers have long, hairy catkins in the early spring. The female catkins are shorter. The fruit is shiny tan to dark brown acorns, 1-inch long, that form in the fall.

FOLIAGE: White oak has my favorite tree foliage. The leaves are deeply cut and rounded on the edges. They are alternate, simple, deciduous, and 5–9 inches long with 7–11 lobes. It tends to hold its leaves well into the winter. Some people consider this a maintenance problem. Summer foliage color is deep green to slightly blue-green. Fall color will range from wine red to orange red.

BARK: The bark is light gray to reddish brown. It develops shallow fissures with age but retains its light color even at maturity.

CULTURE: White oak is easy to grow in acid-to-neutral soils. It is fairly drought tolerant and requires little fertilizer.

PROBLEMS: Unfortunately, this tree will not grow adequately in the black and white soils of north and central Texas. It must have deep, neutral-to-acid sandy loam.

PROPAGATION: White oak is grown from acorns planted immediately after they are released from the tree in the fall and are still fresh. White oak is difficult to transplant due to its deep taproot that develops early on young seedlings.

INSIGHT: White oak is without doubt one of our state's most beautiful trees. The wood is heavy, hard, and durable and used to make railroad ties, wine and other barrels, and flooring. It is also used for firewood and boat building. It has an attractive grain. **Gamble oak** (*Quercus gambellii*) is a strong look-alike but grows in alkaline and blackland soils. It is smaller, 15–25 feet tall, and native to the mountains of the Trans-Pecos.

Willow oak fall color.

Willow oak foliage.

Oak, Willow

COMMON NAMES: Willow Oak, Pin Oak, Peach Oak, Swamp Willow Oak

BOTANICAL NAME: *Quercus phellos*

PRONUNCIATION: KWER-kus FELL-oss

FAMILY: Fagaceae (Beech Family)

TYPE: Deciduous shade tree

HEIGHT: 80–100 feet

SPREAD: 40–60 feet

FINAL SPACING: 30–50 feet

NATURAL HABITAT AND PREFERRED SITE: The deep, sandy, acid, moist soil of east Texas is the primary habitat. Willow oak can grow in clays or loams and is often seen along stream bottoms and frequently flooded drainage ways. It will grow in deep clay soils but not above white limestone rock.

IDENTIFICATION: Willow oak is a graceful tree that is pyramidal when young but spreads with a rounded crown with age. It has narrow, delicate leaves.

FLOWERS AND FRUIT: The flowers are borne in the spring. Male and female flowers are separate but on the same tree (monoecious) and are not showy. The fruits are small acorns, $^2/_5$ inch long, that grow singly or in pairs and mature in 2 years.

FOLIAGE: The alternate, simple, deciduous, golden leaves have yellow fall color. They are 3–5 inches long and $^1/_4$–$^1/_2$ inch wide with a bristled tip.

BARK: The bark is greenish to reddish brown when young. It becomes gray and smooth after a few years and develops into a slightly furrowed and textured bark with age, especially at the base of large trees.

CULTURE: Willow oak needs the moist, acid, sandy soils of east Texas and other parts of the state. It will not grow in the alkaline soils, especially where white limestone is present. It requires plenty of moisture but minimal fertilization. Pest problems are few.

PROBLEMS: Nutrient deficiency and chlorosis can result from its being planted in the improper soil.

PROPAGATION: It is grown from fresh acorns just released from the tree in the fall.

INSIGHT: Its acorns are a favorite of several forms of wildlife. Willow oak is easily confused with its close relatives, the laurel oak and water oak.

Russian olive.

Russian olive foliage.

Olive, Russian

COMMON NAMES: Russian Olive, Oleaster
BOTANICAL NAME: *Elaeagnus angustifolius*
PRONUNCIATION: eel-ee-AG-nus an-gus-ti-FOAL-ee-us
FAMILY: Elaeagnaceae (Oleaster Family)
TYPE: Deciduous tree
HEIGHT: 20–30 feet
SPREAD: 15–20 feet
FINAL SPACING: 15–20 feet
NATURAL HABITAT AND PREFERRED SITE: Native to southern Europe and west and central Asia, it adapts well to any well-drained soil, from sand to heavy clays and from acid to alkaline conditions. Russian olive can stand fairly high levels of soil alkalinity and can grow at relatively high altitudes.
IDENTIFICATION: Russian olive is a distinctive, small tree with silver or gray leaves. It can be thorny or thornless. If the lower branches are allowed to remain, the tree develops into a dense, shrubby form.
FLOWERS AND FRUIT: Small, yellow or silvery flowers bloom in the summer followed by small drupes, which mature from August to October. The flowers are very fragrant. Early summer flowers appear around June, scattered on the branches in clusters. The flowers are perfect. The fruits mature in August through October and are approximately ⅜–½ inch long and oval in shape. They are silvery gray,

becoming yellow to tan with maturity. The seed is hard and oval and has a ridge.
FOLIAGE: The leaves are simple, alternate, and bright green to silver with brown dots on the lower surface. There is little fall color.
BARK: The young stems are covered with silvery scales. The stems and bark become reddish brown and lose the scales, eventually becoming rough and vertically striped with shallow furrows. The branches may or may not have thorns, depending on the rate of growth and the seed source. Spines can be as long as 2 inches and quite thick.
CULTURE: Russian olive is easy to grow but relatively short-lived. It will do well in most well-drained soils, is drought tolerant, has few pest problems, and has low fertilizer requirements. It does respond to healthy soils, fertilizer, and watering during drought periods.
PROBLEMS: Too much water can cause several root fungal diseases. Root diseases resulting from environmental problems can be countered with the Sick Tree Treatment (see Appendix 3).
PROPAGATION: It is grown from seed, cuttings, or grafting. The fruit should be gathered in the fall when it first begins to separate from the tree. For best results, stratify the seed for 90 days at 41°F to break the dormancy (wake the seed up).
INSIGHT: There are some so-called improved cultivars such as 'Cardinal' and 'Red King' that have red fruit.

Wild olive at the Alamo.

Wild olive foliage and flowers.

Olive, Wild

COMMON NAMES: Wild Olive, Mexican Olive, Anacahuita, Texas Olive, Flor De Anacahuite, Nacahuite, Nachuitl

BOTANICAL NAME: *Cordia boissieri*

PRONUNCIATION: KOR-dee-ah BOIS-see-err-ee

FAMILY: Boraginaceae (Borage Family)

TYPE: Small evergreen tree

HEIGHT: 15–25 feet

SPREAD: 10–15 feet

FINAL SPACING: 10–15 feet

NATURAL HABITAT AND PREFERRED SITE: Wild olive grows in the far southern tip of Texas in the counties along the Rio Grande. It is adaptable as far north as San Antonio but will freeze to the ground there in harsh winters.

IDENTIFICATION: This is the beautiful tree just to the left of the front door of the Alamo in San Antonio. It is a rounded evergreen tree with dramatic, white flowers and velvety leaves.

FLOWERS AND FRUIT: The flowers are large, trumpet-shaped, and brilliant white with yellow throats, 2–3 inches wide. They form in football-sized clusters and appear year round but are the most profuse in the spring and early summer. The white fruit is sweet and eaten by wildlife and livestock. It is a round drupe, 1 inch long, shiny white to pale yellow, turning yellowish brown. There is a single, spindle-shaped seed that is about ⅜ inch long.

BARK: Young twigs are brown to grayish and fuzzy. The bark turns darker gray, tinged with red, and gains a heavier texture with age.

FOLIAGE: The leaves are velvety soft to the touch, 4–5 inches long, approximately 2–4 inches wide, light to medium green with brown fuzz on the underside.

CULTURE: Wild olive needs a lot of water to get established but is drought tolerant once established.

PROBLEMS: Freeze damage can occur anywhere north of San Antonio.

PROPAGATION: Wild olive can be grown from seed, which is collected and planted immediately after maturing in the fall.

INSIGHT: The fruit is reported to be sweet, pulpy, and edible, although warnings exist that it causes dizziness when eaten in excess. A jelly made in Mexico from the fruit is reported to be a remedy for coughs, and the leaves are used as a traditional home cure for rheumatism and bronchial problems.

Orchid tree.

Orchid Tree

COMMON NAMES: Orchid Tree, Anacacho Orchid Tree, Crow Foot

BOTANICAL NAME: *Bauhinia congesta* (syn. *B. lunarioides*)

PRONUNCIATION: baw-HIN-ee-ah kun-JESS-tah

FAMILY: Fabaceae (Legume, Bean, or Pulse Family)

TYPE: Deciduous small tree for understory

HEIGHT: 6–10 feet

SPREAD: 6–10 feet

FINAL SPACING: 10–12 feet

NATURAL HABITAT AND PREFERRED SITE: Although rare in Texas, orchid tree is found in the canyons and arroyos of the Anacacho Mountains in Kinney County and in landscapes in the southern part of the state. It can stand temperatures down to 10°F and does well in the Austin, Houston, and San Antonio climates. It is marginal in the Dallas/Fort Worth area. It will grow in a wide range of well-drained soils from clay and rocky soils to sandy loams. It is best used as an understory tree and seems to like limestone conditions.

IDENTIFICATION: Orchid trees are usually multi-trunked and deciduous and have beautiful, light green leaves that are divided at the base into 2 leaflets. These interesting trees have showy flowers in the spring and yellow fall color.

FLOWERS AND FRUIT: The orchid-like flowers are white or pale pink with long stamens (male reproductive parts). The fruit is a flattened legume, 1–3 inches long, containing 1–4 oblong, smooth, flattened, brown seeds. The pods twist open and quickly drop the seed when ripe and dry.

FOLIAGE: The leaves are quite distinctive. They appear to be one broad, deeply cleft, hoof-shaped leaf, although each is actually two leaflets. Each leaflet is ½–1½ inches long.

BARK: Thin and gray when young, the bark becomes brown, darker, and rougher in texture with age.

CULTURE: Orchid tree easily grows in any well-drained soil if protected from harsh winter temperatures. It is drought tolerant and needs little fertilizer or pest control.

PROBLEMS: Freeze damage is possible in the northern half of the state. It is best to plant it in protected spots.

PROPAGATION: Collect the seed pods in the summer when they have turned brown but before they open. Air dry the pods a few days, dust with natural diatomaceous earth, and store in glass in a cool place if necessary. The seed can be planted without treatment outdoors in the ground or in containers the following spring after the last frost. Look for germination within 3 weeks and transfer the seedlings to 1-gallon containers when they have 4–6 true leaves.

INSIGHT: Orchid tree is a terrific specimen tree. Even if you live in the northern part of the state, try it in pots and move it to a protected area in the winter.

Texas palms in Corpus Christi.

Dwarf Texas palm.

Palm, Texas

COMMON NAMES: Texas Palm, Texas Palmetto, Mexican Palmetto, Rio Grande Palmetto, Victoria Palmetto, Palma De Micharos, Palmetto

BOTANICAL NAME: *Sabal mexicana* (syn. *S. texana*)

PRONUNCIATION: SAY-ball mex-ee-CON-ah

FAMILY: Arecaceae (Palm Family)

TYPE: Ornamental tree

HEIGHT: 20–50 feet

SPREAD: 5–8 feet

FINAL SPACING: 8–10 feet

NATURAL HABITAT AND PREFERRED SITE: Texas palm is native to the southern tip of Texas but will adapt to landscape sites as far north as the Dallas/Fort Worth area.

IDENTIFICATION: Texas palm is a small palm tree with large, fan-shaped leaves forming a rounded crown and a single trunk. For 8–10 years the tree grows into a large clump before the trunk starts to appear at the base.

FLOWERS AND FRUIT: The flower stalks are 6–8 feet long and form drooping clusters. The flowers are small, white or greenish, and fragrant, and they bloom from March to April. The fruits are dull black to dark purple, hang down in showy clusters, and are sweet and edible. Seeds are dark brown and shiny, and one edge is often flattened.

FOLIAGE: Large and dramatic, the leaves reach up to 3 feet in diameter with spineless stems. They are blue-green in color.

BARK: The bark is reddish brown with prominent leaf scars. Leaf bases cling to the trunk, forming a distinctive cross-hatched appearance. These leaf scars will often shed as the tree ages.

CULTURE: Texas palm is slow-growing with an enormous root system, which makes it rather hard to transplant after the plant is large. It is easy to grow in a wide range of soils as far north as the Dallas/Fort Worth area.

PROBLEMS: Freeze damage occurs in the far northern part of the state.

PROPAGATION: It is grown from seed planted immediately after it matures.

INSIGHT: Texas palm is the only tree-sized palm native to Texas. Several Texas palms were planted in 1936 at the State Fairgrounds in Dallas for the Texas Centennial. They survived until the severe winter of 1983 and 1984 killed the plants to the ground. They did return. Almost all of the exotic palms were completely killed during this winter.

Washington palm in El Paso—another commonly used palm in Texas.

Palmetto, Saw

COMMON NAMES: Saw Palmetto, Sabal Palm
BOTANICAL NAME: *Serenoa repens*
PRONUNCIATION: ser-ah-NOAH RAY-penz
FAMILY: Arecaceae (Palm Family)
TYPE: Fan palm tree
HEIGHT: 3–7 feet usually, sometimes up to 25 feet
SPREAD: 6–8 feet
FINAL SPACING: 8–10 feet
NATURAL HABITAT AND PREFERRED SITE: Native from South Carolina to Florida and across the Gulf coast, it grows in a wide range of soils. It likes full sun to partial shade.
IDENTIFICATION: Saw palmetto has blue-gray-green leaves that are about 2 feet wide. It is a shrubby, clumping palm, sometimes with almost no distinct stem.
FLOWERS AND FRUIT: Early summer flowers are branched, white, and fragrant and are followed by dusky, 1-inch, red to brownish black berries. It has the typical palm, shredded-looking bark with old stems remaining attached for some time.
FOLIAGE: It has large, blue-gray-green leaves on strong leaf stems. Each blade ends in two sharp points.
BARK: The stem is short and often partially underground. It branches freely. The trunk is covered with leaf bases and brown fibers.
CULTURE: Saw palmetto grows easily in a wide range of soils but likes sandy soils best. It is hardy to about 10°F. It is a tough, drought tolerant plant but is difficult to transplant. After establishment it is very easy to grow and can be grown in containers. Extremely salt tolerant, it grows in almost any soil including extremely low fertility sands. It does not respond much to fertilizer.
PROBLEMS: Getting the plant established is a problem. Transplanting is difficult due to its large root system. Another problem is freeze damage in the northern part of the state. Palmetto weevils that occasionally attack can be controlled easily with Garrett Juice (see Appendix 2) plus garlic/pepper tea.

Saw palmetto.

PROPAGATION: Saw palmetto is grown from fresh seed planted immediately after harvest.
INSIGHT: Saw palmetto has become a very important culinary and medicinal plant. The flowers are a significant source of honey. Extracts from the berries are now used as a treatment for noncancerous enlargement of the male prostate gland. It is an excellent small palm for the garden or for large pots. Saw palmetto is a great landscape palm, especially for the southern half of the state, and should be grown more for both its medicinal and landscape value.

Parasol tree.

Parasol tree foliage and fruit.

Parasol Tree

COMMON NAMES: Parasol Tree, Chinese Parasol Tree, Chinese Varnish-Tree, Phoenix-Tree, Bottle-Tree, Chinese Bottle Tree, Japanese Varnish Tree, Phoenixtree

BOTANICAL NAME: *Firmiana simplex*

PRONUNCIATION: fir-me-AHN-ah SIM-plex

FAMILY: Sterculiaceae (Chocolate or Cacao Family)

TYPE: Deciduous shade tree

HEIGHT: 30–60 feet

SPREAD: 30–40 feet

FINAL SPACING: 20–50 feet

NATURAL HABITAT AND PREFERRED SITE: A native of Japan and China, it is cultivated in the United States. It escaped to various parts of the south. It grows well in a wide variety of soils from sand to heavy clays.

IDENTIFICATION: This distinctive, upright tree has smooth, green bark, a rounded crown, very large leaves, and dramatic seeds that mature in the fall.

FLOWERS AND FRUIT: Yellowish green flowers bloom in June or July, followed by showy, brown fruit. The flowers are terminal panicles, 4–12 inches long, with male and female plants on the same tree (monoecious).

FOLIAGE: The leaves are alternate, simple, and deciduous. Fall color is yellow. The leaves are large, 5–18 inches long, with usually 3 blades. They are dull green and slightly hairy above and below.

BARK: It has unusual smooth, green bark, even on the mature tree trunks.

CULTURE: Parasol tree is easy to grow in a wide range of soils, given a moderate amount of moisture and fertilizer. It is relatively drought tolerant.

PROBLEMS: Few serious problems exist other than that the tree has weak wood and is relatively short-lived. Some people think it is too coarse. I think it is an interesting-looking tree, although I wouldn't plant a lot of them.

PROPAGATION: It is easy to grow from seed planted fresh immediately after it matures. Seed can be saved at cool temperatures for some period of time.

INSIGHT: Parasol tree is easy to grow from seed. It can become a pest from seedlings popping up all over the garden unless the beds are heavily mulched.

Parasol tree has a smooth, green trunk.

Parkinsonia.

Parkinsonia

COMMON NAMES: Parkinsonia, Jerusalem Thorn, Retama, Horsebean, Cloth-of-Gold, Crown-of-Thorns, Barbados Fence Flowers, Palo Verde, Mexican Palo Verde

BOTANICAL NAME: *Parkinsonia aculeata*

PRONUNCIATION: park-kin-SOH-nee-ah ak-you-lee-AH-tah

FAMILY: Fabaceae (Legume, Bean, or Pulse Family)

TYPE: Deciduous tree

HEIGHT: 12–30 feet, up to 40 feet

SPREAD: 15–20 feet

FINAL SPACING: 12–15 feet

NATURAL HABITAT AND PREFERRED SITE: A native along the Rio Grande in the Rio Grande Valley, it will adapt to a wide range of soils. It can grow in wet soils but is extremely drought tolerant and will do very well up through central Texas.

IDENTIFICATION: This graceful, airy tree has long, thin compound leaves, yellow summer flowers, and green bark. It is heavily armed with thorns.

FLOWERS AND FRUIT: Fragrant, yellow flowers bloom in the spring or throughout the summer, especially after rains. The racemes are 5–6 inches long. The pea-shaped flowers persist for at least a week. The fruits form as slender, brown pods, 2–4 inches long, and are constricted between the seeds. The seeds are green, turning brown at maturity.

FOLIAGE: The leaves are compound with tiny leaflets. The overall leaf is 8–16 inches long. Leaflets are only ⅓ inch long or less. The leaf midrib, branches, and twigs are green, so they also provide photosynthesis.

BARK: The bark is thin, smooth, and green. On older trunks it turns reddish brown with small scales.

CULTURE: Parkinsonia is easy to grow in a wide range of soils, even in high salt conditions. It can grow as far north as Dallas but risks freeze damage there during severe winters. It grows best in moist, deep soils but is strongly drought tolerant. During drought it sheds the small leaflets, leaving only the midribs of the leaves, which are green and can continue to manufacture necessary sugars for survival. Fast-growing when young, it is relatively short-lived. It tolerates moist soil but doesn't like sopping, heavy, wet clay soils.

PROBLEMS: Freeze damage is possible in the northern half of the state. Seedlings can become somewhat of a problem by sprouting up all over the place.

PROPAGATION: It is easy to grow from cuttings or seed, but acid or physical scarification treatment is needed to aid germination. Causing physical damage, such as filing the seed coat and/or soaking the seed in liquid humate or seaweed, can also aid germination.

INSIGHT: It is probably risky to invest a lot of money in this plant for use north of Austin.

Flowering peach in full bloom.

Flowering peach foliage.

Peach

COMMON NAMES: Peach
BOTANICAL NAME: *Prunus persica*
PRONUNCIATION: PROO-nus PURR-si-cah
FAMILY: Rosaceae (Rose Family)
TYPE: Deciduous ornamental or fruit tree
HEIGHT: 10–15 feet, up to about 25 feet
SPREAD: 10–15 feet
FINAL SPACING: 15–30 feet
NATURAL HABITAT AND PREFERRED SITE: Peach is native to China but adapts well to a wide range of soils as long as they are well-drained.
IDENTIFICATION: Peaches are spreading, ornamental, and fruiting trees that have early spring flowers of all colors followed by either ornamental or edible fruit.
FLOWERS AND FRUIT: Colorful flowers form in the early spring in a wide range of colors from white to pink to various shades of red. The flowers bloom before the leaves sprout in March through May. Trees that produce showy flowers produce almost no fruit at all. The edible-peach trees form a delicious, soft, fuzzy-covered fruit in the mid to late summer. The fruit is actually a drupe, generally maturing from July through October. Fruit color, shape, and size will vary depending on the cultivar. Peach fruit is delicious and the flowers are also edible.

FOLIAGE: The leaves are simple, alternate, elongated, and sometimes clustered. They are thin, 3–6 inches long, and bright green. Fall color is usually yellow. The leaves have a fine sawtooth margin and tend to drop early.
BARK: Smooth with a metallic, silver-gray, or brown appearance when young, the bark develops a heavier texture with age. Mature trees will develop furrowed bark.
CULTURE: Flowering peach trees are easy to grow for a wonderfully colorful flower display in the spring.
PROBLEMS: Peach trees are attacked by a variety of pests because they are not well-adapted. Flare-ups of insects and disease can be knocked back with Garrett Juice (see Appendix 2) plus garlic and potassium bicarbonate. Insect pests can also be controlled with fire ant control mixture used as a spray or other citrus-based products. Trees in severe stress with lots of problems should be treated with the Sick Tree Treatment (see Appendix 3).
PROPAGATION: To get the fruit desired, propagation must be done by cuttings. To get a "who knows what" peach, plant seed. Softwood cuttings and grafting of cultivars also are done.
INSIGHT: This is an excellent plant for attracting beneficial insects. There are many varieties that I recommend for Texas. Consult *Texas Organic Vegetable Gardening* by Garrett and Beck.

Bradford pear fall color.

Pear, Bradford

COMMON NAMES: Bradford Pear, Ornamental Pear, Callery Pear

BOTANICAL NAME: *Pyrus calleryana* 'Bradford'

PRONUNCIATION: PIE-rus cal-er-ee-AH-nah

FAMILY: Rosaceae (Rose Family)

TYPE: Deciduous ornamental tree

HEIGHT: 25–30 feet

SPREAD: 15–20 feet

FINAL SPACING: 10–20 feet

NATURAL HABITAT AND PREFERRED SITE: The ornamental pears are native to China but are well-adapted to a wide range of soils, provided there is good drainage and full sun.

IDENTIFICATION: Bradford pear is an upright, deciduous tree with white flowers in the spring and red fall color. The crown of the tree is usually quite uniform and symmetrical-looking, like a big, oval lollipop.

FLOWERS AND FRUIT: Spring flowers emerge before the leaves form. The white flowers are showy but have a somewhat unpleasant odor. The flowers are perfect (male and female parts in the same flower). The fruit is ornamental only and ripens in the late summer through fall. It is no larger than a coffee bean, ½ inch in diameter. Fall color can range from orange to scarlet red.

FOLIAGE: The leaves are heart-shaped with rippled edges. Fall color is red and in most years quite spectacular. The leaves are alternate, simple, 2–3 inches long, and roughly triangular with an irregular, sawtooth margin.

BARK: The young bark is smooth, light to medium gray or brown. It develops heavier texture and darker color with age. Mature trunks are shallowly furrowed with an irregular bark pattern.

CULTURE: Bradford pear is somewhat easy to grow in most soils except for heavy clays that do not drain well. It responds well to fertilizer and moisture but is easily stressed by excessive soil moisture.

PROBLEMS: Bradford pear and the other ornamental pears are all short-lived and subject to root diseases if the soil is not excellently drained and healthy. The Basic Organic Program (see Appendix 5) can usually keep the trees in good shape. Stressed trees that are going downhill should be treated with the Sick Tree Treatment (see Appendix 3).

PROPAGATION: The ornamental hybrid pears are propagated by stem cuttings. Trees propagated by seed will not come true to form (i.e., won't turn out right). Hybrids can be propagated by grafting or budding. Cuttings are not easy to do successfully.

INSIGHT: There are several ornamental pears. 'Bradford' is the most common. Others include 'Aristocrat,' which has more open branching and is actually a superior tree. 'Capital' and 'White House' are two cultivars that are narrow-growing and have had mixed reviews. I am not a huge fan of any of the ornamental pears unless they are used on a short-term basis for flowers and fall color. They should not be considered a long-term tree investment.

The mother plant of these hybrids, **Callery pear** (*Pyrus calleryana*), which does have thorns, is a superior plant. This tree's root system is used as the root stock for many of the commercial fruit trees. Callery pear has more open branching and more of a tree form. It will live longer and have considerably fewer problems than the other ornamental pears.

Bradford pear foliage in the fall.

Aristocrat pear.

Bradford pear branching structure.

Callery pear.

Pear, Common

COMMON NAMES: Common Pear, Pear, Peara
BOTANICAL NAME: *Pyrus communis* (syn. *P. pyrifolia*)
PRONUNCIATION: PIE-rus COM-you-nis
FAMILY: Rosaceae (Rose Family)
TYPE: Deciduous fruit tree
HEIGHT: 15–25 feet
SPREAD: 10–15 feet
FINAL SPACING: 15–20 feet
NATURAL HABITAT AND PREFERRED SITE: A native of Europe and west Asia, it will adapt to various soils, preferring sandy soils to sandy loams as well as good moisture and excellent drainage.
IDENTIFICATION: Common pear is an upright to spreading tree with early, white flowers followed by colorful summer fruit.
FLOWERS AND FRUIT: White flowers bloom in the spring prior to leaf emergence. These are followed by edible summer fruit. The flowers bloom from March to May. The fruit ripens from July through October.

FOLIAGE: The leaves are simple, alternate, and deciduous with primarily yellow fall color.
BARK: Metallic gray to medium brown when young, the bark develops a heavier texture with age.
CULTURE: Pears are fairly easy to grow, especially for fruit trees. Having a successful fruit crop is harder.
PROBLEMS: Fire blight is the most common pest, which can be avoided by cutting back on nitrogen fertilizer. Use the Basic Organic Program (see Appendix 5) and spray with Garrett Juice (see Appendix 2) plus potassium bicarbonate and/or garlic tea.
PROPAGATION: Collect seed at maturity when the fruit is ripe and use cold stratification at 32°–45°F for 60–90 days. Hybrids can only be propagated to come true to form from stem cuttings. For specific variety recommendations, refer to *Texas Organic Vegetable Gardening* by Garrett and Beck.
INSIGHT: My personal favorites are the Asian pears. They are round, thin-skinned, and incredibly delicious. They are a little harder to keep healthy in Texas but worth the trouble.

National and more importantly "state" champion pecan tree in Weatherford, Texas.

Pecan champ in the dead of winter from a different angle.

Pecan

COMMON NAMES: Pecan, Nogal Morado, Nuez Encarcelada

BOTANICAL NAME: *Carya illinoinenis*

PRONUNCIATION: CARE-ee-ah ill-ih-noy-NEN-sis

FAMILY: Juglandaceae (Walnut Family)

TYPE: Deciduous nut and shade tree

HEIGHT: 80 to over 100 feet

SPREAD: 60–100 feet

FINAL SPACING: 30–60 feet and a 60 × 60-foot grid in orchards is ideal. Closer spacing used to be recommended but proved to be a mistake.

NATURAL HABITAT AND PREFERRED SITE: Pecan is native to the eastern half of Texas—all areas except the High Plains and the Trans-Pecos. It is well-adapted to a wide range of soils, although it prefers the deep, moist, sandy loam soils. In a landscape situation, it will grow in sand or heavy clays.

IDENTIFICATION: This large-growing, graceful shade tree has a rounded crown. It tends to be open at the top. It produces edible nuts in the fall and so-so yellow fall color.

FLOWERS AND FRUIT: Male flowers appear as drooping catkins. Female flower clusters show just before leaf emergence. Both sexes appear on the same tree at the same time (monoecious). The male catkins are 5–6 inches long, and the female flowers appear in short, terminal spikes. The fruit (pecan nuts) ripens in the fall in clusters of 3–11. The husks split into 4 sections and often stay on the tree after the nuts have fallen. Pecan nuts are a wonderful, natural food high in vitamin E.

FOLIAGE: The leaves are alternate and compound, 12–20 inches long, and have yellow fall color. There

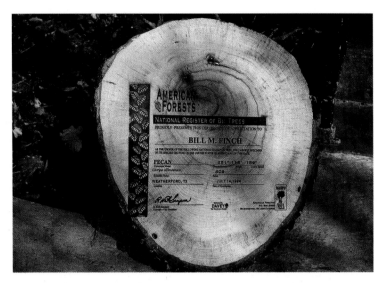

Official plaque acknowledging the national champion status of our Texas pecan tree.

are normally 19 leaflets that are 3–8 inches long. Terminal leaflets tend to be larger than the leaflets closer to the stem.

BARK: The bark is thick, light brown or gray to reddish brown, with narrow, irregular fissures. The bark becomes flattened and scaly with age.

CULTURE: Pecan trees are easy to grow in a wide range of soils. They respond to moderate fertilization, although heavy, high nitrogen fertilization can lead to many pest problems. Pecans are relatively drought tolerant, but moisture is important in the summer as the nuts are forming. Zinc is often recommended as a foliar spray, but I have found it unnecessary when using the Basic Organic Program (see Appendix 5). Buffered and proper levels of zinc exist in many of the natural organic products, including fish emulsion, seaweed, Garrett Juice (see Appendix 2), humates, etc. Plus the program allows tied-up nutrients in the soil to be released and made available to the plants.

PROBLEMS: Hickory shuckworm, pecan casebearer, and webworms are the most common pests that pop up, but they are all able to be controlled under the Basic Organic Program (see Appendix 5). Pecan trees are somewhat messy in a residential setting, but they are certainly worth the trouble.

PROPAGATION: Pecans are easy to grow from seed (the nuts). They should be planted immediately on release from the trees in the fall. The only problem is keeping the squirrels from digging them up.

INSIGHT: Pecan is the state tree of Texas and a great shade tree choice. Native trees and hybrids with

Pecan foliage and fruit.

small nuts such as 'Kanza' and 'Caddo' are the best choices. Everyone that understands trees, including the Texas State Forest Service and the A&M Extension System, are now recommending the native pecans and the smaller nut trees instead of the large paper-shell hybrids. This is because the smaller nut and native trees are healthier trees, are more long-lasting, and have fewer problems. Also the quality of the meat and oil from the nut is superior.

Persimmon, Common

COMMON NAMES: Common Persimmon, Persimmon, Eastern Persimmon, Possumwood, Date Plum, Jove's Fruit, Winter Plum

BOTANICAL NAME: *Diospyros virginiana*

PRONUNCIATION: dye-OSS-pear-os ver-gin-ee-AN-ah

FAMILY: Ebenaceae (Persimmon or Ebony Family)

TYPE: Deciduous edible fruit tree

HEIGHT: 40–70 feet

SPREAD: 30–40 feet

FINAL SPACING: 30–40 feet

NATURAL HABITAT AND PREFERRED SITE: It grows wild in east Texas and other spotty areas of the state. Persimmon is very much at home in a wide range of soils from sandy to deep gumbo, alkaline clays.

IDENTIFICATION: Common persimmon has a variety of overall looks from dense and symmetrical to open and spreading. It has beautiful, orange fruit in the fall, yellow to orange fall color, and spreading, often crooked or drooping branching.

FLOWERS AND FRUIT: It flowers from April to June. Male and female flowers are on separate trees (dioecious), are greenish yellow, and are not showy. The fruit is sweet and edible when ripe but extremely astringent when unripe. It will ripen from August through February depending on its location in the state. Early or late fruit is generally smaller than the fruit that ripens about the time the leaves fall from the trees. The fruits are generally ¾–1½ inches long and contain 4–8 flat seeds that are leathery and about ½ inch long. The fruit is bright pink to orange when ripe. Only the female trees have the fruit.

FOLIAGE: The leaves are deciduous, simple, and alternate. They are 3–6 inches long with smooth margins, shiny, dark green above, and a paler color below. They are also somewhat hairy on the underside. Fall color shows very early in the season. Fall color is from yellow to pink to orange and some years is spectacular. The shiny summer foliage has a graceful, drooping appearance.

BARK: The bark is brown to black with deep, heavy fissures.

CULTURE: Common persimmon is easy to grow in any well-drained soil. It needs minimum fertilizer and is relatively drought tolerant. It is difficult to transplant from the wild.

PROBLEMS: Webworms attack unhealthy trees in the summer. The fruit is messy, especially if the tree is planted near paved surfaces. Releasing trichogramma wasps and using the Basic Organic Program (see Appendix 5) will prevent most of the insect pests.

Common persimmon foliage and fruit.

PROPAGATION: Common persimmon is grown by planting seed from mature fruit. Germination is increased by soaking the seed in water 2–3 days before planting. Seed can be planted in the spring or the fall. Common persimmon can also be propagated by root cuttings that are 6–8 inches long and approximately ⅓ inch in diameter. Grafting and budding can also be done. Seed will also respond well to being cold stratified for 30–60 days at 36°–41°F and then sowed outdoors in the early spring.

INSIGHT: Persimmon wood is known for its toughness, strength, hardness, and ability to absorb shock. It has been used to make billiard cues, spools, bobbins, and wooden golf club heads in the past. The fruit is very important for wildlife.

Common persimmon fall color.

Japanese persimmon foliage and fruit.

Persimmon, Japanese

COMMON NAMES: Japanese Persimmon

BOTANICAL NAME: *Diospyros kaki*

PRONUNCIATION: dye-OSS-pear-os KAH-ki

FAMILY: Ebenaceae (Persimmon or Ebony Family)

TYPE: Deciduous fruit tree

HEIGHT: 20–30 feet

SPREAD: 20–30 feet

FINAL SPACING: 15–30 feet

NATURAL HABITAT AND PREFERRED SITE: Native to China and Japan, it adapts to a wide range of soils here in Texas, as long as there is moisture in the soil and good positive drainage at the same time.

IDENTIFICATION: Japanese persimmon fruit is smaller than our common persimmon fruit but is larger than our Texas persimmon fruit. The leaves are large and the fruit is apple-sized.

FLOWERS AND FRUIT: The spring flowers are inconspicuous. The fruit is large, edible, orange-red in the fall, and 2–4 inches in diameter. It is rounded and sometimes egg-shaped, depending on the cultivar. It is seedless for the most part. Japanese persimmon fruit ripens on the tree after the leaves have fallen.

FOLIAGE: The leaves are alternate, simple, 3–7 inches long, and oval- to heart-shaped. They have smooth margins and are generally thick, shiny, and dark green. Fall color can be quite showy and ranges from yellows to oranges to reds.

BARK: Light brown to medium brown when young, the bark gains a darker and heavier texture as the tree matures.

CULTURE: Japanese persimmons grow well in most well-drained soils but cannot take wet feet or poor drainage. They respond to fertilization, mulching, and other parts of the Basic Organic Program (see Appendix 5). Pruning is done, as with most trees, for your benefit, not the tree's. This tree is fairly difficult to transplant but is easy to establish bare-rooted or as a container-grown plant.

PROBLEMS: Japanese persimmon is sometimes attacked by disease and insect pests, but most attacks are cosmetic and can be controlled or prevented with the Basic Organic Program (see Appendix 5).

PROPAGATION: Propagation is done by grafting selected cultivars onto common persimmon seedlings.

INSIGHT: 'Ureka' is a flat-shaped fruit cultivar on small, easy-to-grow trees. 'Hachiya' is a medium-sized tree with large, cone-shaped, colorful, seedless fruit. 'Tanenashi' is an excellent, moderately productive tree. 'Tamopan' produces a flattened fruit with a ring constriction near the middle. 'Fuyu' and 'Fuyugaki' are nonastringent choices that can be eaten even slightly green without the pucker. They have the texture of an apple and are also self-pollinating. 'Izu' is another nonastringent selection that has been recently introduced to the Dallas market and is supposedly more cold tolerant.

Texas persimmon.

Texas persimmon foliage and fruit.

Texas persimmon trunk.

Persimmon, Texas

COMMON NAMES: Texas Persimmon, Mexican Persimmon, Black Persimmon, Chapote

BOTANICAL NAME: *Diospyros texana*

PRONUNCIATION: dye-OSS-pear-os TEX-ann-ah

FAMILY: Ebonaceae (Persimmon or Ebony Family)

TYPE: Small fruit tree, evergreen in the most southern parts of the state but deciduous from San Antonio north

HEIGHT: 20–40 feet

SPREAD: 15–20 feet

FINAL SPACING: 15–20 feet

NATURAL HABITAT AND PREFERRED SITE: Texas persimmon is found primarily in south Texas to central Texas, growing in a wide range of soils. It is quite drought tolerant and needs excellent drainage.

IDENTIFICATION: It is an ornamental tree that is intricately branched and has smooth, beautiful bark with small, leathery leaves and small, edible fruit in the fall.

FLOWERS AND FRUIT: The flowers are approximately 1 inch long, greenish white, and somewhat bell-shaped. Female and male flowers appear on different plants (dioecious). The fruit is a round, ¾–1-inch persimmon, which is black when ripe and has sweet, edible pulp. The fruits are crowded with seeds, making some people wonder if they are worth eating.

FOLIAGE: The leaves are small, 1–2 inches long, and leathery. The undersides are often fuzzy, and the edges are often slightly rolled under. They have very little fall color.

BARK: The bark is brown to gray and smooth, but the outer bark peels off, revealing a lighter-colored inner bark. The trunks and branches somewhat resemble crape myrtle or madrone with their beautiful, exfoliating outer surfaces.

CULTURE: Texas persimmon is a slow-growing plant but is easy to grow. It requires a minimum amount of fertilizer and is quite drought tolerant. It can even grow in rocky soil areas.

PROBLEMS: The only problems I have seen with Texas persimmon are poor availability in the nursery trade and freeze damage in the northern portions of the state. Pest problems are few.

PROPAGATION: It is easily grown from seed by planting immediately after seed matures in the fall. Apply cold stratification through the winter and plant in the spring. It can also be easily transplanted from the wild.

INSIGHT: Texas persimmon fruit has been used in Mexico to dye animal hides, and the wood is used to make tool handles and lathe products as well as salt shakers because of its moisture-absorbing ability. It has been said that the fruit can cause constipation in livestock.

Austrian pine.

Austrian pine foliage.

Pine, Austrian

COMMON NAMES: Austrian Pine
BOTANICAL NAME: *Pinus nigra*
PRONUNCIATION: PIE-nus NI-gra
FAMILY: Pinaceae (Pine Family)
TYPE: Evergreen tree
HEIGHT: 30–60 feet
SPREAD: 20–30 feet
FINAL SPACING: 15–20 feet
NATURAL HABITAT AND PREFERRED SITE: It is native to central and southern Europe and Asia.
IDENTIFICATION: Austrian pine is a slow-growing, thickly foliaged pine tree. It keeps its foliage all the way to the ground unless it is pruned away. The thick branching creates a mounded appearance.
FLOWERS AND FRUIT: The female flowers are inconspicuous. The male flowers or catkins are noticeable but nothing spectacular in the spring. The fruit is a light brown, woody cone borne singly or in clusters.
FOLIAGE: The leaves are fairly short, stiff, dark green needles, 3–6 inches long, in bundles of 2. They tend to be curved or twisted and tufted at the ends of the branches.
BARK: The bark is medium to dark brown with a heavy texture.

CULTURE: Austrian pine is an easy-to-grow pine tree in most of Texas, even in the black alkaline soils, as long as the drainage is good. It responds well to fertilization and needs moderate amounts of water.
PROBLEMS: Occasional chlorosis can be overcome using the Basic Organic Program (see Appendix 5) or for severe problems the Sick Tree Treatment (see Appendix 3). Austrian pine has resistance to pine tip moth but may occasionally get the pine twig blight. Soil treatment with horticultural cornmeal normally cures disease pests. According to Whitcomb's *Know It and Grow It*, herbicide vapors are causing a decline of Austrian pines over most of the United States. He no longer recommends the species. I would suggest that we no longer allow the herbicides to be used, especially since they are totally unnecessary.
PROPAGATION: It can probably be grown from seed, although I have never done it. Nursery transplants are the common method of growing the plant.
INSIGHT: Austrian pine is more symmetrical and has more twisted or curved needles than **Japanese black pine** (*Pinus thunbergii*). Austrian pine also holds its needles longer and gives a denser internal appearance then the Japanese species.

Eldarica pine foliage and flowers.

Pine, Eldarica

COMMON NAMES: Eldarica Pine, Mondell Pine, Afghan Pine

BOTANICAL NAME: *Pinus eldarica*

PRONUNCIATION: PIE-nus ell-DAR-eh-kah

FAMILY: Pinaceae (Pine Family)

TYPE: Evergreen tree

HEIGHT: 30–40 feet

SPREAD: 15–20 feet

FINAL SPACING: 12–20 feet

NATURAL HABITAT AND PREFERRED SITE: As one of the common names above implies, this tree is a desert tree, native to southern Russia, Afghanistan, and Pakistan. It will grow well for a few years in a wide range of soils in Texas if the drainage is good. Although it is fairly well-adapted to west Texas, it is dying out in the higher rainfall areas of the state.

IDENTIFICATION: Eldarica pine is an upright, fast-growing pine with medium green needles. It normally keeps its foliage all the way to the ground.

FLOWERS AND FRUIT: Inconspicuous flowers are followed by seed-bearing cones.

FOLIAGE: It has typical pine foliage but seems to have a somewhat duller appearance than that of other pines.

BARK: The bark is medium to dark brown with a medium heavy texture.

CULTURE: Eldarica pine is fast-growing and does fairly well the first 5–10 years in any soil that is well-drained. It is drought tolerant. In fact, it is totally intolerant of rainfall above 20 inches a year or regular irrigation from an irrigation system. It responds well to fertilizer, but too much can contribute to root disease problems.

PROBLEMS: This tree is dying out in the eastern part of the state. Unfortunately, the decline and death happen after the tree has reached some maturity. Root diseases start to hit and take the tree out rather quickly once the soil pathogens attack the root system. The problem can be abated with the use of horticultural cornmeal and the Sick Tree Treatment (see Appendix 3), but Mother Nature is going to eventually get her way. Eldarica pine is a desert tree—it is not adapted to high rainfall or irrigation areas.

PROPAGATION: It can probably be grown from seed, although I have never done it. Nursery transplants are the common method of growing the plant.

INSIGHT: Eldarica pine is fairly well-suited to west Texas and unirrigated sites. See other pine entries here for better selections.

State champion eldarica pine at the USDA Research Center in Knox City.

Japanese black pine.

Japanese black pine foliage and spring candles.

Pine, Japanese Black

COMMON NAMES: Japanese Black Pine
BOTANICAL NAME: *Pinus thunbergii*
PRONUNCIATION: PIE-nus thun-BERG-ee-eye
FAMILY: Pineaceae (Pine Family)
TYPE: Evergreen ornamental tree
HEIGHT: 30–60 feet
SPREAD: 20–30 feet
FINAL SPACING: 15–20 feet
NATURAL HABITAT AND PREFERRED SITE: Native to Japan, it is reasonably well-adapted to Texas to the deeper soils—especially the acid, sandy soils.
IDENTIFICATION: Japanese black pine is an irregularly shaped pine tree that is somewhat pyramidal when young but becomes more oval and unevenly spreading with age.
FLOWERS AND FRUIT: The female flowers are inconspicuous. The male catkins are noticeable in the spring. It is monoecious—both male and female flowers are on the same tree. The fruit is a light brown, woody cone, 1½ –2½ inches long.

FOLIAGE: The dark green needles are 3–4 inches long in bundles of 2. They are straight, rarely twisted, and harsh to the touch.
BARK: The bark is medium to dark brown with a heavy texture.
CULTURE: Japanese black pine is fairly easy to grow in deep soils, but it particularly likes neutral-to-slightly-acid soils. It does not do well over white rock and gets weaker every year in that situation. It does respond to fertilizer and moisture but is fairly drought tolerant.
PROBLEMS: Chlorosis occurs in the alkaline soils. Pine tip moth and other typical pine problems develop once the tree is in stress. Adding large amounts of compost, Texas greensand, and lava sand can help reverse soil problems. Beneficial insects are an effective control of insect pests.
PROPAGATION: It is grown from seed. Gather the cones in the fall and cure them at room temperature for 1 month, then plant in sandy loam soil.
INSIGHT: Japanese black pine is not quite as good a choice for alkaline soils in Texas as the Austrian pine but is better than the straight-trunked, east Texas pines in those situations.

Loblolly pine.

Slash pine.

Pine, Loblolly

COMMON NAME: Loblolly Pine, Old Field Pine
BOTANICAL NAME: *Pinus taeda*
PRONUNCIATION: PIE-nus TIE-dah
FAMILY: Pineaceae (Pine Family)
TYPE: Evergreen tree
HEIGHT: 80–100 feet
SPREAD: 20–30 feet
FINAL SPACING: 20–30 feet
NATURAL HABITAT AND PREFERRED SITE:
Loblolly pine is the most numerous pine in Texas. It is found throughout the Piney Woods and the far eastern side of the state. It grows in low areas primarily but adapts to more well-drained sites quite well.
IDENTIFICATION: Loblolly pine is the fastest-growing of all the southern pines. It even outgrows

the slash pine. Because of its rapid growth, it is the most widely planted pine in Texas for timber purposes.
FLOWERS AND FRUIT: The male flowers are yellowish, about 1 inch long, and arranged in spiral clusters at the ends of the branches. The female flowers are yellowish and about ½ inch long at the branch tips. The cones are approximately 2–6 inches long and light reddish brown, ripening in the fall. Scales on the cones are only occasionally armed and are reddish brown.
FOLIAGE: The needles are almost always in groups of 3, 5–9 inches long, and light to medium green.
BARK: The bark is scaly and nearly black when young, becoming reddish brown with age.
CULTURE: Extremely fast-growing and easy to grow in acid, sandy soil, it does not do well at all in alkaline soils, especially white rock. It responds to fertilizer,

Short leaf pine in Tyler.

Aleppo pine in Houston.

Slash pine foliage.

although over fertilization and use of pesticides is the cause of the typical pine tree pest problems.

PROBLEMS: Loblolly pine is susceptible to fusarium gall rust, southern pine beetle, and ice storm damage.

PROPAGATION: Propagation is done from seed.

INSIGHT: Loblolly pine is widely planted and one of the most important timber trees in Texas. The name *loblolly* means "mud holes" and refers to its ability to grow in wetter soils. Other pines in this category include **slash pine** (*Pinus elliottii*), which is a native of the southeastern states. Also often planted commercially in Texas, the slash pine closely resembles loblolly pines but differs by having glossy, brown cones on short stalks. The cone scales are armed with curved spines. **Short leaf pine** or **yellow pine** is *P. echinata*, and **long leaf pine** is *P. palustris*. **Aleppo pine** (*P. halepensis*) is one of the most commonly used pines in the Houston area. It will suffer freeze damage in the northern part of the state.

Ponderosa pine in Dallas.

Pine, Ponderosa

COMMON NAMES: Ponderosa Pine, Western Yellow Pine
BOTANICAL NAME: *Pinus ponderosa*
PRONUNCIATION: PIE-nus pon-der-ROE-sah
FAMILY: Pinaceae (Pine Family)
TYPE: Evergreen tree
HEIGHT: 80–100 feet
SPREAD: 20–30 feet
FINAL SPACING: 20–30 feet
NATURAL HABITAT AND PREFERRED SITE: It grows primarily in the Chisos Mountains, but there are some growing in the Dallas/Fort Worth area. It appears to be a tree that can adapt to a wide range of soils as long as the drainage as good.
IDENTIFICATION: This dramatic pine tree has a narrow, open crown, tall, straight trunk, and needles borne in tufts on the ends of the branches.
FLOWERS AND FRUIT: The flowers form in the spring from April to June. Male inflorescences are long and yellow. Female cones are paired, clustered, and dark red. The fruit forms as a large cone in the late summer, from August through September. The cones are 3–6 inches long. The seeds that release soon after the cone opens are about ¼ inch.
FOLIAGE: The leaves are borne in tufts at the ends of the branches. The needles are in clusters of 2 or 3 or sometimes as many as 5. Young foliage is dark green. Older needles become yellowish to blue-green. Needles are 4–11 inches long and smell like citrus when crushed.
BARK: The bark is dark brown to almost black when young. It turns reddish with maturity and becomes deeply furrowed. A vanilla smell is detectable when you are closely inspecting the bark.
CULTURE: Ponderosa pine is usually found at high altitudes in the mountains, but the tree does seem to adapt to well-drained soils in other parts of Texas.
PROBLEMS: Parasitic dwarf mistletoe is the most commonly mentioned pest but can be controlled with the Sick Tree Treatment (see Appendix 3).
PROPAGATION: It is propagated by seed.
INSIGHT: Seeds and young foliage are eaten by several species of wildlife.

Texas pistache.

Pistache, Texas

COMMON NAMES: Texas Pistache, Texas Pistachio, American Pistachio, Wild Pistachio, Lentisco

BOTANICAL NAME: *Pistachia texana*

PRONUNCIATION: pis-TA-see-ah tex-AN-ah

FAMILY: Anacardiaceae (Sumac or Cashew Family)

TYPE: Small semi-evergreen to evergreen tree

HEIGHT: 10–40 feet

SPREAD: 10–15 feet

FINAL SPACING: 15–20 feet

NATURAL HABITAT AND PREFERRED SITE: It grows in the canyons of the Edwards Plateau and the cliffs near the junction of the Rio Grande and Pecos rivers in west Texas. It also grows in streambeds and likes rocky limestone soils.

IDENTIFICATION: Texas pistache is a small, bushy evergreen tree that has small leaflets and is often a multi-trunked plant.

FLOWERS AND FRUIT: Clusters of white flowers are borne in the spring before the new leaves emerge. The sexes are separate on separate trees (dioecious). The fruits are single-seeded, are about ¼ inch long, and start out red and turn dark blue or black at maturity. The fruit is an inedible, nutlike drupe.

FOLIAGE: The new leaves are reddish, later turning dark green and glossy. The foliage is evergreen, 2–4 inches long, with 9–19 leaflets that are ½–1 inch long.

BARK: The bark on the twigs is reddish and slightly hairy, later turning brown to gray with age.

CULTURE: Texas pistache is easy to grow in well-drained soil, is drought tolerant, and needs a minimum amount of fertilizer. It needs protection in the winter in the northern part of the state.

PROBLEMS: It will freeze in the northern part of the state in severe winters and does not like heavily irrigated or high rainfall areas.

PROPAGATION: It can be grown from seed planted immediately after collection in late August through September. It is beneficial to put the seed briefly in water after harvest to separate the viable from the dead seed. The viable seed will float. Fresh seed will germinate quickly. Dried seed must be stratified for 30–60 days at about 41°F prior to sowing outdoors in the spring or planting in a greenhouse during the winter.

INSIGHT: It has been reported that the Texas pistache can be successfully budded onto the root stock of **Chinese pistachi**o (*Pistachia chinensis*).

Chinese pistachio in the fall.

Pistachio, Chinese

COMMON NAMES: Chinese Pistachio, Chinese Pistache
BOTANICAL NAME: *Pistachia chinensis*
PRONUNCIATION: pis-TA-see-ah chi-NEN-sis
FAMILY: Anacardiaceae (Sumac or Cashew Family)
TYPE: Deciduous shade tree
HEIGHT: 40–70 feet
SPREAD: 50–70 feet
FINAL SPACING: 20–50 feet
NATURAL HABITAT AND PREFERRED SITE: A native from Afghanistan to China and the Philippines, it appears to have naturalized in some areas of northeast Texas. It is well-adapted to a wide range of soils with the exception of solid white rock and poorly drained areas.
IDENTIFICATION: A spreading, deciduous shade tree with colorful berries on female plants, it has usually spectacular fall color that ranges from yellows to deep reds. It has a rounded overall shape.
FLOWERS AND FRUIT: Male and female flowers grow on separate trees (dioecious) on bare stems. They are reddish brown and not particularly showy.

Female Chinese pistachio with fruit in the late summer.

Chinese pistachio fall color.

Chinese pistachio spring flowers.

The fruits are small, round, reddish to purple, dry drupes that appear on heavily branched panicles in the fall. They are found only on female trees. When the berry production is heavy, the tree seems to be in some stress because part of the foliage turns yellow and defoliates, especially after a dry summer.

FOLIAGE: The compound leaves, alternate, 8–10 inches long, have usually 10–16 leaflets. Fall color can range from yellow and brown to a spectacular range of yellows, salmons, reds, and deep maroons. All the colors can be on one tree at the same time, and in some years the trees will be just one dramatic color.

BARK: The bark is tan when young, becoming darker and more heavily textured with age.

CULTURE: Chinese pistachio is an easy-to-grow introduced tree that adapts to a wide range of soils. Solid white rock and wet soils should be avoided. Excellent drainage is critical. It does respond to fertilization, although it does not need a heavy amount and is relatively drought tolerant. When young it is an awkward, unattractive tree. Just be patient—it will fill out within the first few years of growth and become a beautiful tree.

PROBLEMS: Chinese pistachio often has a weak trunk system with a weak crotch. If one side of this weak system is not eliminated, the tree can split straight down the middle. Tip growth will sometimes burn in the early summer from too much water or salty conditions.

PROPAGATION: Chinese pistachio is easy to grow from seed, now naturalizing in parts of Texas. The plant is difficult to root from cuttings and grafts.

Split trunk is a common problem with Chinese pistachio.

INSIGHT: Pistachio nuts do not come from this tree but rather from *Pistachia vera*, which is a small tree that grows to about 30 feet in height. It is a little harder to grow and can freeze in harsh winters, especially in the northern part of the state. It is a desert plant and cannot stand much water. **Texas pistache**, (*Pistachia texana*) is our Texas native.

Mexican plum.

Mexican plum spring flowers.

Plum, Mexican

COMMON NAMES: Mexican Plum, Big Tree Plum, Inch Plum

BOTANICAL NAME: *Prunus mexicana*

PRONUNCIATION: PROO-nus mex-ee-KAHN-ah

FAMILY: Rosaceae (Rose Family)

TYPE: Small to medium-sized, deciduous, flowering and fruiting tree

HEIGHT: 20–30 feet

SPREAD: 15–20 feet

FINAL SPACING: 15–20 feet

NATURAL HABITAT AND PREFERRED SITE: Mexican plum grows in most of the eastern half of Texas in a wide range of soils, in full sun or as an understory tree. It appears in fence rows and free-standing in open areas.

IDENTIFICATION: Mexican plum is a good-looking ornamental tree with white spring flowers, orange fall color, beautiful, exfoliating bark, and an irregular branching structure.

FLOWERS AND FRUIT: The flowers are fragrant and white, ¾–1 inch in diameter, and they bloom in the early spring before the leaves. The fruit matures from midsummer through the fall, sometimes becoming completely mature in September. The round, 1-inch, edible, thick plums are used for jellies and jams more than for eating fresh. Mature fruits are a dark purplish red with a whitish surface bloom.

FOLIAGE: The leaves are alternate, simple, and deciduous. Fall color ranges from yellow to a beautiful orange color. The leaves are 2–4 inches in length, smooth, and dark green above and lighter beneath. They are sometimes folded over and look as though they are drooping from lack of water.

BARK: The bark is tight and metallic gray when young, becoming scaly and rough with age. Older trees have lovely, brown, papery, exfoliating, or scaly bark. Mature bark becomes very rough and deeply furrowed.

CULTURE: Mexican plum is an easy-to-grow ornamental tree that is drought tolerant, requires little fertilizer, and does well in sun or shade.

Mexican plum late summer fruit.

Mexican plum fall color.

PROBLEMS: A few insects chew on the leaves occasionally, but the tree doesn't have major pest problems when planted in fairly healthy, well-drained soil. It is rather difficult to transplant from the wild except for very small trees.

PROPAGATION: It is grown primarily from seed planted fresh immediately after harvest in the fall. Seed can be cleaned and stratified at 41°F for 60–90 days before planting in the spring. Mexican plum can also be grown from dormant hardwood, softwood, semi-hardwood, and root cuttings. Semi-hardwood and softwood cuttings made in the summer root the easiest. For landscaping it's best to plant container-grown trees.

INSIGHT: **Common edible plum** (*Prunus salicinia*) is a fairly easy fruit tree to grow in well-drained soils that have been made healthy with the Basic Organic Program (see Appendix 5). These trees grow from 15–20 feet and are one of the easiest of the fruit trees to grow. Appendix 5 also includes a section on fruit trees. Plums, like other fruit trees grown in Texas as food crops, have a variety of insect and disease problems when the soil is not healthy. Healthy soil is the key. Some of the best plum varieties for Texas are 'Methley,' 'Morris,' 'Bruce,' and 'Santa Rosa.' **Purple plum** (*P. cerasifera*) is a purple-foliage ornamental tree that has pink blooms in the spring. I no longer recommend this plant because it just simply doesn't live long enough to be a good investment.

Common plum.

Purple plum.

Texas redbud in the late summer.

Native redbud spring flowers.

Redbud

COMMON NAMES: Redbud, Eastern Redbud, Judas Tree

BOTANICAL NAME: *Cercis canadensis*

PRONUNCIATION: SER-sis kan-a-DEN-sis

FAMILY: Fabaceae (Legume, Bean, or Pulse Family)

TYPE: Small deciduous tree

HEIGHT: 20–30 feet, up to 40 feet

SPREAD: 20–30 feet

FINAL SPACING: 15–20 feet

NATURAL HABITAT AND PREFERRED SITE: It is found in the eastern third of Texas from the Piney Woods into northeast and central Texas and across the center of the state. Redbud will grow in a wide range of soils in full sun or as an understory tree.

IDENTIFICATION: The overall look is of a small tree with a spreading and rounded to irregular crown. Eastern redbud is the largest of the redbuds and is usually single-trunked.

FLOWERS AND FRUIT: Flowers in various shades of lavender, purple, or white bloom in the early spring before the leaves start to emerge. The flowers are about ½ inch in length and occur in clusters of 4–8 on older branches. They often form along the trunk. The fruit forms in clusters of flattened, papery pods that range in length from 2–4 inches and ripen in the fall. The dark, shiny seeds inside are about ¼ inch long. The pods remain on the tree throughout the winter.

FOLIAGE: The leaves are alternate, simple, and deciduous with a yellow fall color that is usually less than spectacular. They are 3–5 inches long, dark green on top, lighter-colored on the bottom, distinctively heart-shaped, and dull in texture.

BARK: The tight and thin bark ranges from light gray-brown when young to reddish brown, turning a darker gray to almost black with age. The trunk eventually becomes scaly, separating into narrow ridges with maturity.

CULTURE: Redbud is easy to grow in a wide range of soils from sandy to alkaline white limestone rock. The plant is drought tolerant and doesn't need a lot of fertilizer, although it responds to a good fertilization program.

Spring flowers of white redbud.

Mexican redbud.

PROBLEMS: Borers, leaf rollers, and other minor insects attack trees that are in stress. Leaf miners can also be a minor problem.

PROPAGATION: Redbud is easily grown from seed. Collect the pods in the fall when they first mature. Pea weevils can find them and attack during the winter if they are left on the tree. Much of the seed will be infertile. Collect a large quantity of seed and separate the good from the bad by throwing the seed in water. Sound seed will sink; poor seed will float. Air dry the seed and store in sealed containers at room temperature for 1 year. Store at 41°F if the seed is to be kept longer. Seed can be scarified with acetic acid or a strong vinegar solution. Then stratify at 41°F for 30–60 days. Seed will generally germinate in 3 weeks. Cuttings can be taken from juvenile wood or root sprouts in the late spring and summer. Softwood and semi-hardwood cuttings are somewhat difficult to root.

INSIGHT: Mexican redbud (*Cercis canadensis* var. *mexicana*) generally grows to 20 feet in height and is multi-trunked. It likes the hard alkaline soils of west Texas. Its leaves are smaller than those of Texas redbud and are crinkled around the edges. The cultivar 'Oklahoma' is apparently bred from this tree. **Texas redbud** (*Cercis canadensis* var. *texensis*) is common in the thin calcarious soils of central Texas up to west of the

Redbud fruit in the winter.

Dallas/Fort Worth area. Its leaves are thicker, either dull blue and leathery or shiny and dark green on top. Its twigs and leafstalks are smooth, whereas the Mexican redbud twigs and leafstalks are hairy.

Dawn redwood in the winter showing upright branching.

Dawn redwood foliage.

Redwood, Dawn

COMMON NAMES: Dawn Redwood

BOTANICAL NAME: *Metasequoia glyptostroboides*

PRONUNCIATION: met-ah-see-KWOY-ah glip-toe-stro-BOY-dis

FAMILY: Cupressaceae (Cypress or Redwood Family)

TYPE: Deciduous conifer

HEIGHT: 80–100 feet

SPREAD: 25–35 feet

FINAL SPACING: 20–40 feet

NATURAL HABITAT AND PREFERRED SITE: China is the native habitat, but dawn redwood adapts to a wide range of soils from sand to clay. It even seems to tolerate alkaline, rocky soils better than bald cypress.

IDENTIFICATION: Dawn redwood is a narrow, pyramidal, upright-growing deciduous conifer. The most distinguishing feature is that the branches grow upward rather than perpendicular as do those of the bald cypress.

FLOWERS AND FRUIT: Male and female flowers are on the same tree (monoecious). The male flowers are in clusters on the ends of the branches. The female flowers are smaller and insignificant. The fruit is a rounded cone that forms in the late summer through fall.

FOLIAGE: The medium green, opposite, simple, needle-like leaves are similar to those of the bald cypress. They turn coppery to rust color in the fall.

BARK: The bark is relatively smooth and light tan to reddish brown, shallowly furrowed, peeling off in vertical strips.

CULTURE: It does not become brown and look stressed in the late summer as does the bald cypress.

PROBLEMS: Stem canker can be a problem, but it is simply a result of environmental stress. Under the Basic Organic Program (see Appendix 5) and in relatively healthy and moist soil, this tree does extremely well in most of Texas. Expect some chlorosis and foliage burn when it is planted in shallow soils on top of white rock.

PROPAGATION: It is propagated by seed after treatment as explained in the entry "Cypress, Bald."

INSIGHT: An ancient tree that is very durable, it should be planted more in Texas. It is considered a living fossil like the ginkgo tree.

Sassafras tree in the winter.

Sassafras starting its fall color.

Sassafras

COMMON NAMES: Sassafras, White Sassafras

BOTANICAL NAME: *Sassafras albidum*

PRONUNCIATION: SASS-ah-frass al-BEE-dum

FAMILY: Lauraceae (Laurel Family)

TYPE: Deciduous tree

HEIGHT: 20–50 feet

SPREAD: 25–30 feet

FINAL SPACING: 15–30 feet

NATURAL HABITAT AND PREFERRED SITE: Sassafras lives in east Texas sandy, acid soils. It does not adapt to any other soil. Sassafras is frequently found along fence lines where the seeds have been planted by birds.

IDENTIFICATION: This medium-sized deciduous tree has beautiful, red fall color and spicy, aromatic bark and leaves.

FLOWERS AND FRUIT: Male and female flowers form on separate trees. The female flowers are larger. The flowers bloom in the spring as the new leaves emerge. The greenish yellow flowers are only about ¼ inch wide in branched clusters 2 inches long. The fruit matures in the late summer. It is ¼–½ inches in diameter and round to oblong in shape. It is shiny,

blue-black, single-seeded, and fleshy and grows on coral stalks about 1½ inches long. Sassafras fruits are a favorite of several species of wildlife.

FOLIAGE: The leaves are alternate, simple, and deciduous, 3–6 inches in length. Three distinct leaf forms are the most common: the simple shape, the single-lobed or mitten style, and the 3- or occasionally 5-lobed variation. All three leaf shapes can be found on the tree at the same time. The leaves are dark green on top, paler beneath. Fall color can range from orange to pinks and salmons to dark reds.

BARK: The bark is reddish brown and thin when young. It becomes thicker and develops a heavier texture and gray appearance.

CULTURE: Sassafras is easy to grow as long as you have nice, sandy, acid soil. In that situation it grows quickly, especially when young. It spreads by rhizomes to create mottes or groves. It is very sensitive to physical disturbance in the root system.

INSIGHT: Dried sassafras leaves are used to make filé, a Creole ingredient used in gumbos and other dishes. The bark is used to flavor rootbeer and to make sassafras tea. The bark does, however, contain safforal, which is now considered to cause cancer. The bark has been banned as an ingredient in food by the FDA.

Soapberry in full bloom in the spring.

Soapberry

COMMON NAMES: Soapberry, Western Soapberry, Wild Chinatree, Wild Chinaberry, Indian Soap Plant, Jaboncillo

BOTANICAL NAME: *Sapindus drummondii*

PRONUNCIATION: sap-IN-dus druh-MUN-dee-eye

FAMILY: Sapindaceae (Soapberry Family)

TYPE: Deciduous tree

HEIGHT: 40–50 feet

SPREAD: 20–30 feet

FINAL SPACING: 15–20 feet

NATURAL HABITAT AND PREFERRED SITE: It lives in all of the vegetative areas of Texas in a wide range of soils. It also adapts to various garden soils as long as they are well-drained. Soapberry is found along streams, at the edges of woods, and in fence rows. It is sometimes confused with the pecan tree because of the texture and look of its compound leaves. As opposed to pecan, it is a short-lived tree.

IDENTIFICATION: Soapberry is an upright to spreading, medium-sized tree with a rounded crown at maturity. It has white flowers in the spring, chinaberry-like fruit in the fall, light-colored bark, and slightly weeping branches.

FLOWERS AND FRUIT: The flowers form from May to June in large, showy panicles, 5–10 inches long. The fruit forms in the fall, September to October, and is round, fleshy, white to yellowish, and translucent. Male and female flowers occur on separate trees (dioecious). Each fruit contains one shiny, black seed. The yellow-orange fruit is fairly showy and usually stays on the tree through the winter. It is rich in saponin, which was used by Native Americans as a cleansing agent. Handling the fruits has been known to cause dermatitis in some people.

FOLIAGE: The leaves are compound, alternate, and deciduous. They grow up to 18 inches in length with 4–19 leaflets. The leaflets are 1½–4 inches long and are sometimes a spectacular yellow-gold in the fall. The foliage is very similar to that of the Chinese pistachio.

BARK: The bark is light tan but gets darker with age, peeling off in thin flakes. The mature color of the bark is a salmon-brown to orange-brown color.

CULTURE: Easy to grow in any well-drained soil, it needs little fertilizer and is drought tolerant. Soapberry spreads vegetatively by rhizomes, forming large groves that are sometimes only one sex.

PROBLEMS: It is short-lived and has brittle wood. Pest problems are minimal. It has never seemed to transplant well into landscape projects.

PROPAGATION: It is easy to grow from seed collected from the trees in the late fall or early winter. Clean seed by soaking it in hot water and rubbing it on a screen to dry, or dry seed with the pulp on and store it in sealed containers in a cool place for up to 1 year. Soapberry has a hard seed coat so scarify it in acid, vinegar, or acetic acid for 3 hours and then stratify at 35°–45°F for 30–60 days prior to planting. There is not much information on propagating soapberry from cuttings. I have never tried it, so you are on your own.

INSIGHT: The berries are still used in Mexico as soap. The flower nectar is believed to be poisonous, and the fruit is not preferred by wildlife. Native Americans have used the fruit much like rotenone to stun fish. Some books say the pulp is mildly poisonous. It is definitely very bitter, making it highly unlikely that anyone would eat enough to cause more than a stomachache.

Soapberry foliage and fruit in the late summer.

Young sweetgum with fall color.

Mature sweetgum with fall color growing in east Texas.

Sweetgum

COMMON NAMES: Sweetgum, Redgum, Whitegum, Star-Leafed Gum, Liquid Ambar, Alligator Tree, Bilsted, Satin Walnut, Gumwood

BOTANICAL NAME: *Liquidambar styraciflua*

PRONUNCIATION: lick-wid-AM-bar sty-rah-SIFF-flu-ah

FAMILY: Hamamelidaceae (Witch Hazel Family)

TYPE: Deciduous tree

HEIGHT: 70–100 feet

SPREAD: 30–40 feet

FINAL SPACING: 20–40 feet

NATURAL HABITAT AND PREFERRED SITE: It likes east Texas sandy, acid soils and other similar areas of the country. Sweetgum will adapt to sand or clay soils as long as they are deep and not associated with shallow, white limestone rock. Sweetgum normally grows in low bottomlands and moist soil areas. It is one of the most common hardwood trees in the east Texas Piney Woods.

IDENTIFICATION: Sweetgum is distinctive in shape and texture and can be easily identified. It is upright, pyramidal, and almost always with a central, long, straight trunk. It has large, star-shaped leaves, beautiful fall color, and distinctive, spiny fruit, which forms in the fall and lasts through the winter.

FLOWERS AND FRUIT: Greenish and unimpressive flowers form early in the spring as leaves emerge. Sexes are separate but on the same tree (monoecious). The fruit forms from September to November. It is a round, spiky fruit, 1–1½ inches in diameter, on long stems. Only 1 or 2 of the flat winged seeds mature; the rest abort. The seeds are small.

FOLIAGE: The leaves are simple, alternate, deciduous, and star-shaped, with 5–7 lobes. Fall color is spectacular, ranging from golden yellow to reds to deep crimsons, maroons, and even purples. The leaves are fragrant when crushed.

BARK: The bark is smooth on the young stems and trunks but becomes rough and deeply furrowed with age, turning brown to gray. The stems often have corky wings, and trunks also have corky spots.

CULTURE: Sweetgum is easy to grow as long as the soil is deep. It grows at a medium rate. It can't stand being above or into white limestone rock but can tolerate

Sweetgum foliage and fall color.

most other situations. Although it prefers deep, sandy, acid soils and plenty of moisture, it responds to good fertilization. It is easy to transplant at most any size.

PROBLEMS: Chlorosis, a so-called iron deficiency, shows up when the tree is planted in dry, rocky soil, especially white rock. It is easily damaged by fire. Some people consider the spiny balls a great nuisance. I kind of like them. Other pests include tent caterpillar, aphids, and spider mites, but those can be controlled easily with the Basic Organic Program (see Appendix 5).

PROPAGATION: It is grown by planting the seed. Collect the fruit from the tree as it turns from green to brown but before it has completely dried. The spiky fruit can be spread out to dry until the seed is released. The seed can be planted outdoors immediately after it is collected or after it is stratified for 1 or 2 months at 41°F. The seed can be stored in a moist medium, such as potting soil, at 41°F for about 30 days. It normally takes 5–10 days at 68°F. Air dry the seed before storing it in sealed bags or containers at about 35°F. Properly stored seed will remain viable for about 4 years. Leafy semi-hardwood cuttings can be rooted under mist in the summer.

INSIGHT: Several bird species like to eat the fruit. Sweetgum is a source of a fragrant gum obtained from the inner bark and the wood. The tree is one of the leading commercial hardwoods. "Improved" cultivars such as 'Palo Alto,' 'Burgundy,' 'Festival,' and 'Autumn Glow' were bred for better color and to be fruitless, but they are not nearly as well-adapted and are not recommended. *Rotunda Loba* is a grafted, seedless cultivar that I do recommend.

Sweetgum fall foliage and fruit.

Sycamore showing its beautiful white bark in the late summer.

Sycamore

COMMON NAMES: Sycamore, American Sycamore, Eastern Sycamore, Buttonwood, Plane Tree, American Plane Tree, Buttonwood Tree, Buttonball Tree, Water Beach

BOTANICAL NAME: *Platanus occidentalis*

PRONUNCIATION: PLAT-ta-nus ox-eye-den-TAL-iss

FAMILY: Platanaceae (Sycamore Family)

TYPE: Deciduous shade tree

HEIGHT: 90 to over 100 feet

SPREAD: As much as 100 feet

FINAL SPACING: Do not plant, unless way out on the farm or ranch by a creek or river.

NATURAL HABITAT AND PREFERRED SITE: Sycamore lives in the eastern half to two-thirds of the state, primarily in river and creek bottoms in deeper soils. It adapts fairly well to a variety of soils.

IDENTIFICATION: Sycamore is a large-growing tree with large, papery leaves and a distinctive bark that flakes off leaving a white smooth underbark. It has round seed pods in the fall. Fall color is nondescript, basically brown.

FLOWERS AND FRUIT: The flowers appear in the spring, from April to May. Male and female flowers are on the same tree (monoecious) and are not very attractive. The flowers are borne in dense, round clusters about ½ inch in diameter on short stalks. The fruit ripens in the fall, from September to October. It is round, 1–1½ inches in diameter, and light brown. It grows on long stems, 3–6 inches long.

FOLIAGE: The leaves are simple, alternate, and deciduous. They are large, 4–12 inches across. They are medium green and paler and hairier on the underside in the summer. They are a poor yellow or brown in the fall and a maintenance problem because they blow around like paper and don't decay very quickly at all.

BARK: The bark is quite distinctive. It is greenish cream to white and sometimes marked with patches of dark green or brown at first. It flakes off later to reveal lighter layers of younger bark. Older trunks are often roughened and fissured. Sycamore has the most spectacular bark of all the trees in the winter.

CULTURE: Sycamore is easy to grow, becoming big trees in short periods of time if the diseases don't hit. They respond to fertilizer but don't need much. They do need plenty of water.

PROBLEMS: Anthracnose, a disease that attacks the leaves and young twigs, is the most commonly referred to problem, but it is not the most serious disease. Bacterial leaf scorch is more serious. It kills large sections of the tree and eventually the entire plant. Lacebugs can also be a problem during the growing season. The Sick Tree Treatment (see Appendix 3) and the long-term Basic Organic Program (see Appendix 5) can keep sycamore trees healthier than any other approach. Sycamore is not a good tree choice unless you like aphids, scale, bagworms, borers, lots of dead limbs falling out of the tree, and short-lived trees.

PROPAGATION: Why would you want to? If you must, seed can stay on the tree through the winter and be planted in the spring. It will germinate readily. Early harvested seed must be stratified for at least 30 days at 41°F before planting in the spring. Sycamore will also root from dormant hardwood or softwood cuttings if kept under a mist.

INSIGHT: Some of the landscape architects in Texas have continued to try to use this plant or its close relatives such as the **plane tree** *(Platanus acerfolia)* or various hybrids. None of them are any good nor should any be designed into any residential or commercial projects. It is very poor tree choice for landscape use. It is a shame this plant is so problematic because the white bark in the winter is spectacular.

Sycamore foliage and fruit.

Chinese tallow fall color and fruit.   Chinese tallow in full bloom.

Tallow, Chinese

COMMON NAMES: Chinese Tallow, Vegetable Tallow
BOTANICAL NAME: *Sapium sebiferum*
PRONUNCIATION: SAY-pee-um seb-eh-FARE-um
FAMILY: Euphorbiaceae (Spurge Family)
TYPE: Deciduous shade tree
HEIGHT: 20–30 feet
SPREAD: 20–30 feet
FINAL SPACING: Do not plant.
NATURAL HABITAT AND PREFERRED SITE:
Native to China and Japan, it adapts and grows well
in any soil but prefers moist soils.
IDENTIFICATION: This medium-sized tree, to a max-
imum height of 30 feet with an equal spread, has a
rounded top and often a twisted trunk. Fall color can
be spectacular some years.
FLOWERS AND FRUIT: Flowers appear on Chinese
tallow in the late spring or early summer. Male and
female flowers grow together in drooping, tassel-like
clusters about 2–3 inches long. The flowers have a
golden yellow color. The fruit ripens in the fall and is
hard and round. It is a 3-lobed, white capsule, containing a single, wax-covered seed about ⅜ inch long.
FOLIAGE: The leaves are alternate, simple, and deciduous. Excellent fall color ranges from yellow to oranges
and reds to deep purples and can be spectacular.
BARK: The bark is gray brown to dark brown and
medium textured.
CULTURE: Relatively easy to grow for a short number
of years in most soils, it responds to fertilization and
moist soil.
PROBLEMS: Freeze damage, borers, cotton root rot,
and all other insects and diseases afflict Chinese
tallow. And the tree is short-lived. Do not plant.
PROPAGATION: Why would you want to?
INSIGHT: Please don't give me a hard time about the
fact that I've recommended this plant in the past. By
the way, the seeds are poisonous.

Texas mountain laurel foliage and fall seed pods.

Texas Mountain Laurel

COMMON NAMES: Texas Mountain Laurel, Mescal Bean
Sophora, Mountain Laurel, Frijollito, Mescal Bean

BOTANICAL NAME: *Sophora secundiflora*

PRONUNCIATION: So-FORE-ah se-kune-di-FLOR-ah

FAMILY: Fabaceae (Legume, Bean, or Pulse Family)

TYPE: Small evergreen tree

HEIGHT: 20–30 feet

SPREAD: 10–12 feet

FINAL SPACING: 8–15 feet

NATURAL HABITAT AND PREFERRED SITE: It
grows wild in the limestone soils of central and west
Texas but adapts to most garden soils.

IDENTIFICATION: Texas mountain laurel is a beautiful, small, bushy evergreen tree with fragrant flowers
in the spring and black seed pods in the fall.

FLOWERS AND FRUIT: Violet, wisteria-like flowers
bloom in the spring, followed by 3–5-inch, hard,
constricted seed pods. The seeds are bright red and
¾–1 inch in diameter.

FOLIAGE: The leaves are medium to dark green,
waxy, and 4–6 inches long with 5–13 leaflets that are
1–2 inches long.

BARK: The bark is dark gray to black. It has narrow
ridges and shallow fissures, and a heavier texture
with age.

CULTURE: Our mountain laurel is slow-growing but
does well in most soils. It grows in full sun or part
shade. It responds well to organic fertilizer and even
soil moisture.

PROBLEMS: There are few pest problems. The foliage
is poisonous to livestock. The red seeds and flowers
are poisonous to humans.

Texas mountain laurel foliage and flowers.

PROPAGATION: It is best to grow Texas mountain laurel
from seed. Plant slightly immature seed that is barely
pink or the mature red seed after scoring the hard
seed coat with a file.

INSIGHT: It is considered a bush but when trimmed
becomes a lovely ornamental tree—one of our most
beautiful, small, native trees. But 1 seed is enough to
cause fatal poisoning. The flowers produce a grape-
like fragrance. They are too strong to use as cut flowers indoors. Bees like the flowers but the honey is
said to be mildly toxic. The beautiful red seeds have
been used to make necklaces and other jewelry.

Tree of heaven foliage and fruit.

Tree of Heaven

COMMON NAMES: Tree of Heaven, Tree of the Gods, Chinese Sumac, Heavenward-Tree, False Varnish Tree, Devil's Walking Stick

BOTANICAL NAME: *Ailanthus altissima*

PRONUNCIATION: eye-LAN-thus all-TISS-a-mah

FAMILY: Simaroubaceae (Quassia Family)

TYPE: Deciduous tree

HEIGHT: 50–100 feet

SPREAD: 20–40 feet

FINAL SPACING: 20–30 feet if you really want to. It comes up from seed all over the place.

NATURAL HABITAT AND PREFERRED SITE: Native to China, tree of heaven has naturalized all over the United States.

IDENTIFICATION: This very upright, fast-growing tree has large compound leaves and distinctive seed pods in the fall and winter.

FLOWERS AND FRUIT: The flowers form in the spring, from April through May, in large, loose panicles, 6–12 inches long. Male and female flowers are on the same tree (monoecious) in upright clusters. They bloom yellow-green soon after the leaves are fully developed in the late spring. The male flowers stink. The female flowers disperse large quantities of seeds that germinate and sprout all over the place.

The fruit forms in the fall, from September to October, in large clusters of propeller-shaped, winged seeds that have a central seed cavity and that hang on the tree for a long time.

FOLIAGE: The leaves are alternate, deciduous, compound, and reddish green, becoming darker green during the growing season. They turn yellow in the fall.

BARK: When young, the bark is smooth and light gray to tan. It becomes a dark gray and slightly rough and fissured with age.

CULTURE: Almost an indestructible tree, it will grow where almost no other vegetation will. It tolerates high heat, poor soils, heavy winds, polluted air, salty soils, limited soil availability, too much or too little water, and other harsh conditions.

PROBLEMS: It can become a real pest by growing so easily from seed and sprouting up all over. Most books say that, unfortunately, tree of heaven has no pests. Its wood is weak and brittle, making it susceptible to ice and wind storms.

PROPAGATION: Propagation is by seed or suckers. This plant is so easy to grow from seed, it will come up in cracks in sidewalks, driveways, parking lots, etc.

INSIGHT: I'm interested in the tree because it is so easy to grow in such harsh conditions. It is a good tool to use to improve the air and soil where no other plants can grow.

Tulip tree in the fall.

Tulip tree in flower in spring.

Tulip Tree

COMMON NAMES: Tulip Tree, Yellow Poplar, Yellow Wood, White Wood, Tulip-Poplar, Saddle Leaf, Canoe Wood, Cucumber Tree, Blue Poplar, Lynn-Tree, Saddle Tree, Hickory-Poplar

BOTANICAL NAME: *Liriodendron tulipifera*

PRONUNCIATION: lir-ee-ah-DEN-dron too-li-PIF-err-ah

FAMILY: Magnoliaceae (Magnolia Family)

TYPE: Deciduous shade tree

HEIGHT: 60–100 feet

SPREAD: 40–50 feet

FINAL SPACING: 30–40 feet

NATURAL HABITAT AND PREFERRED SITE: Native to the eastern United States from the Gulf of Mexico to Canada, tulip tree grows in the rich, moist soils of Louisiana and Arkansas, eastward to Florida, and northward all the way to the northeast part of the United States. It will grow in Texas, especially in the deep soils, although it does have a little trouble in the heat of the summer.

IDENTIFICATION: This straight-trunked, smooth-barked tree has leaves shaped like tulips. It is a large-growing, good-looking tree from an overall and textural standpoint. Generally it has a single trunk, interesting leaves, and yellow fall color. It is capable of becoming huge and has brittle wood.

FLOWERS AND FRUIT: The flowers bloom in April and May. Male and female parts are in the same flowers (called perfect flowers). They are 2–5 inches across and cup-shaped. They are green on the outside with an orange-yellow center. They face upward and are not showy from the ground but attractive close up. The fruit is a dry, cone-like structure that matures in the fall, from September to October, and contains numerous woody, brown scales, 2–3 inches long, and many seeds. Flowers usually don't form until the tree is at least 10–12 years old, although this is accelerated in an organic program (see Appendix 5).

FOLIAGE: The leaves are simple, alternate, and deciduous and display yellow fall color.

BARK: The bark is smooth, light brown to gray, becoming more heavily textured with age.

CULTURE: Fairly easy to grow in Texas, especially in the deep, acid, sandy soils, it has a little trouble above rock, especially the limestone rocks of north and central Texas, but responds well to the organic fertilization program and consistent moisture.

PROBLEMS: Chlorosis and foliage burn in the heat of the summer can cause leaf drop. It has relatively few insect and disease problems.

PROPAGATION: It is grown by seed primarily, although the plant can also be propagated by budding, grafting, or layering.

INSIGHT: Tulip tree, because of its thin bark, is easily damaged by fire. It is not a good tree to plant often in Texas, but a few here and there are interesting.

Rusty blackhaw viburnum.

Viburnum, Rusty Blackhaw

COMMON NAMES: Rusty Blackhaw Viburnum, Black-
haw, Rusty Nanny-Berry, Southern Blackhaw, South-
ern Blackhawy, Dawny Viburnum, Rusty Blackhaw
BOTANICAL NAME: *Viburnum rufidulum*
PRONUNCIATION: vi-BURN-um rue-FID-you-lum
FAMILY: Caprifoliaceae (Honeysuckle Family)
TYPE: Small deciduous tree for sun or shade
HEIGHT: 10–30 feet
SPREAD: 15–20 feet
FINAL SPACING: 10–20 feet
NATURAL HABITAT AND PREFERRED SITE: It has
a wide range of native habitat in Texas including most
of the eastern half of the state as well as in the calcarious hillsides of west Texas. It adapts to a wide range of
soils and sun exposures. It is an excellent choice for
formal landscape projects as well as natural settings.
IDENTIFICATION: It is a small to medium-sized tree
that is full and spreading in full sun but tends to be
upright and more open as an understory in the
shade. Rusty blackhaw viburnum has clusters of
white flowers in the spring and blue-black berries
in the late summer into fall. It sometimes forms
thickets but usually appears as single plants.

FLOWERS AND FRUIT: The flowers form in clusters in
the mid spring after the leaves start to unfold. They
are ¼ inch wide, white, 5-lobed, and highly fragrant.
The fruit ripens in the fall in clusters of dark blue,
football-shaped, edible, fleshy drupes about ⅓–½ inch
long with a flattened, stone-like seed within. The fruit
pulp is sweet and edible with a raisin-like taste.
FOLIAGE: The leaves are about 3 inches long, glossy,
opposite, and deciduous. They are dark green in the
summer and beautiful pink to red to dark purple in
the fall. The leaves are hairy underneath.
BARK: Smooth gray at first, it darkens with age to
almost black with a distinctive blotchy or checkered appearance.
CULTURE: Rusty blackhaw viburnum is an easy-to-
grow ornamental tree that should be used much
more. It responds well to fertilizer and irrigation but
is also quite drought tolerant.
PROBLEMS: It has very few pest infestations. This is
practically a maintenance-free tree.
PROPAGATION: It is easily grown by seed or by semi-
hardwood cuttings taken in the summer or early fall.
INSIGHT: This is one of my favorite small trees and
should be planted considerably more in Texas in both
sun and shade. It is beautiful from spring to hard

Rusty blackhaw viburnum foliage and late spring flowers.

Rusty blackhaw viburnum foliage with fall color.

Arrowwood viburnum foliage and fall color.

frost in the late fall. Another good choice is **arrow-wood viburnum** (*Viburnum dentatum*), also known as southern arrow wood, mealy tree, with-rod, and with-wood. This tree has triangular, serrated leaves and will grow in a range of soils, although it prefers sandy loams, and it does well in full sun to filtered light. It grows to a height of 8–15 feet and has clusters of small, white flowers in the spring, which are followed by bluish black drupes in the late summer into the fall.

Vitex

COMMON NAMES: Vitex, Lilac Chaste Tree, Sage Tree, Monk's Pepper Tree, Wild Pepper, Indian Spice, Abraham's Balm, Hemp-Tree, Wild Lavender, Tree of Chastity, Chaste Lamb-Tree

BOTANICAL NAME: *Vitex agnus-castus*

PRONUNCIATION: VIE-teks AG-nus-CAST-us

FAMILY: Verbenaceae (Vervain Family)

TYPE: Small deciduous tree

HEIGHT: 20–30 feet

SPREAD: 20–25 feet

FINAL SPACING: 15–20 feet

NATURAL HABITAT AND PREFERRED SITE: Native to southern Europe and western Asia, it has become naturalized in northeast and central Texas, especially in moist soil areas.

IDENTIFICATION: This small tree is either single-trunked or multi-stemmed with a wide-spreading crown. The trunks are usually crooked or leaning. It has long-lasting summer color from white or purple flowers.

FLOWERS AND FRUIT: It has purple or white flowers in the early summer and yellow fall color. The flowers form in the late spring but may continue to bloom sporadically throughout the summer. They form

Purple vitex flower and foliage.

White vitex in full bloom.

Mature vitex.

terminal spikes up to 7 inches long and are blue, purple, white, and sometimes even pink. The fruit matures in the fall as upright, round, woody, brown to black, terminal drupes about ⅛–⅙ inch wide and with a 4-celled stone. The fruit is strongly scented like the leaves.

FOLIAGE: The leaves are compound with 3–9 leaflets. They are fragrant when crushed.

BARK: Thin, smooth, and light gray when young, the bark becomes fissured and darker gray with age.

CULTURE: Vitex is easy to grow in most well-drained soils and is drought tolerant.

PROBLEMS: The only thing I've seen is freeze damage in the northern part of the state. Sometimes deadwood needs to be trimmed out. Deadwood problems can be alleviated to a great extent by using the organic program and the Sick Tree Treatment (see Appendix 3) for trees in stress.

PROPAGATION: Pick the dry fruit in the fall and clean by maceration and by floating the hulls away. Treat to break dormancy by stratification in moist sand, soil, or peat at 41°F for 90 days. Vitex can also be grown from layers and softwood cuttings kept humid or under mist.

INSIGHT: The fruits have been used as a pepper substitute. White flowering vitex has been considered a method of preserving chastity. According to *Texas Trees: A Friendly Guide* by Cox and Leslie, an oil can be made from the seeds to provide sedative properties. A tea made from the leaves is said to have anti-aphrodisiac properties and reportedly was used by monks to help them remain chaste. The leaves can be used to spice foods and a perfume is made from the flowers. Vitex should not be used as a primary tree on landscape projects, farm, or ranch, but certainly should be used as a colorful and interesting secondary tree.

Walnut foliage and fruit.

Walnut

COMMON NAMES: Walnut, Black Walnut, American Black Walnut, Eastern Black Walnut
BOTANICAL NAME: *Juglans nigra*
PRONUNCIATION: JEW-gluns NI-gra
FAMILY: Juglandaceae (Walnut Family)
TYPE: Deciduous nut tree
HEIGHT: 50–80 feet
SPREAD: 40–50 feet
FINAL SPACING: 30–50 feet
NATURAL HABITAT AND PREFERRED SITE: Walnut is native to the eastern third of Texas. It is fairly well-adapted to a wide range of soils, from sandy to heavy clays, in much of Texas. It likes deep, rich, moist soil and does fairly well in the acid, sandy soils of east Texas. It also likes calcium soils. It does not like growing on thin soils on top of limestone rock.

IDENTIFICATION: Walnut is an upright deciduous tree with yellow fall color, large compound leaves, and dark gray to black, heavily textured bark. The tree has an open branching structure.

FLOWERS AND FRUIT: The flowers are male and female on the same tree (monoecious) and not showy. The fruit ripens in the fall, from September through October, solitary or clustered. The husk is yellowish green and thick and contains an extremely hard, bony, dark brown to black nut. The husk does not split open when ripe. The meat is sweet, edible, and nutritious.

FOLIAGE: The leaves are compound, 1–2 feet long, light to medium green, and deciduous. It has yellow fall color. The leaflets are more evenly sized than pecan and hickory leaves. There will be 11–23 leaflets per leaf.

BARK: Dark and smooth when young, the bark becomes very dark, heavily fissured, and alligator-looking with age.

CULTURE: Relatively easy to grow in deep soils that have plenty of moisture and good drainage, walnut tolerates alkaline soil but prefers a neutral soil.

PROBLEMS: Walnut is susceptible to stress related to dry weather and dry soils. Walnut is alleopathic to nearby plants. This means the tree contains a substance that prevents the growth of seedlings, including other walnuts, from coming up near the parent tree. The substance responsible is called juglone, a tannic acid. The substance is especially damaging to plants in the nightshade family (Solanaceae), such as tomatoes, peppers, potatoes, and tobacco. Walnut sawdust has been used in the past to treat fire ant mounds, and a brown dye can be obtained from the husk of the fruit. Walnut is also capable of causing skin rashes to sensitive people.

PROPAGATION: Nuts should be gathered in the fall or early winter after the husks have begun to turn black. They can be eaten or planted. Dormancy can be broken by cold stratification for 60–120 days at 34°–41°F. Some people say that walnut can be germinated by removing the husks and simply mashing the nuts into garden soil with your foot. This sounds easy and worth a try. Improved cultivars of walnuts are propagated by grafting and budding onto established root stocks.

INSIGHT: Walnuts are hard to shell but worth the trouble because the meat is delicious and full of nutrients. **English walnut** (*Juglans regia*) is native to Europe but not well-adapted here in Texas, although

Walnut.

Little walnut foliage and fruit.

it does fairly well under an organic program (especially in sandy, acid soil). **Little walnut** (*Juglens microcarpa*) is also referred to as Texas walnut, Texas black walnut, river walnut, nogal, and namboca. The little walnut is a multi-trunked, small tree growing to about 30 feet high. It adapts more easily than does regular walnut to various soils in Texas and should be grown more. The nuts are smaller, only ½ to ¾ inch in diameter, but have very high quality meat and excellent taste. All walnut leaves and fruit are strongly scented when bruised. Walnut wood is highly desirable for use in furniture construction, cabinetwork, veneers, gunstocks, and other products.

Wax myrtle.

Wax myrtle foliage and fall fruit on female tree.

Wax Myrtle

COMMON NAMES: Wax Myrtle, Wax-Myrtle, Bayberry, Southern Bayberry, Candleberry, Tallow Shrub, Southern Wax Myrtle, Waxberry, Spice Bush, Sweet Oak

BOTANICAL NAME: *Myrica cerifera*

PRONUNCIATION: MY-ruh-kuh sir-RIFF-eh-ruh

FAMILY: Myricaceae (Wax Myrtle or Bayberry Family)

TYPE: Small to medium-sized, evergreen ornamental tree.

HEIGHT: 10–15 feet

SPREAD: 10–12 feet

FINAL SPACING: 8–12 feet

NATURAL HABITAT AND PREFERRED SITE: Wax myrtle grows in swamps and moist woodlands, on shores of streams and lakes, and in the wet grasslands of the Piney Woods. In general, it grows from east Texas through central Texas. Wax myrtle will adapt in a garden or landscape situation and to sandy or acid soils if given reasonable moisture and just a moderate amount of fertilizer.

IDENTIFICATION: This small, multi-stemmed tree has delicate evergreen foliage that is a light green in color.

FLOWERS AND FRUIT: The golden yellow and green flowers are short, scaly, and erect. The female and male flowers grow on different plants (dioecious) from March through April. They are small, inconspicuous, and spike-like catkins. The fruits of the female plants are small, blue berries or drupes that are clustered along the stems.

FOLIAGE: Wax myrtle has small, alternate, resinous, medium green leaves. The aromatic leaves have fine, yellow, glandular dots, especially on the underside, which are fragrant when the leaves are crushed.

BARK: The bark is smooth-textured, light to medium gray. The texture gets heavier with age.

CULTURE: Wax myrtle will adapt in a garden or landscape situation to sandy or acid soils if given reasonable moisture and a moderate amount of fertilizer. Wax myrtle is easy to grow in any well-drained soil. It is moderately fast-growing and spreading and drought tolerant.

PROBLEMS: Problems include brittle wood, suckers, and freeze damage in the northern part of the state.

PROPAGATION: Seeding can be done by sowing outdoors in the fall or stratifying the seed for 60–90 days at 34°–41°F. Natural germination occurs in the spring following the seed fall. Cuttings can be rooted from softwood or semi-hardwood cuttings, and the plant can also be successfully transplanted either balled, burlapped, or bare-rooted in the winter.

INSIGHT: This genus has the ability (as do legumes) to fix atmospheric nitrogen through root nodules. Birds and other wildlife like the berries. **Dwarf wax myrtle** (*Myrica pusilla*) does well in Texas also.

Black willow.

Willow, Black

COMMON NAMES: Black Willow, Swamp Willow, Gooding Willow, Western Black Willow, Southwestern Black Willow, Sauz, Linheimer Black Willow, Gulf Black Willow, Scythe-Leaf Willow, Pussy Willow

BOTANICAL NAME: *Salix nigra*

PRONUNCIATION: SAY-lix NI-gra

FAMILY: Salicaceae (Willow Family)

TYPE: Deciduous tree

HEIGHT: 40–80 feet

SPREAD: 20–30 feet

FINAL SPACING: 20–30 feet

NATURAL HABITAT AND PREFERRED SITE: It grows all over Texas—anywhere there is any moisture in the soil. It adapts to a wide range of soils from sand to heavy clays.

IDENTIFICATION: Black willow is an upright willow, open-trunked, with a regular crown, typical willow leaves, and yellow fall color.

FLOWERS AND FRUIT: The flowers are yellow catkins, about 1 inch long, and appear in the early spring. Male and female flowers appear on separate plants (dioecious). The fruits are light brown capsules, $1/4$ inch or less in length, and appear in the late spring and early summer. They contain many tiny seeds covered with silky hairs. The fruit forms from May through June. Flowers form from April through May. Neither are showy.

FOLIAGE: The leaves are simple, alternate, and deciduous. Color is yellow in the fall.

BARK: The reddish brown to black bark has moderately heavy fissures, flat ridges, and thick scales. It becomes shaggy with age, and is rich in tannin.

CULTURE: Black willow is easy to grow in most soils as long as there is ample moisture. It does respond to fertilization. It is a short-lived tree—rarely living more than 20 years. Black willows can grow as much as 4 feet in 1 year.

PROBLEMS: The primary shortcoming is its short life, even when healthy. Borers attack plants in stress. Other insects feed on the foliage of ill trees. Black willows are weak trees, subject to wind damage, and they have shallow, destructive root systems.

PROPAGATION: Collect the seed as soon as the capsules dry and turn from green to yellow-brown. The small, black seed starts to lose viability immediately and so should be planted quickly after collection. No pretreatment is required. Germination occurs 12–24 hours after sowing. This is also one of the easiest of all plants to root from stem cuttings. Hard-wood cuttings taken in the late winter to early spring will root almost 100%.

INSIGHT: Black willow is the largest and most wide-spread of the Texas willows. Black willow is considered a fast-growing junk tree, but it has its place in wet soil areas. I wouldn't plant many of them, but they are useful if they grow naturally on the site. Other willows include **weeping willow** (*Salix babylonica*), a graceful, fast-growing tree that is almost evergreen in the southern half of the state. It is easy to grow but very short-lived. **Corkscrew willow** (*Salix matsudana* 'Tortuosa') has upright growth with interesting, twisted limbs and branches. It again is relatively short-lived but a very interesting landscape tree. Willows are functional to use as erosion control. Black willow wood is soft, light, and weak but is used to make boxes and artificial limbs as well as for fuel. At one time it was used to make a high grade charcoal for gunpowder. The narrow branches are flexible and are used in weaving baskets and making wicker furniture. Willow branches have also been used as divining rods. Willow water, which supposedly works as a rooting hormone liquid, is made by soaking pencil-length pieces of willow in water for 24 hours.

Corkscrew willow.

Black willow foliage.

Weeping willow foliage.

Weeping willow.

Desert willow foliage and flowers.

Willow, Desert

COMMON NAMES: Desert Willow, Flowering Willow, Willow Leaf Catalpa, Desert Catalpa, Flore De Mimbre, Bow Willow

BOTANICAL NAME: *Chilopsis linearis*

PRONUNCIATION: KY-lop-sis lin-ee-ERR-iss

FAMILY: Bignoniaceae (Catalpa or Trumpet Vine Family)

TYPE: Small deciduous tree

HEIGHT: 25–35 feet

SPREAD: 15–25 feet

FINAL SPACING: 15–25 feet

NATURAL HABITAT AND PREFERRED SITE: Its natural habitat is the Trans-Pecos and Edwards Plateau of west Texas. It adapts to a wide range of soils, but drainage is critical. It will not survive in heavily watered or high rainfall areas. It would not do well in deep east Texas.

IDENTIFICATION: Desert willow is a small, open, lacy tree with beautiful summer flowers, yellow fall color, and decorative seed pods.

FLOWERS AND FRUIT: The flowers form in showy clusters on the tips of the branches on new wood. Flowers can resemble trumpets, bells, or lips. They are fragrant and predominantly light pink to light violet, although some plants with pure white flowers exist. Desert willow blooms from the late spring to early fall (June to October), depending on rainfall. The fruits are long, narrow capsules, 5–8 inches long, containing flat, hairy, winged seeds, typical of catalpa.

FOLIAGE: Desert willow foliage can be opposite or alternate. The leaves are long, narrow, pointed, and 3–10 inches long. They are light to medium green and often sticky to the touch.

BARK: Smooth when young, the bark turns dark brown, ridged, and scaly as the tree matures.

Desert willow.

CULTURE: Desert willow is easy to grow in any soil that is well-drained, but it cannot stand constantly moist soil or wet feet. Disease organisms in the root system will take it out. Trees that are in trouble should be treated with the Sick Tree Treatment (see Appendix 3) and have the water reduced if possible.

PROBLEMS: It is susceptible to root rot from over watering. It's also not easy to find in the nursery industry.

PROPAGATION: Gather the seed from late summer through fall when the pods have dried and turned brown but before they have split open and released the light, feathery seed to be blown by the wind. Seed loses viability quickly in storage but can be kept over the winter in the refrigerator. It is best to plant the seed immediately on collection. Soaking the seed in a mild solution of vinegar before planting will increase germination time. As with most trees, avoid heavy applications of fertilizer. Cuttings can be rooted from semi-hardwood cuttings taken from the current year's growth in the late summer or from dormant cuttings in the winter. It is best to keep the cuttings under intermittent mist.

INSIGHT: Desert willow branches have been used to weave baskets. Its wood is light and brittle but durable and has been used by Native Americans for making bows as well as used for fence posts and fuel. Desert willow is a good bee plant. Simpson in his book *A Field Guide To Texas Trees* says that the tree is attractive when grown to its full height but also when pruned back heavily and kept at 3–10 feet high.

Witch hazel foliage with fall color.

Witch Hazel

COMMON NAMES: Witch Hazel, Winter Bloom, Spotted-Alder, Tobacco-Wood, Pistachio, Snappy Hazel, Witch-Elm

BOTANICAL NAME: *Hamamelis virginiana*

PRONUNCIATION: ham-a-MAY-liss vir-gin-ee-AYN-ah

FAMILY: Hamamelidaceae (Witch Hazel Family)

TYPE: Deciduous ornamental tree.

HEIGHT: 10–20 feet

SPREAD: 8–10 feet

FINAL SPACING: 8–10 feet

NATURAL HABITAT AND PREFERRED SITE: It grows wild in east Texas and central Texas, usually near creeks and streams as an understory plant. It adapts to various soils and does well in landscape situations or in the herb garden. It likes full sun to partial shade.

IDENTIFICATION: Witch hazel is a shrubby plant or small, open-growing tree. It grows to a maximum height of about 20 feet, with single or multiple trunks and an irregularly shaped top. The foliage and flowers are distinctive, and the fall color is usually quite good.

FLOWERS AND FRUIT: Golden yellow flowers bloom in the fall and winter after the leaves have fallen. The flowers of some species have a red or purple cast near the base. The fruit and flowers form simultaneously. The fruit ripens in the second season. The seeds form inside woody capsules and are torpedo-shaped, black, and shiny. Often seeds are shot out when the capsule dries, sometimes traveling several yards from the mother plant.

FOLIAGE: The leaves are alternate, deciduous, and 2–6 inches long. They have an uneven base. In the summer they are deep olive green on top with prominent principal veins and paler and hairy underneath. Fall color is golden yellow.

BARK: Deep brown and smooth when young, the bark becomes scaly with maturity, often having blotches and horizontal markings.

CULTURE: Witch hazel is an easy-to-grow plant in various well-drained soils. It works very well as an understory plant but can take full sun as well.

PROBLEMS: Few exist, other than scarce availability in the nursery trade.

PROPAGATION: Plant seed just before or as they are ejected. It is best to get them just before the capsules split open. Seed may be stored for a year at 41°F or stratified in sand or peat at 41°F for about 90 days. Soaking the seed in hot water prior to stratification is said to help germination. Some seed does not germinate until the second year. Witch hazel is also propagated by layering.

INSIGHT: Witch hazel is a wonderful little tree that should be planted more often. The name comes from the fact that dousers, or diviners, like to use this plant for finding water. The seeds are edible and the leaves are used in herb teas. The seeds are also excellent bird food.

BIBLIOGRAPHY

Cox, Paul W., and Patty Leslie. *Texas Trees: A Friendly Guide*. Corona Publishing Company, San Antonio, 1999.

Diggs, George M. Jr., Barney L. Lipscomb, and Robert J. O'Kennon. *Shinners & Mahler's Illustrated Flora of North Central Texas*. Botanical Research Institute of Texas and Austin College, Fort Worth, 1999.

Garrett, J. Howard. *Howard Garrett's Plants for Texas*. University of Texas Press, Austin, 1996.

Garrett, J. Howard, and C. Malcolm Beck. *Texas Organic Vegetable Gardening*. Gulf Publishing Company, Houston, 1998.

Garrett, John Howard. *Plants of the Metroplex*. University of Texas Press, Austin, 1998.

Nokes, Jill. *How To Grow Native Plants of Texas and the Southwest*. Gulf Publishing Company, Houston, 1986.

Simpson, Benny J. *A Field Guide to Texas Trees*. Lone Star Books, Houston, 1999.

Susser, Allen. *The Great Citrus Book*. Ten Speed Press, Berkeley, California, 1997.

Tull, Delena. *Edible and Useful Plants of Texas and the Southwest: A Practical Guide*. University of Texas Press, Austin, 1999.

Valder, Peter. *The Garden Plants of China*. Timber Press, Portland, Oregon, 1999.

Vetress, J.D. *Japanese Maples*. 2nd ed. Timber Press, Portland, Oregon, 1992.

Vines, Robert A. *Trees, Shrubs, and Woody Vines of the Southwest*. University of Texas Press, Austin, 1990.

Wasowski, Sally. *Native Texas Plants*. Gulf Publishing Company, Houston, 1988.

Whitcomb, Carl E. *Establishment and Maintenance of Landscape Plants*. Lacebark, Inc., Stillwater, Oklahoma, 1987.

Whitcomb, Carl E. *Know It and Grow It*. Lacebark, Inc. Publications and Research, Stillwater, Oklahoma, 1996.

EASY REFERENCE LIST FOR TREES

EVERGREEN TREES

Anacua
Cedar
Citrus
Cypress, Italian (see Cypress, Arizona)
Holly
Magnolia
Oak, Live
Olive, Wild
Palm, Texas
Pine
Texas Mountain Laurel
Wax Myrtle

TREES WITH FALL OR WINTER BERRIES FOR WILDLIFE

Carolina Buckthorn
Cherry Laurel
Chinaberry
Dogwood
Holly, Yaupon
Madrone
Possumhaw (see Holly, Yaupon)
Soapberry
Viburnum, Rusty Blackhaw
Wax Myrtle

TREES THAT PRODUCE EDIBLE FRUIT

Citrus
Crabapple
Jujube
Mulberry, Red
Peach
Pear
Pecan
Plum, Mexican
Walnut

FLOWERING TREES

Anacua
Bird of Paradise
Black Locust
Buckeye
Camphor Tree
Catalpa
Cherry, Black
Chitalpa (see Catalpa)
Crabapple
Crape Myrtle
Dogwood
Eve's Necklace
Fringe Tree
Golden Raintree
Goldenball Lead Tree
Hawthorn
Magnolia
Olive, Wild
Orchid Tree
Parkinsonia
Peach
Pear
Plum, Mexican
Redbud
Soapberry
Texas Mountain Laurel
Tulip Tree
Viburnum, Rusty Blackhaw
Vitex
Willow, Desert

YELLOW FALL COLOR

Ash
Black Locust
Bois d'Arc
Buckeye, Mexican
Crape Myrtle
Elm
Eve's Necklace
Ginkgo
Golden Raintree
Linden
Maple, Caddo
Maple, Coralbark
Maple, Green Japanese (see Maple, Japanese)
Maple, Japanese
Mulberry, Red
Oak, Bur
Pecan
Persimmon
Pistachio, Chinese
Redbud
Soapberry
Sweetgum
Tulip Tree
Walnut
Willow

ORANGE FALL COLOR

Ash, Texas
Carolina Buckthorn
Maple, Big Tooth
Maple, Caddo
Maple, Chalk
Maple, Japanese
Pistachio, Chinese
Plum, Mexican
Sweetgum

RED FALL COLOR

Ash, Texas
Crape Myrtle
Dogwood
Maple, Japanese
Oak, Shumard Red
Pear
Pistachio, Chinese
Sweetgum
Tallow, Chinese
Viburnum, Rusty Blackhaw

WORST TEXAS TREES

In addition to the good tree choices for Texas, it's important to identify the bad choices. Here they are:

Arizona ash is short-lived and a heavy water user, has destructive roots, is subject to several insect and disease problems, and will suffer freeze damage.

Chinese tallow freezes back every hard winter in the northern part of the state and has lots of insect and disease problems.

Cottonwood trees are stately and beautiful when healthy but are a bad investment. They are short-lived, have brittle wood, and are subject to wind damage and insects (especially borers). Also the female plants produce messy cotton that clogs air conditioners.

Siberian elm is the worst choice of all. It is incorrectly called Chinese elm. It gets severe elm leaf beetle infestation every year and is susceptible to Dutch elm disease. Wind damage due to weak wood is also a problem.

Honey locust continues to be used by some people, but borers love it, and it just never seems to be healthy here. It also has extremely vicious thorns.

Hackberry is just a big weed. It is short-lived and plagued by insects and diseases.

Mimosa is another real dog. Although beautiful when healthy, it never is. The root system is ravenous and destructive, devouring water and soil nutrients. The tree is highly vulnerable to insects and diseases.

Fruitless mulberry is the most overused junk tree. It shades the ground too heavily, uses too much water, and is the target of several insects and diseases. Its root system is highly destructive to lawns, walks, driveways, and pipes. It is also short-lived.

Pin oak grows well in acidic sandy soil but is a disaster in alkaline clay soils. It crossbreeds with other oaks and creates problems. Red oaks that accidentally cross with pin oak will always be yellow and sick in alkaline soils.

Poplars in general are fast-growing, unhealthy trees and should be avoided. The have lots of insect and disease problems.

Silver maple is a lousy tree. It is usually chlorotic (yellow from trace mineral deficiency), is subject to insects and diseases, and has weak, brittle wood.

Sycamore trees are gorgeous when healthy, but disease problems are wiping them out. Bacterial leaf scorch is the primary culprit.

Italian cypress trees are prone to freeze damage, insect problems, and diseases.

Working *with* nature is the key to successful tree growing. Trying to use problem trees is fighting nature because these plants just don't like it here in Texas and will never be successful. Some of them don't like it anywhere. Stick with recommended varieties and enjoy your trees and the birds in them.

GUIDE TO MAKING HOMEMADE ORGANIC REMEDIES

The mixtures included here are recommended as solutions
to certain problems described in the book.

MANURE COMPOST TEA

This is an effective foliar spray because it includes many mineral nutrients and naturally occurring microorganisms. Fill any container half full of compost and finish filling it with water. Let the mix sit for 10–14 days and then dilute and spray on the foliage of any and all plants. The amount of dilution depends on the leachate, down to 1 part compost liquid to 4–10 parts water. The ready-to-use spray should look like iced tea. Be sure to strain the solids out with old pantyhose, cheesecloth, or floating row-cover material. Full-strength tea makes an excellent fire ant mound drench when mixed with 2 ounces molasses and 2 ounces citrus oil per gallon.

GARLIC-PEPPER TEA INSECT REPELLENT

In a blender with water, liquefy 2 bulbs of garlic and 2 cayenne or habanero peppers. Strain away the solids. Pour the garlic-pepper juice into a 1-gallon container. Fill the remaining volume with water to make 1 gallon of concentrate. Shake well before using and add ¼ cup of the concentrate to each gallon of water in the sprayer. To make garlic tea, simply omit the pepper and add another bulb of garlic. For additional power, add 1 tablespoon of seaweed and 1 tablespoon of molasses to each gallon. Always use plastic containers with loose-fitting lids for storage.

Dirt Doctor's Potting Soil

5   parts compost
4   parts lava sand
4   parts granite sand
3   parts peat moss
2   parts cedar flakes
1   part soft rock phosphate
1   part earthworm castings
½   wheat bran/cornmeal soil amendment
¼   part Texas greensand

This is a very powerful potting soil and needs no additional fertilizer. It is also too strong to use for most interior house plants. A very strong argument could be made that the best potting soil in which to start trees from seed is the natural soil of the area. When trees are started in this way, the transplant shock is zero, and the trees adapt and establish very quickly. Trees planted from natural soil pots in the fall, assuming they are planted with the natural methods and watered well over time, rarely die or need additional supplemental water.

Garrett Juice

My recommended basic organic foliar spray is available commercially. Or you can make your own. Mix the listed ingredients in a gallon of water.

Garrett Juice (ready to spray):

1   cup manure-based compost tea
1   ounce molasses
1   ounce natural apple cider vinegar
1   ounce liquid seaweed

For disease and insect control add:

¼   cup garlic tea or
¼   cup garlic/pepper tea or
1   ounce of orange oil

For homemade fire ant killer add:

2   ounces of citrus oil

The ready-to-use solution should not have more than 2 ounces of orange oil per gallon.

Garrett Juice Homemade Concentrate

1   gallon compost tea
1   pint cider vinegar
1   pint liquefied seaweed
1   pint blackstrap molasses

Mix all ingredients together. For spraying, use 1½ cups of concentrate per 1 gallon of water. Note: 1 pint = 2 cups = 16 ounces.

Tree Trunk Goop

Mix in water and paint on trunks: ⅓ natural diatomaceous earth, ⅓ soft rock phosphate, and ⅓ manure compost. Paint onto cuts, borer holes, or other injuries on trunks or limbs. Reapply if it is washed off by rain or irrigation. Don't worry about it washing off. It is an excellent organic fertilizer for the soil.

APPENDIX 3

SICK TREE TREATMENT

My answer to most tree problems started with a solution I proposed to save a red tip photinia that was dying of root disease. The technique was successful and evolved into the Sick Tree Treatment. We have learned more, and the recommendations have continued to improve. Here are the reasons for, and details of, the current improved program for trees that are infected with cotton root rot, oak wilt, or any other fungal disease.

Oak wilt is a devastating fungal disease of native and introduced red oaks and live oaks. Texas A & M and the Texas Forest Service recommend a program of trenching to separate the roots of sick trees from those of healthy trees, cutting down sick and nearby healthy trees, and injecting a toxic chemical fungicide called Alamo directly into the

trunks or root flares of the trees. I don't recommend this program because it does nothing to address the cause of the disease. Trees succumb to insect pests and diseases because they are in stress and sick. Mother Nature then sends in the clean-up crews. The bugs and pathogens are just doing their job—trying to take out the unfit plants. Most sickness is environmental—too much water, not enough water, too much fertilizer, the wrong kind of fertilizer, ill-adapted plant varieties, and/or over planting single species and creating monocultures (such as is the case with American elms in the northwest and red oaks/live oaks in certain parts of Texas).

The plan is simple. Keep trees in a healthy condition so their immune systems can resist infection and disease. It has been noticed by many farmers and ranchers that the disease doesn't bother some trees—especially those that are mulched and those where the natural habitat under the trees has been maintained. There's only anecdotal evidence so far, but we have seen excellent results from the following organic program that is called the Sick Tree Treatment:

1. Remove all soil that is above the actual root ball with a rake or hire an arborist to use an air spade. Prune away any girdling roots.
2. Aerate the root zone heavily. Start between the drip line and the trunk and go far out beyond the drip line. A 7–12-inch depth for the aeration holes is ideal but any depth is beneficial. An alternative is to spray the root zone with a living-organism product such as Bio-Innoculant or AgriGro.
3. Apply Texas greensand at about 40–80 pounds per 1,000 square feet, lava sand at about 40–80 pounds per 1,000 square feet, cornmeal at about 10–20 pounds per 1,000 square feet, and sugar or dry molasses at about 5 pounds per 1,000 square feet. Cornmeal is a natural disease fighter and sugar is a carbon source to feed the microbes in the soil.
4. Apply a 1-inch layer of compost, followed by a 3–5-inch layer of shredded native tree trimmings. Native cedar is the best source for mulch. In turf use a 1-inch layer of horticultural cedar flakes.
5. Spray foliage and soil monthly or more often if possible with Garrett Juice (see Appendix 2). For large-scale farms and ranches, a one-time spraying is beneficial if the budget doesn't allow ongoing sprays. Adding garlic tea to the spray is also beneficial while the tree is in trouble.
6. Stop using high nitrogen fertilizers and toxic chemical pesticides. Pesticides kill the beneficial nematodes and insects. Fake fertilizers are destructive to the important mycorrhizal fungi on the roots.

A premix of all these materials is now available from the organic suppliers.

If you've already had trees die, you can use the wood for firewood and mulch. Since the fungal mats form on red oaks only, not on live oaks, the live oak wood can be used for firewood without any worry of spreading the oak wilt disease. Red oak wood needs to be stacked in a sunny location and covered with clear plastic to form a green-house effect to kill the beetles and fungal mats. When oaks are shredded into mulch, the aeration kills the pathogens and eliminates the possibility of disease spread. That goes for all species.

About the nitidulid beetle—is this beetle the only vector of the oak wilt disease? I doubt it. I would also suspect mechanical damage to tree trunks, wind, squirrels, hail, sapsuckers, and other insects. Fire ants seem to prefer weaker trees over others and could also be part of the disease-spreading problem.

The Sick Tree Treatment has not yet been proven by any university (and probably won't be), even though the evidence continues to stack up. The key seems to be improving the health of the soil and thus the population of beneficial fungi on the root system. Spraying the foliage during the rebuilding of the soil and root system provides trace minerals for the plant that can't yet come in through the roots. This program is not just for oak wilt. It works for most environmental tree problems and all tree types. The point here is that if it works for oak wilt, it will work even more effectively for less deadly tree conditions. If your tree problem is a result of poor tree selection, I can only help you in the future. Choose more wisely next time.

TREE PESTS

AND

REMEDIES

Anthracnose—This fungal disease attacks and turns sycamore leaves brown, although the leaves remain on the tree. It is not normally fatal. Spray Garrett Juice (Appendix 2) plus garlic tea on emerging new foliage in the early the spring. Apply the Sick Tree Treatment (Appendix 3). Sprays of Bordeaux mix, potassium bicarbonate, garlic, and neem are also effective. The best control is to avoid planting sycamores.

Aphids—These small, sucking insects exist in a wide range of sizes and colors. They primarily attack the young foliage of stressed plants. Spray with a strong water blast. Add Garrett Juice (Appendix 2) for even better pest control. Release beneficial insects—ladybugs, brachonid wasps, and green lacewings. Giant bark aphids require no treatment at all.

Bacterial leaf scorch—A fatal disease of sycamores and other plants, it causes a browning between the veins of the leaves. It kills limbs from the tips and moves back quickly. It is often incorrectly diagnosed as anthracnose.

Bagworms—These defoliating insects attack several tree species. Hand-remove the bags and apply the Sick Tree Treatment (Appendix 3).

Release trichogramma wasps and green lacewings. As a last resort spray Bt (Bacillus thuringiensis) product, adding 2 tablespoons (1 ounce) of molasses per gallon of spray.

Ball moss—This is not a serious problem other than cosmetic. It can be controlled by spraying a mixture of $\frac{1}{3}$ cup baking soda or potassium bicarbonate per gallon of water. Like mistletoe ball moss does tend to attack trees as their health declines.

Beetles—Some beetles attack trees that are in stress. Spray Garrett Juice (Appendix 2) plus citrus oil for problem infestations, but make sure the beetle in question is harmful because many are beneficial. Apply beneficial nematodes to the soil for additional help.

Borers—Borers are the larvae of beetles and only attack trees in stress. Some of the causes of tree stress include pruning wounds, high nitrogen, synthetic fertilizers, weed-eater damage, sun scald, soil compaction, chemical damage, and planting ill-adapted trees. Improve the soil health and the immune system of the plants by using the Basic Organic Program (Appendix 5). Run stiff wire into borer holes to kill the active larvae. Treat the trunks with Tree Trunk Goop (Appendix 2) after putting nematodes into the holes.

Canker—This stress-related disease of trees and shrubs causes decay of the bark and wood. Cankers have to start with a wound through the bark. Healthy soil and plants are the best solution. Use Tree Trunk Goop (Appendix 2) on the injured spots, improve the environmental conditions, and apply the Sick Tree Treatment (Appendix 5). Fungicides do not work on this disease. Hypoxolyn canker is a common disease of stressed post oaks and occurs especially after droughts or long rainy seasons. The brown spores rub off easily and the bark sloughs off the trunks. No treatment is necessary other than improving the immune system of the tree. This is the #1 disease seen on post oaks.

Caterpillars—All the larvae of moths and butterflies eat plant foliage. Some are more troublesome than others. Release beneficial insects and especially encourage and protect native wasps. Green lacewings are also quite effective.

Chlorosis—This condition is caused by trace mineral deficiency. Iron scarcity is usually blamed, but the cause can be the lack of several trace minerals or magnesium. To cure, improve trace mineral availability by applying Texas greensand, humate, lava sand, organic fertilizer, and foliar feeding.

Construction damage—Construction activity causes compaction of the soil, which kills beneficial microbes and root hairs. Prevent it— don't allow it—by using physical barriers. Build strong fences so contractors cannot access the root zone.

Cotton root rot—This fungal disease common in alkaline soils attacks poorly adapted plants. The best preventative is healthy soil with a balance of nutrients and soil biology. Solutions include adding sulfur to the soil at 5 pounds per 1,000 square feet. Products that contain sodium will sometimes help. Cornmeal and living-organism products will also help.

Elm leaf beetle—The larvae and adult beetles eat the green from the leaves, leaving the leaf with a skeletonized appearance. Plant better quality trees. Spray if necessary with *Bacillus thuringiensis* 'San Diego'. Spray according to the label directions at dusk. Add 1 tablespoon molasses per gallon of spray.

Entomosporium leaf spot—A fungal disease of photinia, hawthorns, and other related plants, it primarily hits large monoculture plantings. This fungal leaf spot can be controlled by improving soil conditions and avoiding susceptible plants. This disease is most active in the spring and fall. Use the Sick Tree Treatment and try to avoid watering the foliage.

Fire blight—This is a bacterial disease of plants in the rose family in which blossoms, new shoots, twigs, and limbs die back as though they have been burned. Leaves usually remain attached but often turn black or dark brown. Prune back into healthy tissue and disinfect the pruning tools with a 3–5% solution of hydrogen peroxide. Spray plants at the first sign of disease with Garrett Juice (Appendix 2) plus garlic and neem. Consan 20 and agricultural streptomycin are also effective controls. Kocide 101 is a copper-based fungicide often recommended. The best recommendation is to spray Garrett Juice (Appendix 2) plus garlic, treat the soil with horticultural cornmeal, apply the Sick Tree Treatment (Appendix 3), and reduce the nitrogen fertilizer. High nitrogen, synthetic fertilizers are the primary cause of this disease.

Forest tent caterpillars—These pest caterpillars attack trees in the late spring or early summer. The damage is generally more cosmetic than destructive. Release trichogramma wasps and as a last resort spray Bt (*Bacillus thuringiensis*) at dusk. Add 1 tablespoon molasses per gallon. The caterpillars can also be killed with a mix of orange oil, compost tea, and molasses.

Fungal leaf spot—See **Entomosporium leaf spot**

Galls—There are many different kinds of galls primarily caused by wasp, fly, and aphid insects. They are usually more of a cosmetic problem than damaging. Insects "sting" a plant, which causes a growth that the insect uses as a home for its young. The gall serves as a shelter and food supply. Although unsightly, most galls are not considered very damaging. The natural control is biodiversity. The healthy plants seem to have fewer galls. Improve the general health of trees using the Basic Organic Program (Appendix 5).

Grasshoppers—Especially severe during drought seasons, grasshoppers are one of our most troublesome pests. Plant lots of plants to establish strong biodiversity. Feed the birds regularly to keep lots of them on the property. Broadcast *Nosema locustae* per the label instructions. Spray a particle film product such as a generic kaolin clay or the EPA-approved product Surround WP.

Herbicide damage—Most, if not all, of the toxic chemical herbicides can cause tree problems. The contact killers and the pre-emergents can kill the beneficial fungi and the feeder roots of trees. The symptoms can look remarkably similar to oak wilt. That may be exactly what we are seeing in some oak wilt areas.

Juniper dieback—This fungal disease of cedars and junipers is also called "twig dieback." The spores look like a yellow worm oozing out of the plants. Treat by pick pruning, rather than sheering the whole plant, and mulching.

Lacebugs—Lacebugs suck leaves from the underside, causing brown specks. Black waste material will also be visible. Spray Garrett Juice (Appendix 2) plus neem oil product. Apply per the label instructions. Add citrus oil at 2 ounces per gallon for serious infestations.

Leaf miners—These small insect larvae tunnel through leaf tissue, leaving whitish trails. Spray Garrett Juice (Appendix 2) plus garlic tea. They cause only minor damage and there is usually no need to treat them.

Leaf spot—This is a cosmetic disease of oak and elm. No control is needed.

Lightning damage—If your tree gets hit, keep your fingers crossed. Install lightning protection to prevent future damage. There are two kinds of lightning damage. When the lightning travels along the outside of the tree in the rainwater, bark is knocked off but damage is usually minimal. If the lightning goes through the center of the tree, the bark is blown off and the tree is a goner.

Loopers—These moth larvae eat plant foliage but are easily controlled by releasing trichogramma wasps. Apply Bt product per the label instructions at dusk. Add 1 tablespoon of molasses per gallon of spray.

Mealybugs—Adults and nymphs suck the juice from new growth. Spray Garrett Juice (Appendix 2) plus neem or citrus oil and apply the Sick Tree Treatment (Appendix 3).

Mistletoe—This tree parasite attacks sick, stressed trees. Physical removal of the mistletoe and improving soil health are the long-term controls. Remove entire infested limbs where practical. Apply black pruning paint to large wounds and apply the Sick Tree Treatment (Appendix 3).

Nematodes—Root knot nematodes are plant-damaging soil organisms. Till or fork citrus pulp into the soil prior to planting or gently work the pump into the root zone of existing trees.

Oak leaf blister—A rare disease that needs no control, it usually results from a heavy rainy season. The leaves change from light green to a light brown, dry blister. The disease only appears in isolated spots on the tree.

Oak wilt—Apply the Sick Tree Treatment (Appendix 3). Oak wilt attacks red oaks and live oaks especially when they occur in large monocultures and are treated with synthetic fertilizers and pesticides. The disease on red oaks first shows up when greasy green leaves turn brown starting on the ends. This is usually seen on one limb at a time. Live oak leaves have veinal necrosis (brown veins and green in between). Some leaves will be dead on the last half. Red oaks have sweet-smelling, fungal mats on the trunks. Dutch elm disease is closely related to oak wilt. I do not recommend injecting fungicides into trees, and I don't recommend removing healthy trees that are near sick trees. The chemical injection hurts the tree, wastes money, and doesn't address the real problem. This procedure has been pushed by Texas A&M and the Texas Forest Service for many years, and I have yet to have anyone report that the fungicide injections ever saved a single infected tree.

Peach tree curl—This disease causes deformed leaves and can affect the quality and quantity of the fruit crop. Spray Garrett Juice (Appendix 2) plus garlic tea in the fall. Treat the soil with horticultural cornmeal. Use the organic fruit and pecan tree program (Appendix 5).

Pecan nut casebearers—The larvae of these small moths damage the pecan nut production by feeding on the small nutlets as they develop. Release trichogramma wasps every two weeks during the spring. The first release should be made at leaf emergence. A little damage from the moth is actually beneficial by reducing heavy nut production. This keeps the weight of the nuts from breaking the limbs and will help the tree have larger nuts.

Pine tip blight—A pine disease that forms black bumps on the needles, it resembles pine tip moth and can be controlled with the Sick Tree Treatment (Appendix 3).

Pine tip moth—Larvae of the moths feed on and damage the buds of pine trees. This common problem of Christmas tree farms can be easily controlled with the Basic Organic Program (Appendix 5) and the release of trichogramma wasps.

Powdery mildew—This fungal disease is a white or gray, powdery growth on the lower leaf surface and flower buds. Leaves turn yellow on the top. Controls include baking soda spray, potassium bicarbonate spray, neem, garlic,

and horticultural oil. Spray Garrett Juice (Appendix 2) plus garlic tea for the best long-term results. Treat the soil with horticultural cornmeal and use the entire Sick Tree Treatment (Appendix 3) for serious problems. This disease can cause long-term weakness when it occurs early in the growing season. This common fungal disease is increased by humidity but is actually deterred by water. Spraying neem every 7 days is the best treatment for severe cases.

Rust—This fungal disease forms an orange stain on the surface of foliage. Pustules form on the undersides of the leaves. This is mostly a cosmetic disease but can be treated with Garrett Juice (Appendix 2) with garlic or potassium bicarbonate.

Sapsuckers—These beautiful birds attack and severely damage stressed trees. Spray the trunks with garlic-pepper tea (Appendix 2), apply the Sick Tree Treatment (Appendix 3), and treat wounds with Tree Trunk Goop (Appendix 2).

Sooty mold—This black fungal growth appears on the foliage of plants infested with aphids, scale, or whiteflies. It is caused by the honey-dew (excrement) of the insect pests. The best control is to release beneficial insects to control the pest bugs. Also spray Garrett Juice (Appendix 2) plus garlic. Treat the soil with horticultural cornmeal and use the entire Sick Tree Treatment (Appendix 3).

Spider mites—These small mites attack plants that aren't able to absorb water properly. Too much or too little water can be the culprit. Adjust the watering schedule. Release green lacewings and predatory mites. Spray Garrett Juice (Appendix 2) or garlic-pepper tea with seaweed as needed. Seaweed spray by itself will work—spider mites hate seaweed.

Tree decline—A generic term referring to a sick, declining tree, this is not a specific disease but rather a result of planting an ill-adapted tree, construction damage, drought, lightning, salt fertilizer, chemicals, contamination, etc.

Webworms—Webworms are the larvae of moths. Release trichogramma wasps and spray with Garrett Juice (Appendix 2) plus garlic. Add neem or citrus oil for strong infestations. Use Bt (*Bacillus thuringiensis*) as a last resort. Spray with 1 tablespoon molasses per gallon at dusk.

Wet wood—Bacterial wet wood shows up as an oozing cell sap that appears as a white, frosty material that attracts insects. Increase the tree's health so it can wall off the problem area. Use the Sick Tree Treatment (Appendix 3).

Wind damage—Don't over prune. Remember that heavy pruning is weakening and detrimental to tree health. Pruning is done for your benefit, not the tree's benefit.

Xylella—Also called xylem limited disease, it plugs the vascular system of elms, oaks, sycamores, pecans, and other trees. It looks like heat stress damage and can be easily diagnosed by lab tests. Apply the Sick Tree Treatment (Appendix 3).

JOHN HOWARD GARRETT'S BASIC ORGANIC PROGRAM

1. **Soil testing**—Send soil samples to Texas Plant and Soil Lab in Edinburg, Texas (956-383-0739), for organic recommendations. Another way to test the soil is to dig a cubic foot of soil and sift it back into the hole. If you don't see about 10 earthworms, you need to do more of what's listed below.

2. **Planting**—Prepare new planting beds by scraping away existing grass and weeds, adding a 4–6-inch layer of compost, lava sand at 40–80 pounds per 1,000 square feet, organic fertilizer at 20 pounds per 1,000 square feet, and horticultural cornmeal at 10–20 pounds per 1,000 square feet. Till to a depth of 3 inches into the native soil. Excavation and the addition of ingredients such as concrete sand, topsoil, and pine bark are unnecessary and can cause problems. More compost is needed for shrubs and flowers than for ground cover. Add Texas greensand to black and white soils and high-calcium, lime-to-acid soils. Soft rock phosphate is an effective amendment for all soils.

3. **Fertilizing**—Apply an organic fertilizer 2–3 times per year. During the growing season, spray turf, tree and shrub foliage, trunks, limbs, and soil at least monthly with Garrett Juice (see Appendix 2). Add lava sand annually at 40–80 pounds per 1,000 square feet.

4. **Mulching**—Mulch all shrubs, trees, and ground cover with 3–5 inches of shredded tree trimmings or shredded hardwood bark to protect the soil, to inhibit weed germination, to decrease watering needs, and to mediate soil temperature. Mulch vegetable gardens with 8 inches of alfalfa hay, rough-textured compost, or shredded native tree trimmings. Avoid Bermuda hay because of the possibility of broadleaf-herbicide contamination. Shredded native cedar is the best of all mulches.

5. **Watering**—Adjust the schedule seasonally to allow for deep, infrequent waterings in order to maintain an even moisture level. Start by applying about 1 inch of water per week in the summer and make adjustments from there. Water needs will vary from site to site and from season to season. Add 1 tablespoon natural vinegar per gallon when watering in containers, unless the water is already acidic.

6. **Mowing**—Mow weekly, leaving the clippings on the lawn to return nutrients and organic matter to the soil. The general mowing height should be 2½ inches or taller. Put occasional excess clippings in the compost pile. **Do not ever bag clippings. Do not let clippings ever leave the site.** Mulching mowers are best if the budget allows. Do not use line trimmers around trees.

7. **Weeding**—Hand-pull large weeds and work on soil health for overall control. Mulch all bare soil in beds. AVOID SYNTHETIC HERBICIDES, especially pre-emergents, broadleaf treatments, and soil sterilants. These are unnecessary toxic pollutants. Spray broadleaf weeds as a last resort with full-strength vinegar and citrus mix or remove them mechanically. Commercial organic herbicides are now on the market.

8. **Pruning**—Remove dead, diseased, and conflicting limbs. Do not over prune. Do not make flush cuts. Leave the branch collars intact. Do not paint cuts except on red oaks and live oaks in oak wilt areas when spring pruning can't be avoided. Remember that pruning cuts hurt trees. Pruning is done for your benefit, not for the benefit of the trees.

9. **Compost making**—Compost, nature's own living fertilizer, can be made at home or purchased ready to use. A compost pile can be started any time of the year in sun or shade. Anything once living can go in the compost—grass clippings, tree trimmings, food scraps, bark, sawdust, rice hulls, weeds, nut hulls, and animal manure. Mix the ingredients together and simply pile the material on the ground. The best mixture is 80% vegetative matter and 20% animal waste, although any mix will compost. Since oxygen is a critical component, the ingredients should be a mix of coarse and fine-textured material to promote air circulation through the pile. Turn the pile once a month if possible. Turning more often speeds up the process but releases nitrogen to the air. Another critical component is water. A compost pile should be roughly the moisture of a squeezed-out sponge to help the living organisms thrive and work their magic. Compost is ready to use as a soil amendment when the ingredients are no longer identifiable. The color will be dark brown and the texture soft and crumbly, and it will smell like the forest floor. Rough, unfinished compost can be used as a topdressing mulch around all plantings.

10. **Manure compost tea**—See Appendix 2 for recipe and instructions.

11. **Controlling insects—Aphids, spider mites, whiteflies, and lacebugs:** Release ladybugs and green lacewings regularly until natural populations exist. Garrett Juice (see Appendix 2) and/or garlic-pepper tea (see Appendix 2) are effective controls. Use strong water blasts for heavy infestations. **Caterpillars and bagworms:** Release trichogramma wasps. Spray *Bacillus thuringiensis* (Bt) as a last resort. **Fire ants:** Drench mounds with Garrett Juice (see Appendix 2) plus citrus oil and release beneficial nematodes. **Grasshoppers:** Eliminate bare soil, apply beneficial nematodes, and then dust or spray with one or more of the following: self-rising flour, natural diatomaceous earth, or fire ant control formula. Encourage biodiversity and feed the birds. **Grubworms:** Beneficial nematodes and general soil health is the primary control. **Mosquitoes:** Use *Bacillus thuringiensis* 'Israelensis' for larvae in standing water. Spray citrus oil or garlic-pepper tea (see Appendix 2) for adults. Lavender, vanilla, citronella, and eucalyptus also repel adult mosquitoes. **Slugs, snails, fleas, ticks, chinch bugs, roaches, and crickets:** Spray or dust diatomaceous earth products and crushed red pepper. Citrus oil also kills these pests. See Appendix 4 for more pests and remedies.

12. **Controlling diseases—Black spot, brown patch, powdery mildew, and other fungal problems:** The best control is prevention through soil improvement, avoidance of high nitrogen fertilizers, and proper watering.

Spray Garrett Juice (see Appendix 2) plus garlic and/or neem. Baking soda or potassium bicarbonate can also be added. Treat the soil with horticultural cornmeal at about 20 pounds per 1,000 square feet. Alfalfa meal and mixes containing alfalfa are also good disease fighters.

13. **Garlic-pepper tea insect repellent**—See Appendix 2 for recipe and instructions.

14. **Garrett Juice (foliar spray and soil drench)**—See Appendix 2 for recipe and instructions.

15. **Dirt Doctor's potting soil**—See Appendix 2 for recipe and instructions.

ORGANIC PECAN AND FRUIT TREE PROGRAM

Pecan trees and fruit trees can be grown organically and, no, you don't have to spray toxic pesticides. Plant adapted, small nut varieties like Caddo, Kanza, and the native pecans. Plant the trees in wide, rough-sided holes, backfill with soil from the hole (no additions), settle the soil with water (no tamping), add a 1-inch layer of lava sand and compost mix, and finish with a 3–5-inch layer of coarse-textured native cedar mulch. Do not stake, wrap the trunk, or cut back the top. Those who say to dig a small, round hole are wrong. Mechanical aeration of the root zone of existing trees is beneficial, but tilling, disking, or plowing destroys feeder roots and should never be done. Pecans should never have bare soil around them. The root zone should always be covered with mulches and/or native grasses and legumes.

Fertilizing Program for Pecans and Fruit Trees

Round #1 February 1–15: Use organic fertilizer at 20 pounds per 1,000 square feet (i.e., use Garden-Ville, GreenSense, Bradfield, Bioform Dry, MaestroGro, Sustane, or natural meal), lava sand at 80 pounds per 1,000 square feet, and wheat bran/cornmeal soil amendment at 50 pounds per 1,000 square feet.

Round #2 June 1–15: Use organic fertilizer at 10 pounds per 1,000 square feet and Texas greensand at 40–80 pounds per 1,000 square feet (or soft rock phosphate at the same rate if in acid soils).

Round #3 September 15–30: Use organic fertilizer at 10 pounds per 1,000 square feet and sul-po-mag at 20 pounds per 1,000 square feet.

Note: If soil health has been achieved by round #2, round #3 can be omitted.

Large-scale pecan orchards can use livestock manure or compost at 1–2 tons per acre per year. Also establish green-manure cover crops. Lava sand and other rock powders can be applied any time of the year. Then foliar feed with Garrett Juice twice monthly.

Pest Control Program

Add the following to Garrett Juice (see Appendix 2) and spray as needed:

Garlic tea—¼ cup per gallon.

Citrus oil, orange oil, or d-limonene—1 ounce per gallon as a spray, 2 ounces per gallon as a drench.

Potassium bicarbonate—1 rounded tablespoon per gallon for diseases.

Liquid biostimulants—Use Agrispon, AgriGro, Medina, Bio-Innoculant or similar product per label instructions.

Neem—Use per label directions for serious pest problems.

Fish emulsion—1–2 ounces per gallon for additional nutrients (this may not be needed when using compost tea).

Spray Schedule

1st spraying: at pink bud. The first two sprayings should contain Garrett Juice (see Appendix 2) and garlic tea.

2nd spraying: after flowers have fallen. Schedule additional sprayings as time and budget allow. For the best results spray every two weeks but at least once a month.

3rd spraying: about June 15.

4th spraying: last week in August.

Insect Release

Trichogramma wasps—Weekly release of 10,000–20,000 eggs per acre or residential lot starting at bud break for 3 weeks.

Green lacewings—Weekly release of 4,000 eggs per acre or residential lot for 1 month.

Ladybugs—Release 1,500–2,000 adult beetles per 1,000 square feet at the first sign of shiny honeydew on foliage.

Very little pruning is needed or recommended. Maintain cover crops and/or natural mulch under the trees year round. Never cultivate the soil under pecan and fruit trees.

GLOSSARY

Adapted tree—A tree native to the geographical area and soil type or an introduced tree that accepts the new conditions and grows well in the long term.

Air root pruning—The natural killing of plant roots as they grow out of the bottom of a bottomless container. The roots are killed or pruned away by the exposure to air.

Allelopathy, allelopathic—The harmful effect by one plant species upon another. Some plants produce phytotoxic compounds that inhibit the germination or growth of other plants.

Alternate host—A second plant species that is required to help host the entire life cycle of an insect pest or disease.

Alternate leaves—Leaves where one leaf or other structure is borne per node, contrasting with opposite or whorled leaves.

Bract—A modified leaf that is often colorful or decorative and resembles a flower. Some function as flowers by attracting pollinators.

Bud break—That time in the early spring when buds first begin to open.

Budding—A propagation or grafting technique where buds from one plant are attached to another plant.

Calcarious—The term used to describe soil that is very high in calcium, such as the highly limestone soils of the arid southwest.

Catkins—The unshowy male and female flowers of a tree such as oak and pecan.

Chlorotic (chlorosis)—The yellowing or blanching of leaves and other parts of plants, usually caused by mineral deficiencies, sometimes but not always an iron deficiency. Leaf veins often remain green.

Cold hours—The number of hours a dormant plant must be exposed to temperatures that are below a certain point for the plant to properly set fruit.

Come true (as in "the plant won't come true")—To return to the exact genetic makeup of the parent plant. This always happens with stem cuttings and only sometimes with seed.

Compound leaves—Leaves with several leaflets. Pecan, walnut, and pistachio have compound leaves.

Cultivar—A variety or variation of a cultivated plant.

Cypress knees—The specialized root structures of the bald cypress that grow vertically above water or moist soil. It is thought that these structures aid the oxygen/carbon dioxide exchange in the roots.

Damping off—Fungal diseases that attack and quickly kill small seedlings (e.g., *Pythium, Fusarium, Rhizoctonia*).

Deciduous—Refers to plants that lose their leaves in the winter.

Dioecious—Refers to plants that have male and female flowers on separate plants.

Drupe—A one-seeded fruit with a fleshy interior and smooth outer skin. Plums and cherries are examples of drupes.

Evergreen—A plant that remains green throughout the winter.

Grafting—The art of joining two plants together so they will unite and grow as one plant.

Greensand—A marine deposit called glauconite, which is iron potassium silicate, an excellent source of trace minerals. Texas greensand contains 19–20% iron.

Hardwood cuttings—Dormant cuttings made in the winter from mature stems after the previous growing season.

Inflorescence—A flower cluster.

Introduced tree—A tree that is introduced from another part of the world; not native.

Layering—The process of vegetatively propagating plants by causing adventitious roots to form on a stem that is still attached to the parent plant. The rooted stem is then detached to grow on its own.

Leaf margin—The edge of the leaf.

Liquid humate—A liquid form of leonardite shale or low grade lignite coal that is an excellent source of carbon, humic acid, and trace minerals. It can be used as a soil drench or a foliar feeding material.

Maceration—The process of physically removing the soft pulpy tissue of fleshy fruits.

Monoculture—The cultivation or mass planting of a single plant species.

Monoecious—Refers to plants with staminate (male) flowers and pistillate (female) flowers on the same plant, but lacking perfect flowers.

Mott—A small isolated clump of trees, usually of the same species and usually occurring in open areas of grassland.

Native tree—A tree that grows wild in the specific area in question.

Neem—A botanical pest control product that is made from the seed of the tropical neem tree of India and Burma.

Nipple gall—A small gall caused by insects (a common occurrence on hackberries).

Nutlet—Diminutive of nut, refers to any nut-like fruit or seed.

Opposite leaves—Leaves where there are two leaves at each node on opposite sides of the axis.

Ovate leaves—Leaves that are egg-shaped with the widest part at the base.

Panicles—Branched inflorescences or clusters with flowers on the branches of the primary central stem.

Perfect flower—A bisexual flower that has both stamens and pistils.

Petiole—The leafstalk that supports the blade.

Pinnate leaf—A compound leaf having leaflets along both sides of the central stem.

Pubescent—Refers to plant parts that are fuzzy or hairy.

Raceme—An unbranched inflorescence or flower cluster on an elongated axis.

Rhizome—An underground stem with nodes and scale leaves.

Root cutting—A small piece of root used for the purpose of starting new plants asexually.

Samara—A dry, indehiscent (not splitting open), winged fruit. It can be one-seeded as in ash or two-seeded as in maple.

Saponin—Soap-like molecules that lower the surface tension of water solutions. They are highly toxic to cold-blooded animals and are used to stun fish.

Scale—Any small, thin, usually dry leaf or bract such as the parts of a pine cone.

Set (as in "to set flowers or fruit")—Refers to the successful impregnation of the female flower resulting in the formation of fruit.

Softwood cutting—A cutting of juvenile or green herbaceous wood during the growing season or cutting made early in the season from new growth.

Specimen tree—A special tree that is used as a focal point in the garden.

Stem cutting—A cutting of the twig or terminal (end) growth of a plant. Stem cuttings are usually 6–8 inches long. The lower leaves are removed and the cutting is plunged into moist potting soil. It is misted for ideal conditions and is successful when roots form on the cut end.

Stratification—The storage of seed at a certain temperature and humidity for a period of time for the purpose of aiding germination.

Sucker—A growth from the base of a plant either above or below ground level. It also refers to shoots growing from the roots of parent plants.

Terminal—Refers to plant growth at the top of a plant or at the ends of twigs, stems, or limbs.

Tomentose—Refers to plant parts covered with short, soft, curly, densely matted, or entangled hairs.

Trifoliate—Having three leaves.

Unisexual flowers—Flowers having only one sex, either stamens or pistils.

Whorled—Having a ring of leaves or other plant parts radiating from a node.

Xeriscape—A term used for water-saving gardening.

Index

Boldface numbers indicate the primary information about the plant.